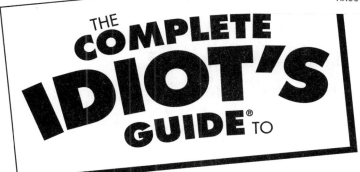

THE
COMPLETE
IDIOT'S
GUIDE® TO

The Akashic Record

by Dr. Synthia Andrews, ND, and Colin Andrews

ALPHA

A member of Penguin Group (USA) Inc.

We would like to dedicate this book to the children who inherit the earth, specifically our own children: Mandy Butcher, Erin Infantino, and Adriel Infantino.

ALPHA BOOKS

Published by the Penguin Group

Penguin Group (USA) Inc., 375 Hudson Street, New York, New York 10014, USA

Penguin Group (Canada), 90 Eglinton Avenue East, Suite 700, Toronto, Ontario M4P 2Y3, Canada (a division of Pearson Penguin Canada Inc.)

Penguin Books Ltd., 80 Strand, London WC2R 0RL, England

Penguin Ireland, 25 St. Stephen's Green, Dublin 2, Ireland (a division of Penguin Books Ltd.)

Penguin Group (Australia), 250 Camberwell Road, Camberwell, Victoria 3124, Australia (a division of Pearson Australia Group Pty. Ltd.)

Penguin Books India Pvt. Ltd., 11 Community Centre, Panchsheel Park, New Delhi—110 017, India

Penguin Group (NZ), 67 Apollo Drive, Rosedale, North Shore, Auckland 1311, New Zealand (a division of Pearson New Zealand Ltd.)

Penguin Books (South Africa) (Pty.) Ltd., 24 Sturdee Avenue, Rosebank, Johannesburg 2196, South Africa

Penguin Books Ltd., Registered Offices: 80 Strand, London WC2R 0RL, England

International Standard Book Number: 978-1-59257-996-9
Library of Congress Catalog Card Number: 2009941615

13 14 15   11 10 9 8

Interpretation of the printing code: The rightmost number of the first series of numbers is the year of the book's printing; the rightmost number of the second series of numbers is the number of the book's printing. For example, a printing code of 10-1 shows that the first printing occurred in 2010.

Printed in the United States of America

Note: This publication contains the opinions and ideas of its authors. It is intended to provide helpful and informative material on the subject matter covered. It is sold with the understanding that the authors and publisher are not engaged in rendering professional services in the book. If the reader requires personal assistance or advice, a competent professional should be consulted.

The authors and publisher specifically disclaim any responsibility for any liability, loss, or risk, personal or otherwise, which is incurred as a consequence, directly or indirectly, of the use and application of any of the contents of this book.

Most Alpha books are available at special quantity discounts for bulk purchases for sales promotions, premiums, fund-raising, or educational use. Special books, or book excerpts, can also be created to fit specific needs.

For details, write: Special Markets, Alpha Books, 375 Hudson Street, New York, NY 10014.

Publisher: *Marie Butler-Knight*
Editorial Director: *Mike Sanders*
Senior Managing Editor: *Billy Fields*
Executive Editor: *Randy Ladenheim-Gil*
Development Editor: *Lynn Northrup*
Senior Production Editor: *Janette Lynn*
Copy Editor: *Lisanne V. Jensen*

Cartoonist: *Richard King*
Cover Designer: *Kurt Owens*
Book Designer: *Trina Wurst*
Indexer: *Johnna VanHoose Dinse*
Layout: *Brian Massey*
Proofreader: *John Etchison*

Contents at a Glance

Part 1:   **Cosmic Record Keeping**   1

1   The Etheric Library   3
The Akashic Record is a library of all events—past, present, and future. This chapter looks at myths and legends from history and the science of today to understand the purpose and ability of the Record.

2   We Are the Librarians   19
Everyone can access the Akashic Record. This chapter tells you about famous Akashic Record readers and how they worked. It also tells you why you might want to access the Record and how.

3   Written in the Record   33
Everything about your personal journey and that of the universe is written in the Record. This chapter reveals some of the personal information you might find.

4   Akashic Contracts   47
All the people in your life are part of your purpose for being here. This chapter explains what relationships mean to your growth and what types of relationships we have.

5   Destiny, Fate, and Free Will   65
How is the future written in the Record if it hasn't happened? Theories of free will and how it relates to preplanned lessons are explored.

Part 2:   **Pieces of the Akashic Puzzle**   **79**

6   The Unknown Past   81
Legends of past lands and Earth mysteries such as how the pyramids were built are explained by readings from the Akashic Record.

7   Akashic Inspiration   93
The Akashic Record provides inspiration for science, art, and technology. This chapter reveals where this inspiration comes from and shares some inspired breakthroughs from famous people.

8 Clues to Your Akashic Past   107
*Want to know what your past lives were and how they
show themselves in your life today? This chapter gives you
tools for recognizing your past life influences.*

9 Healing the Akashic Past   123
*Unfinished business from the past, old trauma, and
limiting attitudes and beliefs can be eliminated through
Akashic Record healing. This chapter gives you simple
exercises for healing the past.*

Part 3:   The Akashic Present   139

10 Discovering Your Path and Purpose   141
*Everyone is here for a reason. Discovering yours benefits
your relationships, career, and personal growth.*

11 Choosing Your Life Circumstances   155
*Who you were in the past affects who you are today. This
chapter brings continuity between your past lives and
present situation.*

12 Past Loves, Future Partners   167
*Do you wonder if you knew your current love partner
before? This chapter looks at the type of love relationships
we have and how to recognize them.*

13 Akashic Challenges   181
*We agree to the challenges in our life, even the most
difficult. This chapter tells you how and why.*

Part 4:   Akashic Imprints   193

14 Afterlife in the Akashic Field   195
*We do not cease to exist after death. This chapter shares
insights into what the afterlife is like, where you go, and
what you learn.*

15 The Physics of the Future   205
*Quantum physics helps to understand the mechanism of the
Akashic Record and how the future can be seen before it
happens.*

16 Future Passages   217
*Akashic readers, ancient prophecies, and psychics have
made predictions for the future. This chapter looks at what
they say and how we shape our future.*

17 The Akashic Realms   231
*The Akashic Record contains many dimensions of reality.
Here is a mix of ancient text and modern science to explain
them.*

Part 5:   **Keys to the Library**   **243**

18 Tapping Your Psychic Abilities   245
*We all have the ability to tap into the record. This chapter
helps you develop your abilities to access the information you
desire.*

19 Accessing Your Record   259
*Akashic readers and intuitives can help you access your
personal record. This chapter tells you about different kinds
of readers, how to find them, and how to get the most from
your sessions.*

20 Evolution of the Record   273
*The Akashic Record is not static. It's growing and evolving
as we are. This chapter provides insight into the paradigm
shift underway and the new reality we are awakening to.*

Appendixes

A Glossary   285
B Resources   291
   Index   301

Contents

Part 1:   Cosmic Record Keeping   **1**

1   The Etheric Library   **3**

What, How, and Where?..4
   What: Defining Akasha 4
   How: Imprinting Memory 5
   Where: No Single Place 5
Akashic Purpose...6
   Wisdom of the Ages 6
   Personal Soul Record...7
   Universal Consciousness 8
Legends of the Records..9
   Ancient Civilizations 9
   Hindu Philosophy...9
   Theosophy 10
   Modern Mystics 10
   Method and Means 11
Why Consult the Record? 11
   Clues to Your Path and Purpose 12
   Have You Lived Before?...12
   Karmic Lessons and Rewards 13
   Understanding Relationships 13
Science and the Akashic Record..13
   Energy Fields and Frequency 14
   Morphic Fields 15
   Quantum Holography...16

2   We Are the Librarians   **19**

Readers of the Record...20
   Madame Blavatsky...20
   Edgar Cayce 21
   Dion Fortune 22
Accessing the Records...23
   Intuition..23
   Meditation...24
   Channeling 25

Astral Projection..25
Remote Viewing..26
Trusting Your Messages 26
At the Gates..27
Attuning to the Gateway 28
Record Keepers..28
Open Sesame 29
Guiding Soul Evolution 30
Increasing the Capacity for Love 30
Accepting Spiritual Identity 31
Stewards of the Earth 31

3 Written in the Record   33
The Journey..33
The Path of Consciousness 34
The Path of the Soul...35
Your Unique Purpose, Path, and Destiny 35
Reincarnation 36
Theory and Principles..36
Historical Perspective 37
Misconceptions About Reincarnation...................37
Karma and the Akashic Record...............................38
Creating Karma...38
Karmic Score Card..38
People Karma 39
Transmuting Karma 40
The Karmic Shadow...40
Out of the Mouths of Babes 41
Dr. Ian Stevenson..42
Shanti Devi...42
The Story of James Leininger 43
Erin's Story 44
Future Journeys...45

4 Akashic Contracts   47
Akashic Relationships 47
The Purpose of People 49
Key Issues..49
Moving On 51

Love Links...51
    Soul Mates 52
    Twin Souls 52
    Unrequited Love 53
    Difficult Relationships 54
    Lack of Relationship 55
Family Ties...56
    Parents...56
    Siblings...57
    Children 58
Spiritual Contracts..58
    Guidance from Above 59
    Working for the Higher Good 59
    Clearing Mass Karma 60
Strangers and Journeymen.......................................61
    Boss and Employee 62
    Petty Tyrants...62

5 Destiny, Fate, and Free Will   65

Group Karma 65
    Soul Groups..66
    Friends and Company 67
    Pacts..67
    Vows..69
    Nations..69
Timing Is Everything 70
The Challenges of Today..70
    World Economy 71
    Ecological Challenges.....................................72
    Changing Paradigms 73
    Living in the Quantum Paradigm 73
Possibility and Probability: Looking at the Future 74
    Dean Radin..74
    Web Bot Project 75
    Princeton Global Consciousness Project 76
Free Will vs. Fate 76
    Areas of Control 77
    Power of Choice...77

Part 2: Pieces of the Akashic Puzzle   **79**

6 The Unknown Past   **81**

Legendary Lands..81

   Atlantis 82

   Lemuria 83

   Reconciling Past History 84

Ancient Monuments and Societies 85

   Egyptian Pyramids 86

   Egyptian Sphinx 86

   Mayans 87

   Additional Mysteries 88

Spiritual Beings in the Record 88

   Angels, Archangels, and Guardian Angels 89

   Guides 90

   Ascended Masters 90

   Demons 91

Myths and Elemental Beings 91

7 Akashic Inspiration   **93**

The Place of Visions 94

   Accessing Inspiration 94

   Morphic Resonance...95

Inspired Inventions 95

   Simultaneous Inventions 96

   Dream It, Create It 97

Scientific and Medical Breakthroughs 98

   Thought Experiments 98

   Dreaming the Nobel Prize 99

   Developing Your Mind..99

Inspiration and the Arts...100

   Music of the Muses 100

   Akashic Art 101

   Library Literature 102

People Who Changed History 102

   Gandhi 103

   The Hitler Factor 103

Evolutionary Advancement 104

   Advanced Souls 105

   Indigo, Crystal, and Rainbow Kids..............................105

8 Clues to Your Akashic Past **107**

The Living Past.. 107
 Benefits *108*
 Unintended Consequences............................ *109*
 Keeping Notes *110*
Examining Your Preferences 110
 Time Gates.. *111*
 Geography: Land of Imagination...................... *112*
 Historical Figures *112*
 Art and Architecture *113*
 Fashion Sense *113*
Activities and Inclinations 114
 Child's Play *114*
 Career and Hobbies.................................. *115*
 Personality Types *115*
 The Abilities You Were Born With *116*
Emotional and Physical Terrain............................ 116
 Goose Bumps and Butterflies *116*
 Spiders in the Closets *117*
 Instant Likes and Dislikes *117*
 Passionate Bliss *118*
Recurring Patterns.. 118
 Have You Experienced This Before? *119*
 Instant Recognition *119*
 Dreaming Clues *120*
Putting the Pieces Together 120
 A Case in the Civil War *121*
 Desert Destruction *121*
 Your Story.. *122*

9 Healing the Akashic Past **123**

Healing in the Akasha 123
 The Akashic Imprint.................................. *124*
 Blocks to Growth *125*
 The End of "Bad" Karma.............................. *125*
 Finding Core Imprints *126*
The Healing Process.. 126
 Identify the Issue..................................... *127*
 Find the Cause....................................... *128*
 Expand Your Perspective.............................. *129*

Shift Your Energy 129
Willingness to Grow 129
Walking the Healing Path 130
Physical Healing 130
Situational Healing 132
Healing Relationships 133
Changing Patterns 134
Creative Thinking 135
Intentional Thinking 135
Affirmations 136

Part 3:   The Akashic Present   139

10   Discovering Your Path and Purpose   141
Connecting to Your Purpose 141
Meaning 142
Effectiveness 143
Direction 143
Motivation 144
Support 144
Detecting Your Purpose 144
Key Questions 145
Major Life Events 146
Knacks, Talents, and Strengths 147
What Intrigues You? 147
Purposeful Exercises 148
Simple Access to Your Purpose 148
Purposeful Puzzling 149
Write a Mission Statement 150
Staying on the Path 150
Synchronicity 151
Being "in the Flow" 151
What Resistance May Be Telling You 152
Learning the Language 152
Manifesting Purpose 153

11   Choosing Your Life Circumstances   155
Akashic Preparation: Your Life Plan 156
Guidance and Planning 157
Not What You Do, but How You Do It 157

Assessing Your Success 158
  Internal Measure.. 159
  External Measure... 160
Childhood and Family 161
  Desert Destruction, Continued.................................. 162
  Leper's Soul... 163
  Learning from Your Family...................................... 164
The Greatest Gifts.. 164
  Major Life Events 165
  Gifts and Abilities.. 166

12 Past Loves, Future Partners   **167**

The Growth of Love.. 167
  Finding Wholeness... 168
  Spiritual Mastery... 169
  Progression of Relationships.................................... 169
Karmic Relationships 170
  Characteristics of the Karmic Partnership 171
  Karmic Example 171
  Evolving Relationships 172
Soul-Mate Reunions.. 173
  Soul-Mate Timing 174
  The Perfect Fit?... 174
  The Ultimate Betrayal... 175
  Attracting Your Soul Mate 175
  Recognizing Your Soul Mate 176
Twin Flame Soul Mates 177
  Recognizing Your Twin Soul 177
  Potholes Along the Road 177
Animal Partnerships 178
  Animal Reincarnation 178
  Animal Soul Mates.. 179

13 Akashic Challenges   **181**

Understanding Challenges.. 181
  The Path of Rebalancing 182
  The Path of Duty 183
  The Path of Awareness and Healing.............................. 184
  The Path of Sacrifice 184
  The Path of Service... 185

Health Tests 185

Transmuting Health Karma 186

Illness and Disease 186

Childhood Illness 187

Terminal Illness 188

Personal Crises 189

Financial Ruin 189

Addiction 190

Natural Disaster, War, and Mass Murder 191

Akashic Planning 191

Part 4:   Akashic Imprints   193

14   Afterlife in the Akashic Field   195

Into the Spirit World 195

Readings from the Record 196

Hypnotic Regression 196

Electronic Phenomenon 197

Near-Death Experiences and Resuscitation 198

Akashic Record Life Review 199

Visions of the Future 200

Life Before Rebirth 200

Guides 201

Homecoming 202

Input for Life Planning 203

15   The Physics of the Future   205

Shifting Futures 205

Personal Precognition 206

Divination 207

Changing the Future 208

Akashic Mechanics 208

The Mystery of Particles and Waves 209

Probability and Intention 209

Schrödinger's Cat 210

Holographic Access 211

Akashic Predictions 212

Trusting the Future 212

Cayce's Predictions 213

Reading Your Future 214

16   Future Passages   217

These Are the Times 217
  Battle of the Souls... 219
  New Frequency... 219
What the Future May Hold 220
  Mayan Prophecy 221
  The Predictions of Nostradamus....................................... 222
  Remote Viewers 223
Alternate Futures... 223
  Predictions of Destruction 224
  Intercession 224
  Transformation 225
  Empowerment 225
Creating the Future 226
  The Power of Intention 226
  Intentional Visioning 227
  Positive Action 228
  Aligning to Your Highest Ideal.. 228

17   The Akashic Realms   231

Within the Akashic Record 231
  Traditional Planes of Reality 232
  The Multiverse 233
Perceptions of Reality 234
  Experiencing the Record... 235
  Altered States of Consciousness 235
  Multidimensional Awareness... 236
Alien Intelligence 237
  Ancient Astronauts... 237
  Close Encounters 238
  A Different Explanation... 240
  Government Disclosure... 240
Our Place in the Universe 241

Part 5:   Keys to the Library   243

18   Tapping Your Psychic Abilities   245

Science of the Mind 245
  Psi and Quantum Physics 247
  Non-Locality Within the Akashic Field 248
  Entanglement and ESP.. 248

Learning to Access the Akasha...249
   The Qualities of a Good Reader..250
   Starting Your Approach...250
Remotely Sensing the Akasha...251
   How to Remote View..252
   Establishing Targets..252
   Finding the Target..252
   Viewing the Record...253
Tuning Your Channel..253
   Pros and Cons of Channeling...254
   How to Channel...255
Lucid Dreams..256
   Preparing to Dream...257
   Inducing a Lucid Dream...257
   The Benefits of Lucid Dreaming..258

19 Accessing Your Record   259
Appointment with the Akasha...259
   Who Can Benefit?...260
   Why Have a Reading?..261
   Verifying Truth...261
Past-Life Regression..262
   The PLR Session..262
   Your PLR Experience..263
   Professional Training in PLR...264
   Pros and Cons of PLR...264
   Choosing a Therapist...265
Akashic Record Readings..265
   Experiencing an Akashic Reading...266
   Professional Training for Readers..267
   Pros and Cons of Intuitive Sessions......................................267
   Finding Your Intuitive..267
Akashic Additions...268
   Access Through the Body..269
   Future "Regressions"..269
   Dimensional Access...270

20 Evolution of the Record   **273**

   Directions to the New Reality 273
      The Ancient Ones..274
      Meditating on the New Reality 275
      Interspecies Communication 276
   The Human Design 277
      Synchronous Dimensions...277
      Faster Than Time 278
      Opening Perceptions to Higher Realms...............................278
      Psi Awakening..279
      Connecting with the Divine 279
   Surviving Change 280
      The Growth of Love 280
      A Path with Heart 281
   Road Map to the New Paradigm..281
      Dimensional Consciousness..281
      The Singularity Consciousness...282

Appendixes

   A Glossary   **285**

   B Resources   **291**

       Index   **301**

Introduction

If you've never heard of the Akashic Record, you're not alone. However, you've unknowingly had hundreds of interactions with it through the course of your life. It has undoubtedly inspired you, cautioned you, and guided your path. It has spoken to you through the lucid imagery of dreams or whispered to you in the quiet moments of meditation. It has sparked your imagination and stimulated your core truth.

What is the Akashic Record? It's the memory of the universe, an imprint of events on an all-pervasive field of consciousness called the akasha. The Akashic Record receives the vibrational imprint of everything that has ever happened, is happening, and will ever happen. It's more than the record of the history of humankind; all life is accounted for. Every physical, mental, emotional, and spiritual event, and the response to each event, of all forms of life are part of the Record.

Ancient people have shared a widespread belief in a celestial book, tablet, or library that contains the history of humanity and each soul's journey. In the Bible, it's called The Book of Life. Egyptians called it The Hall of Two Truths. Spiritualists called it the Akashic Record or the Hall of Records. Today, the belief continues in scientific theories of quantum holography, morphic resonant fields, and universal consciousness.

On a personal level, the Akashic Record holds the memory of your soul's journey through this life and your past lives, too. It holds the purpose you came here to fulfill and the path you're walking. The Akashic Record is a chronicle of all that you've ever said, thought, intended, or done, in the past and future. It's the record of your soul's evolution.

Most importantly, the Akashic Record is not static. It grows and evolves as creation grows and evolves. It not only holds the memory of your life, but it also interacts with you—stimulating your essence, healing your past, and providing creative inspiration. It permeates your consciousness and inspires your actions. To what end? Enlightenment. The best part is that the Akashic Record is available to you. You are the librarian; you hold the key.

How to Use This Book

This book has five parts, and each contains essential information for your journey into the Akashic Record. The journey into the Record is a journey into your personal past, present, and future.

Part 1, "Cosmic Record Keeping," provides the fundamentals to understanding the Akashic Record. It explains what the Record is, how it works, and what it has to offer you. You'll learn the laws that govern the Record and the basics of accessing it for yourself.

Part 2, "Pieces of the Akashic Puzzle," delves into the history contained in the Akashic Record. It probes the mysteries of lost civilizations and the akashic influence on history. You'll also explore your own hidden past in the Record and use its wisdom for healing old patterns.

Part 3, "The Akashic Present," explores the relevance of the Akashic Record in your present circumstances. You can investigate your path and purpose and understand the circumstances of your life as revealed in the Record. It also looks at relationships and life challenges and supports you in living an authentic life.

Part 4, "Akashic Imprints," looks at the probabilities of the future, new science, and "life between lives." It explores your ability to read and affect the future through the Record and examines higher realms of existence.

Part 5, "Keys to the Library," provides you with tools to read the Akashic Record through the signs around you, your dreams, and altered mind techniques. You'll have everything you need to use the Record to guide your life.

Akashic Revelations

Throughout this text, we give you tips on finding more information, define terms, and add interesting insights and quotes. Here's what to look for:

Etheric Advisory

These boxes warn you of common pitfalls, dangers, and misconceptions.

Akashic Wisdom

Read these boxes for quotes that illuminate, advise, inspire, and amuse.

Timeless Tips

More information on a subject as well as tips on other relevant topics can be found in these boxes.

Library Links

Interesting tidbits of related information, insights, and connecting thoughts are revealed in these boxes.

def•i•ni•tion

These boxes give you definitions of unusual terms and concepts.

Acknowledgments

We wish to acknowledge those who have encouraged and inspired our interest in the field of consciousness that can be called the Akashic Record; some as friends and acquaintances, and others who have inspired us through their published work.

Friends and acquaintances: Pat Delgado, Prof. Gerald Hawkins, Dr. Jean-Noel Aubrun, Prof. James Hurtak, Prof. Desiree Hurtak, Lynn Gladwin, Edgar Mitchell, Uri Geller, Johanna Sayre, Brian Weiss, Dannion Brinkley, Dr. Simeon Hein, Ron Russell, Iris DeMauro, Dr. Steven Greer, Dr. Gale Ramsby, Susan Ramsby, and John White.

Published works: Dr. Karl Pribram, Dr. David Bohm, Prof. Dean Radin, Dr. Michael Talbott, Prof. Harold Puthoff, Prof. Russell Targ, Fred Holmes Atwater, Edward Dames, Ingo Swan, Grahman Hancock, Dr. Candice Pert, and Prof. Rupert Sheldrake.

In addition, Synthia extends her profound thanks and acknowledgement to the many clients who have opened their hearts and minds with her in the exploration of the akasha and given permission for their stories to be told, with changes of name, in this book.

A special thanks to Susan Ramsby, whose library of metaphysics and science rivals the Akashic Record.

Heartfelt appreciation to executive editor Randy Ladenheim-Gil at Alpha Books, to our agent Marilyn Allen for presenting this opportunity, and to the professionals at Alpha Books/Penguin who worked hard to whip things into shape, especially development editor Lynn Northrup, senior production editor Janette Lynn, and copy editor Lisanne Jensen. Thank you all!

Trademarks

Part

Cosmic Record Keeping

The Akashic Record is a holographic memory bank existing in an etheric field of energy. It's a library of events, emotions, thoughts, and intentions of universal consciousness for the past, present, and even the future! In many ways, it's analogous to a spiritual Internet—a highway of interactive information and record keeping.

In this part, you'll find explanations of the Akashic Record in past legend and modern science. You'll have an opportunity to meet people who read the Record and learn about methods to try it yourself. You'll probably be most interested in the relationship contracts made with your soul mate, siblings, and even strangers. Enjoy the journey; there are many insights along the way!

"You may be here for enlightenment, but you still must keep your voice down!"

Chapter 1

The Etheric Library

In This Chapter

- ◆ What is the Akashic Record?
- ◆ What the Record reveals
- ◆ Our purpose and path
- ◆ The Record through the ages
- ◆ What can the Record offer you?
- ◆ Science says …

Imagine a place where you can find the answer to every question you've ever had. Imagine this place holds a record of every event that's ever happened and ever will happen—anywhere in the universe from the very beginning of time to the "end of days." It holds a record of every planet; every development; every person; and every deed, word, thought, emotion, and intent of each person. It's a place that holds the purpose of life and the path of each individual. Imagine we have access to this record. What if this place were more than imagination? How would that change your world?

What, How, and Where?

The belief in a legendary Hall of Records has existed in ancient cultures across the planet. What's more, we can access the records ourselves—any time—to find the answers to our questions. The Akashic Record has been consulted to understand individual people's path and purpose. It has been consulted to understand the purpose of mass atrocities and the reason why groups of people come together. It has been consulted by those wanting to read the pages of the "end of days," meaning the time when souls complete their journey home.

Library Links
The advent of computer technology demonstrates how massive amounts of information can be stored in very small physical spaces. The ability to compress bytes of information and imprint them on electric circuitry is strikingly similar to accounts of the Akashic Record.

Often described as a dimensional library, the Akashic Record contains all the information in the universe. Of course, the descriptions of the Record are metaphors. Originally called "The Book of Life," images evoked to illustrate the Akashic Record have evolved with technology. Descriptions have gone from being a book, to being a library, a super-computer system, and a non-physical magnetic-type field—and currently, the Record is described as a hologram. As we will see, the Akashic Record encompasses all of these descriptions and more.

What: Defining Akasha

Understanding what the Akashic Record is, where it's located, and why it exists is easier when we understand what the term *akasha* means. Akasha is a Hindu word often translated either as sky, space, or ether. Ether is a non-physical substance that is one of the five natural elements in Hindu philosophy. It is the first element and gives rise to the other four which are earth, air, fire, and water. Akasha has more than one translation because none of the words for it represents the full idea of what it is. However, when all the words are considered together, the full meaning begins to emerge.

def•i•ni•tion

Akasha, translated as ether, is one of the five Hindu natural elements of earth, air, fire, water, and ether. It is a non-physical substance that provides the template for physical form. The **Akashic Record** is a non-physical compendium, or encyclopedia, of the history of the universe that is imprinted on the akasha. It includes all the thoughts and actions of every person throughout time.

Akasha is the space that fills the sky, connecting everything within. It's the etheric substance that physical reality is made of. Author Robert Chaney calls it the "cosmic sky" and defines it as "space on a higher vibrational level." By definition, the akasha provides the template and substance of the material world. All things arise out of the akasha—and through it, all things are interconnected.

The *Akashic Record* is the imprint of our memories in the non-physical substance called akasha. The akasha receives the impressions of everything it contacts, and because it is all pervading and contacts everything, it contains an imprint of all that is. Although such a concept sounds implausible, we will see later in the chapter that the possibility fits well with modern scientific thought.

How: Imprinting Memory

The Record is often depicted as a stone tablet, wall, or monument engraved with symbols and glyphs, or pictograms. Each glyph represents an individual imprint—the memory of event or person. The glyphs are inscribed in light. While this imagery awakens something deep within us, it is an allegory communicating the importance of the Record through symbolic form.

To avoid confusion, we refer to the entire Akashic Record as the Record while the imprint of an individual life or event is a file, or memory.

How memory is stored also relates to the term akasha. The name Akashic Record was introduced by the Theosophists in the early 1900s because it matched their ideas of how the universe works and how the Record is created. The term akasha was chosen because the Theosophists believed the universe was made of an invisible substance. They saw the substance as organized in magnetic fields where physical reality existed as vibrations within the field. The Record was an imprint of energetic vibration on the all-pervading, invisible substance of akasha.

Where: No Single Place

Although we use the metaphor of a library, in reality we know the Akashic Record is not inscribed in tablets or kept in a hall with row after row of books. The Record is not a collection of physical objects but a collection of energy vibrations.

Because the akasha holding the imprints is all pervading, the Akashic Record doesn't exist in a single, specified place. It exists within and around everything. Like a hologram, the entire record is contained within every single atom in the micro or atomic level of reality, and within entire galaxies in the macro or cosmic level. It exists in the mind and heart of every being in existence.

Akashic Purpose

You may be wondering why the memory of everything that ever happened, everyone who ever lived, and everything that was ever felt, thought, or done, would be kept at all. Unless the Record entries are to be used for something, what is the point of keeping them? And if they are used for a purpose, whose purpose is it? This is certainly the most perplexing question and also yields the most interesting answers.

There are only two reasons to keep such a record: to learn from it and perhaps even gain from collective wisdom or to keep account of debts and balances. The Bible describes weighing a man's soul at the end of his life by going through The Book of Life and looking at the record of his deeds. If his good deeds outweigh his bad deeds, he goes to heaven. The Egyptians have a similar story where the deceased heart is weighed against the Shu feather of truth and justice. If the heart is heavy with sin, the person is devoured by demons. If the heart is light with truth, he or she passes into the next world. These are examples of keeping a record for debts and balances.

The Hindu philosophy contains the idea of a record of debts and balances in the concept of *karma*. The word karma actually means action; however, it also states that every action has a consequence (some good and some bad). At the time of death, a person goes through a life review and their karmic debt is determined. The conditions of their next incarnation are decided on the basis of their karmic debt or reward, similar to the Biblical saying, "As you sow, so shall you reap."

def•i•ni•tion

> Karma, a word that translates simply as action, is a Hindu belief that every action has a consequence. Good and bad karma are the results of good and bad actions.

Let's take a look at what we might find in the Record and who or what is keeping track!

Wisdom of the Ages

The greatest loss to humanity is the loss of the history of past civilizations and the wisdom they contained. Consider the knowledge required to build the pyramids of Egypt or calculate the Mayan calendar. Do you wonder what wisdom and knowledge was lost in the Library of Alexandria?

Throughout history, civilizations have come and gone—some with no lasting record of their achievements or even of their existence. Much of what we do know is speculation based on examining ruins and languages we can't fully decode. The loss to our understanding of the universe and of our own growth is immeasurable. The past holds the key to the present and the direction of the future.

Fortunately, the Akashic Record holds all the wisdom of the ages. Some people who read from the Record, such as psychic Edgar Cayce (1877–1945), told the history of lost civilizations such as Atlantis and Lemuria. They revealed details of life in the past we could not possibly know. (You'll learn more about Cayce and other akashic readers in Chapter 2.) You may be one of the people who want to learn to access the Record for this reason. Perhaps you lived in one of these civilizations in the past and have returned to uncover their secrets in today's world. Through the use of the Akashic Record, nothing in history is lost forever.

There are many who think we are at a pivotal time in history—a time when the world as we know it can change forever. Like Atlantis, Lemuria, and other ancient civilizations, are we headed for catastrophe? Are we doomed to repeat mistakes of the past simply because we forgot our history? Perhaps the rising interest in the Akashic Record is an answer to these times, inspiring people to look for the history that can guide our path.

Personal Soul Record

The Akashic Record has a special attraction because it holds the record of our own life journey and soul growth. The process of a life review provides the opportunity for a person to grow and learn. It allows each person to examine his or her life and develop awareness of the impact of his or her actions. We can then understand what lessons we have learned and what ones need repeating.

But why wait for a life review to learn valuable soul lessons? It's easy to fall into the trap of thinking the Akashic Record is static and remote. It is neither. It grows and develops with each input. Because the akasha is all pervading, the Record permeates our subconscious. We are in constant interaction with it as it molds our thoughts and actions and directs our growth in consciousness. The trick is to learn how to tune in and consciously retrieve the information needed to become more aware of the direction we are taking and what is motivating our choices. You'll learn ways to do this in Chapter 2 and find instructions in Chapter 18.

Universal Consciousness

We can easily see that the Akashic Record is a vehicle for growth. But is this vehicle only for humans, or is it a vehicle for something larger?

The Akashic Record extends far beyond individuals and even beyond the human race. It is more than a record of the history of mankind. The Akashic Record also provides a link to spiritual realms. Many seek the presence of angels, guides, and other high-energy beings that are part of every religion and mythology. Every sentient being contributes to the Record, and all consciousness on all levels is contained within it. Every physical event and the response to each event from all forms of life are part of the Record.

If the purpose of the Record is growth and it contains all possible combinations of events and responses, then the Record itself is evolving. It changes with the interactions of all that is within it. Does this mean the Record itself is conscious?

Through the ages, in many religions and philosophies, the idea exists that the universe is an interconnected whole that is ordered, interactive, and conscious. We normally define consciousness as self-awareness, or awareness of our own existence. Does the idea of a conscious universe imply that the universe is self-aware—that it has sentience? Is the Akashic Record just another name for consciousness? We can begin to see that understanding the Akashic Record involves a deeper understanding of the universe as a whole and of consciousness as well.

Akashic Wisdom

A human being is a part of a whole, called by us universe, a part limited in time and space. He experiences himself, his thoughts and feelings, as something separated from the rest—a kind of optical delusion of his consciousness. This delusion is a kind of prison for us, restricting us to our personal desires and to affection for a few persons nearest to us. Our task must be to free ourselves from this prison by widening our circle of compassion to embrace all living creatures and the whole of nature in its beauty.

—Albert Einstein, *The World as I See It* (1949)

Legends of the Records

Every culture makes reference to the existence of a record of the soul's journey or a place to go for spiritual guidance. While we can't claim this is proof they believed in the Akashic Record, reference to some kind of record of knowledge exists in folklore, myth, and legend.

Many think that sages, shamans, priests, and mystics around the world—past and present—have tapped into the Akashic Record for their spiritual guidance and knowledge. Written in Mayan codices are accounts of how the mathematician priests obtained the calculations for their spectacular calendars. In some accounts, they left their bodies and traveled to the heart of the galaxy—receiving information directly from the planetary gods. However, you don't have to be specially designated to access this knowledge. Anyone can be trained, and many people have a special knack for it. Some people are able to do it without any training and often provide readings for others.

Ancient Civilizations

The Judeo-Christian religion called it "The Book of Life," the Egyptians called it the "Hall of Two Truths," and the Theosophists called it the Akashic Record. Different cultures may use different names, but the essence is the same. Although we can't claim that past cultures were definitely accessing the Akashic Record, certainly they consulted oracles for guidance. Accounts of accessing higher knowledge exist with the Celtic Druids, the Tibetan Lamas, Middle Eastern people, the Ancient Mayans, and Native Americans.

We can say that among the Assyrians, Phoenicians, Babylonians, Hebrews, and Greeks was a common belief in the existence of tablets where spiritual wisdom and the Book of Life resided. Hebrew and Christian traditions talk about the Book of Life as holding the name and record of everyone who has lived. However it is described, it seems that many cultures believed in and accessed records for guidance.

Hindu Philosophy

The term akasha comes from Hindu philosophy. Although the Akashic Record is not spoken of in Hindu writings, the belief in karma presupposes a means of taking account of actions and consequences. The Upanishads are the spiritual writings of Hinduism and are believed to be 3,000 years old.

Two aspects of Hinduism have been especially important in the understanding of the Akashic Record:

◆ The awareness written in the Upanishads that self-consciousness is an extension of the consciousness of Brahman, or God. There is no distinction between the two; they are, in fact, continuous (what exists in one exists in the other). Like the Akashic Record, they are interpenetrating.

◆ The Hindu religion focuses on meditation and self-discipline to shift states of awareness for spiritual connectivity. Through these methods, altered states of consciousness can be attained. Everything you need already exists within; all you need to do is shift your awareness to access it.

Theosophy

Theosophists are responsible for opening the door to our current understanding of the Akashic Record by combining the concept of akasha with the long-standing notion of the existence of spiritual records and laws. Theosophists accessed the Akashic Record to uncover mystical knowledge encoded in the non-physical plane of akasha.

Theosophy is a metaphysical philosophy developed by Madame Helena Blavatsky (1831–1891). Blavatsky popularized many ideas prevalent in today's thinking about consciousness and spirituality, and coined the term "Akashic Record." She brought forward ideas of reincarnation, karma, the presence of a higher self, and the idea of universal consciousness. She founded the Theosophical Society to promote her ideas and train people in accessing the Record for themselves. The Theosophical Society still operates today. (Read more about Madame Blavatsky and other New Age pioneers in Chapter 2 and karma and reincarnation in Chapter 3.)

Modern Mystics

There is no shortage today of people who are accessing the Akashic Record to improve people's lives. People from many countries, walks of life, and religious persuasions have found themselves in the presence of greater knowledge. Certainly one of the most famous is Edgar Cayce, the "Sleeping Prophet" from Virginia. More than anyone else, Cayce has brought the Akashic Record into everyday conversation.

Everyone who reads the Record adds to the collective understanding and opens the door further for those who come next. As the whole of the Record is part of each person, each person contributes back to the whole his or her unique, interactive perspective.

Method and Means

An interesting similarity among different cultures is the method and process they use to access the Record. Descriptions include inducing an altered state of consciousness. The person reading the Record typically enters an altered state before they are invited into the Hall of Records.

Here are some examples:

- The Mayans smoked special tobacco and went into trances where they "walked among the stars."

- At the Delphi Oracle in Greece, the priestesses went into a trance before a smoking dais and answered questions.

- The Hindu tradition uses meditation to enter different levels of awareness.

- In the Old Testament, people were "taken up in spirit" to receive instruction from Yahweh.

- Edgar Cayce fell into a sleeping trance.

Whatever the method, an altered state of awareness is part of accessing the Record. We learn more about this topic in Chapters 2 and 18.

> **Library Links**
>
> Attaining an altered state of consciousness doesn't require entering a trance. When we dream, we are in an altered state—and in fact, many people get information from the Record through their dreams. Meditation and contemplation also change brainwave states, altering consciousness.

Why Consult the Record?

Maybe you're curious about the Record and wonder what it has to offer you. At this point, it should be clear that the Akashic Record has a tremendous influence on many aspects of our everyday lives. It influences our feelings and actions, feeds our attitudes and beliefs, and attracts our circumstances, both good and bad.

The Record holds our dreams and inspirations and molds our aspirations. It also contains the patterns that hold us back, creating the challenges we must confront in order to live our lives fully and completely. The goal we are all seeking is to be our authentic spiritual selves.

In determining our way in life, we can find many insights in the Akashic Record. Most of the time, learning to access the Record yourself is a potent tool for empowerment.

However, there are times when having someone else read on your behalf may be a better choice. Some issues are hard for us to see, and an impartial observer can help clarify the information. Also, the Record can elicit powerful emotions. Another person can help you process and grow from the experience.

Let's take a look at some of the many types of information that can be found in the Akashic Record.

Clues to Your Path and Purpose

Certainly, the most common reason people consult the Record is to find their path and purpose in life. Many people have a strong sense that they have a purpose but no idea of what it is or how to find it. Some people know their purpose but feel unable to manifest it. Both situations are especially prevalent for young people right now as changing economic conditions are narrowing options.

What the Record reveals is that everyone is here at the right time and in the right place. No one is an accident, and everyone's life has purpose and meaning. Each period in history has its own specific challenges and opportunities. If you're having a hard time seeing yours, accessing the Akashic Record is a good way to get insight.

Have You Lived Before?

Many people wonder if they have lived more than one life. Maybe you remember things from previous times that you couldn't know unless you were there. Maybe you feel an affinity for a place you've never seen. Reincarnation frequently is part of the information retrieved in Akashic Record readings. Intrinsic to the idea of recording one's journey through life and having a life review is the concept that we will have an opportunity to correct our mistakes and pay our karmic debt.

> **Etheric Advisory**
>
> Seeking information from the Akashic Record can have a profound impact on your life. Becoming responsible for all your actions and circumstances is the ultimate outcome, but reaching this level of integrity can create its own challenges! Approach the Record with respect.

The Akashic Record almost always helps put this life into perspective by providing details from past lives. Past life information helps us understand repeating patterns, the quality of our relationships, and the circumstances of our present life. It also helps us understand the issues and what retribution is underway.

Karmic Lessons and Rewards

The circumstances of our lives are not a judgment of how great our souls are. They are, however, a reflection of lessons we need to learn and inner resources we're trying to develop. Another main reason why people seek readings from the Record is to understand the dynamics at work in their lives. If you've suffered many challenges, you may want to consult the Record to see past patterns and discover what you need to learn to move beyond.

As well as having challenges, each of us comes with gifts and abilities that come easily to us. Not too many people question where their gift comes from or why they have it. They just use it and enjoy having it. However, how many people do you know who have wasted the gifts they were given? The Record can also provide insight into where your gifts have come from and what you are expected to do with them in this lifetime.

Understanding Relationships

This area is certainly the second, if not the first, reason for an Akashic Record consult. The most rewarding experience in life is a true-love relationship where partners feel the utmost respect for and devotion to each other. Believe it or not, these relationships do exist. Whether they are in the cards for you or not is not a matter of whether your karma will allow it; rather, it's a question of whether you're willing to face your fears and grow beyond them. Many times, the reason for not finding your soul mate (who does exist!) is locked in past memories that need healing.

Chapters 4 and 12 reveal more information on soul mate relationships and how to attract yours. Don't make the mistake of thinking soul-mate relationships are perfect; they come with their own set of challenges and rewards.

Of course, love relationships are not the only ones we struggle with. Family dynamics, authority figures, and work relationships may all be areas you want to clarify in an Akashic Record reading. You'll learn more about these relationships in Chapter 4.

Science and the Akashic Record

There is no way science can prove the existence of the Akashic Record. However, as science delves more deeply into our understanding of nature, the idea of a conscious universe becomes more acceptable. In addition, as scientists understand more about the quantum fields that organize matter, vibrational imprints become a reality. Put that together with holographic understanding, and the framework for something like an Akashic Record exists.

Library Links

Many scientists describe receiving inspiration in meditative states. For example, Friedrich August Kekule is the scientist who discovered the circular structure of the benzene molecule. He describes making his discovery after having a vision, or daydream, where he saw a snake seizing its own tail. Was he accessing the Akashic Record?

Obviously, theoretical plausibility does not create proof. However, it is interesting to see the places where science and metaphysics begin to view reality in the same descriptive framework.

Energy Fields and Frequency

The ground-breaking equation of Albert Einstein—$E=MC^2$—forever changed how we view the material world. This equation states that there is no difference between energy and matter except their speed; they are the same things just vibrating at different rates. The continuum of matter into energy that we can measure is called the electromagnetic spectrum.

All that exists in the physical world is an expression of electromagnetic energy. In the following diagram, you can see that everything—houses, people, radioactive material, and more—has its own range of frequency expressed within. Even our organs have a specific frequency, which is the basis of medical tests such as the electrocardiogram (EKG) that records the frequency of the heartbeat and the electroencephalogram (EEG) that records the frequency of brainwaves. Actually, thoughts and emotions express in their own frequencies, too.

Radio	Microwave	Infrared	Visible light	UV	X-ray	Gamma
10^3	10^{-1}	10^{-4}	10^{-6} Wave Length 10^{-7}		10^{-11}	10^{-12}

AM radio	FM radio	Microwave oven	Radar	People	Light bulb	X-ray Machine ◄SOURCES

Soccer field	Baseball House	Flea	Cell Bacteria	Virus Protein	Water molecule	

Longer	Size of Wave Length	Shorter

Everything we can measure exists within the electromagnetic spectrum.

Matter is organized within fields of energy. The field of gravity organizes life forms to grow in an upward direction. Magnetic fields organize magnetized particles along lines of force. Frequency can be coded on carrier waves within an energy field the way a radio station codes the frequency of its programs on radio waves. Another example is the way cell phones code your conversation on microwaves to send them through space. Can our understanding of energy, energy fields, and frequency explain the Akashic Record?

Morphic Fields

The morphic field is a theory of species development proposed by contemporary English biologist Rupert Sheldrake. He suggests that each species exists within its own vibrational niche in an energy field that stores our evolutionary patterns. The morphic field holds a record of everything learned from each member of a species, including humans, and makes up our collective past. Everything learned or experienced by one of us is available to all of us through a process called *resonance*. Morphic fields can be thought of as invisible fields of memory encoded in all living things. This sounds a lot like the Akashic Record, where each memory is stored as a specific vibration.

def•i•ni•tion

Resonance is the transmission and amplification of frequency within a field of energy. You may have experienced this when playing a musical instrument. For example, if you strum the C note on a harp in one octave, all the C notes in all octaves will vibrate.

Sheldrake claims that each time a person has a specific thought or behavior, it becomes easier for the next person to access that vibration or behavior. When enough individuals are tuned in to a piece of information and it has changed their behavior, it becomes prevalent enough to influence the behavior of everyone. This concept is known as the Hundredth Monkey Effect. It purportedly was observed on an island where one monkey began a new food behavior. His behavior was copied by the monkeys around him. Once a certain number of monkeys exhibited the behavior, all monkeys of the species everywhere—even off the island—were seen using the behavior. It's also the idea of critical mass. Once an idea is in use by enough people, everyone suddenly knows it.

How different is this theory from the Akashic Record? The Record is said to store all the emotions, thoughts, theories, ideas, beliefs, actions, and behaviors of every individual in the form of frequency. The Record is interactive, and through resonance, influences our growth and development. Beliefs that are shared by many people have a stronger presence in the Record and influence the action of others. Your record is easier for you to read than someone else's because you are more resonant with it;

Etheric Advisory

The Hundredth Monkey Effect is a popular theory and describes real phenomena; however, the actual study that is the source of the theory has reportedly been exaggerated. Be sure to check all points of view.

however, we can tune in to anything that has ever been recorded. Tuning in to a common theme in the Record boosts our mindset, good or bad. In this way, common themes and beliefs have greater impact on society. This explains both "an idea whose time has come" and mob mentalities.

Sheldrake's theory is that everything—not just people but the entire universe—is learning, and our learning is shared.

Quantum Holography

A helpful construct for thinking about energy fields and consciousness is the hologram. When holograms were discovered, they changed how scientists viewed both the universe and our brain's capacity to process information. The use of holograms has become quite common in our everyday world. We see holographic ID cards, advertisements, stickers, and knick-knacks in every store. They have become so commonplace that we rarely think of what they really are and limit them to simply a three-dimensional photograph.

Akashic Wisdom

Stanford neurophysiologist Dr. Karl Pribram believes memories are encoded not in neurons, or small groupings of neurons, but in patterns of nerve impulses that criss-cross the entire brain in the same way that patterns of laser-light interference criss-cross the entire area of a piece of film containing a holographic image. In other words, Pribram believes the brain is itself a hologram.

—Michael Talbot, *The Holographic Universe* (1992)

To make a holographic photograph, an object is illuminated with a laser beam. A laser beam differs from regular light in that it has a high level of coherence among the light photons. Photon coherence is the reason for a laser's brilliance. A second laser beam is bounced off the reflected light of the first laser beam, creating an interference pattern where the two beams intersect. The interference pattern is captured on film. The developed film looks like a meaningless swirl of lines. When these meaningless swirls are illuminated with a third laser beam, however, a three-dimensional image of the original object appears. Have you ever looked at a Magic Eye picture? They appear to be a series of wavy lines on a page with no meaning. However, when looked at with a certain eye focus they suddenly become three-dimensional pictures. This utilizes the principles of holography with your brain acting as a laser beam and creates the coherence of a three-dimensional picture.

Its three-dimensional quality is not the most important aspect of the hologram. What is most remarkable is how information is contained in the picture. If a holographic picture of an image is cut in half and then illuminated by a laser, you don't have two halves of the picture as you would if you tore an ordinary photograph in half. Instead, each half contains the entire image. If the halves are divided again, each piece still contains a smaller but intact version of the original image. In fact, every part of a hologram contains all the information possessed by the whole.

Holography has changed scientists' views of nature, consciousness, and the universe, as well as the functioning of our brains. It's called nature's information system. It also provides a framework for us to understand the Akashic Record. It seems the more science learns about nature, the more reasonable mystical knowledge becomes!

The Least You Need to Know

- The Akashic Record contains the past, present, and future "memory" of everything and everyone in the universe, including thoughts, actions, emotions, and intent.

- We can all learn to access the Akashic Record because it exists within and around us as it does with everything in the universe.

- Within the Record you can find the wisdom of lost civilizations, your personal soul journey, and universal consciousness.

- The Akashic Record provides insight into your challenges and opportunities, including your love relationships.

- Current scientific models of holography and morphic resonance provide a plausible framework for the existence of the Akashic Record.

Chapter 2

We Are the Librarians

In This Chapter

- ◆ Who are the readers of the Akashic Record?
- ◆ Developing your ability to read the Record
- ◆ Accessing the different levels
- ◆ Your guardians and guides
- ◆ Steps in soul evolution

Many people have dreams of the Akashic Record and being shown the book of their life. Some describe reading about difficult moments in their past from an enlightened perspective that helps them understand its importance to their soul growth. Some see a past life unfold as if watching a movie. All who come in contact with the Record report a similar message: that each of us is responsible for and to our own record and that our personal record will be protected by guides until we are spiritually ready to use the information we find. Our individual record is the greatest tool we have for personal development.

Readers of the Record

People are often as curious about those who can read the Record as they are about what is contained within. There is no mystique, however; the readers are essentially the same as you and me. The difference is that they have developed their intuitive skills and applied them in this area. Some work hard to develop the necessary skills; some discover their ability through some type of trauma or incident of self-discovery; and others are born with these abilities intact from a past life.

In the early nineteenth century, a lot of interest was generated in the Akashic Record. With new metaphysical ideas flourishing in both Europe and America, a number of people entertained the ability to read the Record. They revealed remarkably similar information about the history of the planet and the spiritual development of the soul.

Timeless Tips

To find an Akashic Record consultant today, do an online search for the key words "akashic readers" or look in local publications that deal with natural health, metaphysics, or New Age philosophy. You can find more information on finding a reader in Chapter 19.

Three people—Madame Blavatsky, Edgar Cayce, and Dion Fortune—were leading lights in metaphysics from about 1870 to 1950. They disseminated tremendous amounts of metaphysical and spiritual information that became the basis of the New Age movement. Their lives reflect different methods of reading the Record and different means of attaining the necessary skill. Today, there are hundreds of people who claim to have the ability—but none has revealed more information for individuals and humanity than these three.

While working with the Akashic Record, both Madame Blavatsky and Dion Fortune claimed to be in direct communication with higher beings who provided information and guided their paths. In contrast, Edgar Cayce was a channel who allowed higher beings, including his own higher self, to speak through him. (A person's higher self is his or her spiritual essence that resides in higher realms and has awareness beyond the physical.) Afterward, Cayce remembered nothing of the information he provided.

Madame Blavatsky

Madame Helena Blavatsky was born in Russia in 1831 and from an early age had a strong desire to understand spiritual truth. She spent many years traveling around the world studying religious teachings in many different cultures. She died in England in 1891 after introducing the Western world to Eastern mysticism. According to legend,

Blavatsky was initiated in Eastern philosophy in Tibet where she spent two years receiving training by Tibetan masters.

Madame Blavatsky is considered the pioneer of current metaphysical thought. She cofounded the Theosophical Society in 1875 in New York City to spread her teachings of spiritual law, which included the doctrine of reincarnation and karma, the power of thought, the presence of ascended masters, and of course the existence of the Akashic Record. The word "theosophy" means "knowledge of the divine" and is claimed to be part of ancient wisdom teachings.

Madame Blavatsky developed her ability through meditation and breathing practices. She delved into the Akashic Record to find deeper levels of metaphysical wisdom and knowledge. She wrote many books on universal spiritual laws, the human energy system (chakras and auras), the history of past civilizations, and the development of the soul. Rudolf Steiner, founder of the Waldorf school system, was one of her students and was an accomplished Akashic Record reader. Many of his theories on biodynamic farming, education, and architecture came from the Akashic Record.

Timeless Tips

Madame Blavatsky, Edgar Cayce, Dion Fortune, and Rudolf Steiner all founded educational institutions that are still in existence today. You can contact them through the following websites:

- Theosophical Society: theosophical.org or www.blavatsky.net
- Edgar Cayce's Association for Research and Enlightenment: www.edgarcayce.org
- Society of the Inner Light: www.innerlight.org.uk
- Anthroposophical Society: www.anthroposophy.org

Edgar Cayce

Edgar Cayce was born on a farm in Kentucky in 1877 and died in 1945. He showed unusual abilities throughout his childhood, such as talking to spirits and displaying telepathic abilities. He studied for exams at school by placing books under his pillow at night. In the morning, it's claimed he knew all the information in the book!

Cayce didn't discover the extent of his abilities until 1901, when he developed a severe and long-lasting case of laryngitis. In desperation, he agreed to be put into a hypnotic trance to affect a cure. While in the trance, he uncovered his ability to heal by accessing the Akashic Record. Cayce was raised as a Christian and was devout in his religious beliefs. Initially, it was very hard for him to accept the information revealed through his readings—especially information such as reincarnation that contradicted Bible teachings.

For more than 40 years, Cayce gave readings to thousands of people. He diagnosed and treated illnesses, provided past life readings and future prophecy, described the human energy structures, detailed the history of past civilizations such as Atlantis and Lemuria, and discerned spiritual law. His information was strikingly similar to Blavatsky and Steiner, including information on the existence of the Akashic Record itself. He often called the Record "God's Book of Remembrance," and he claimed it holds the answers to the nature of the universe and each individual's past, mission, and purpose.

Cayce read the Akashic Record by lying down and meditating. He immediately went into a sleeping trance. While in the trance, he channeled higher beings who answered any question put to them on any topic. Upon waking, he had no memory of what transpired, earning him the title "Sleeping Prophet." Other titles he has been given include "Father of Holistic Medicine" and "Father of the New Age." Cayce is without a doubt the most prolific and studied psychic ever.

Dion Fortune

Born in England, Dion Fortune (1890–1946) was a natural intuitive, possessing *clairvoyant* and *clairaudient* abilities at the early age of five. Dion read the Akashic Record in a manner similar to that of Edgar Cayce. Unlike Cayce, however, she did not undergo any trauma that set off her abilities but had access to them at a young age. Also unlike Cayce, she maintained conscious awareness when she accessed the Record and claims to have consciously negotiated the etheric planes. Her technique for reading the Record consisted of willfully projecting her consciousness into the etheric realms, a process known as astral projection.

def•i•ni•tion

Clairvoyance, or inner vision, is the ability to see information through visions or seeing the realms of divine energy. **Clairaudience**, or inner listening, is the ability to hear messages from the spirit realms or inner self.

Accessing the Records

Each of us has access to the Record because we participate in creating it. Realistically, very few of us develop the ability to read the Record. This may be due to the fact that it takes more than skill; it requires a certain degree of spiritual discernment.

The Akashic Record goes beyond theories of energy and matter to a quantum world of vibrational holography and provides the mechanism for extra-sensory perception (ESP) such as telepathy. Reading minds or knowing what is about to happen is possible because we can tune in to the field of vibration within the akasha. In developing the ability to access the Record, people generally develop their psychic skills first, but the Record has more to offer than enhanced abilities. In addition, the akasha can reveal your soul's path, purpose, mission, and destiny. Reading the Record provides intensely significant and life-changing information.

> ### Etheric Advisory
>
> Not everyone who claims to read the Akashic Record is on the level. Watch out for people who say they will solve your problems or direct your decisions. Also, watch out for those who require additional sums of money for every question you have. Always test the information you receive against your own gut feelings. If it feels wrong, it probably is.

Contacting the Record requires engaging your intuition and paying attention to your felt senses through quieting the mind. You can then develop different techniques to connect with the Record. Methods for connecting with the Akashic Record include channeling, astral projection, and remote viewing. After reading about each of these, you may have an idea of which one will work best for you. Before looking at the methods, let's look more closely at understanding intuition and meditation.

Intuition

Intuition is often called the sixth sense. According to astronaut Edgar Mitchell, one of a handful of people who has walked on the moon and seen Earth from space, intuition is actually our first sense. At its most essential level, intuition is the gut feeling that guides our perceptions—the basic nature within us all. It's the hunches and insight we gain not from information but from the feel of a situation.

Intuition is our direct access to the Akashic Record. It comes from a place deep inside that is connected to our own super-consciousness. Our super-consciousness is a small part of universal consciousness. Accessing the Record is possible simply by quieting your mind and going deep inside. By maintaining a focused, receptive, non-judging state of mind, any of us can link to the Record.

Meditation

Meditation is a practice of quieting the mind and shifting from our normal state of awareness to a more focused and internal state of awareness. Changing levels of awareness corresponds to changing brain wave frequencies, or brain states. There are four basic brain states, which we all experience every day:

◆ **Beta** is the brain state we're in during our typical daily activity.

◆ **Alpha** is the state that occurs when our body is deeply relaxed yet our brain maintains a sharp and focused awareness. Alpha is the first state induced in meditation practices.

◆ **Theta** states are deeper, more relaxed states where we lose our sense of being in a physical body and our brain produces visions that seem as if we're living them. We naturally experience theta every day just before falling asleep and just before waking from sleep. With practice, we can induce theta states through meditation. Theta is the most productive state of awareness for accessing the Record.

◆ **Delta** is our typical sleep state and often the accidental result of meditation.

Timeless Tips _____

There are many cool devices that can train you to shift your brain states and level of awareness at will. The Wild Divine is an affordable home computer program that easily teaches you to change your awareness using guided imagery programs combined with biofeedback. This product is highly recommended for the serious beginner! Learn more at www.wilddivine.com.

Generating different brain states is a common practice. For example, stress- and anger-management techniques teach people how to induce alpha states. People are trained to induce delta states for insomnia, and theta states are often induced prior to intuitive work.

There are many practices that allow us to quiet and focus the mind, such as breathing techniques, yoga, meditation, and self-hypnosis. A prerequisite to any technique is attitude and belief. You must be able to set aside your self-critic and allow yourself to be a witness rather than a judge. Allow images and feelings to arise, and follow them rather than judging them.

The following techniques are frequently used to access the Record and all require you to shift your awareness for success.

Channeling

Channeling is the process of allowing a higher intelligence to communicate information through you. People channel ascended masters, angels, their own higher selves, alien intelligence, and spirits who have died—and of course, all exist within the Akashic Record.

The benefit of channeling is that you separate your conscious mind from the information being downloaded, reducing the possible inflection of your own bias. A person can be a conscious channel and be aware of what he or she is saying without control of it, or a trance channel such as Edgar Cayce with no awareness of the information he or she is speaking and no memory of it afterward.

Astral Projection

Astral projection relies on the belief that we are more than a physical body negotiating material reality. We also have subtle energy bodies we use to travel in the world of spirit. The astral body is one of the subtle energy bodies capable of traveling in the astral, or etheric, energy plane.

When you're astral projecting, your awareness leaves your physical body. You may look back and see yourself lying on your bed. The view is often looking down from the ceiling or some other height. Your astral body and your physical body stay connected through a silver cord that is anchored at the umbilicus. Most people see the silver cord, and it gives them a sense of safety—knowing they will never get lost from their body. This out-of-body experience allows your

Timeless Tips

Astral travel can be challenging to learn on your own. An excellent place to receive training is The Monroe Institute in Virginia. They offer safe, guided expertise either as onsite training or through audio programs. You can reach them online at www. monroeinstitute.org.

awareness to travel anywhere, including the Akashic Record, to retrieve information. Dion Fortune used astral projection extensively in her work with the Record.

Many people believe that we all astral project at night in our dreams. Clues that you have been out of your body include feeling paralyzed, hearing a buzzing sound, or feeling vibrations throughout your body. These are signs that you are either getting ready to leave or have just returned. For some people, leaving their body is scary. If you find this to be true for you, remote viewing may be a better choice.

Remote Viewing

Another method for reading the Akashic Record and witnessing events of the past, present, or future is remote viewing. This technique was developed at the Stanford Research Institute and has been used in CIA intelligence-gathering programs. Actually, it's a form of clairvoyance that is induced through a simple protocol.

Timeless Tips

There are many places you can go to learn remote viewing techniques. One of our favorite programs is through Dr. Simeon Hein and Ron Russell. You can see their training schedule at www.mountbaldy.com/mbi/.

This is an easy and safe technique. It doesn't require leaving your body or giving another being the use of your body to transmit information. Instead, it relies on connecting with your holographic nature. In a hologram, all the information in the whole exists in each part. You have inside yourself all the information about everything in the universe. Accessing it is a technique. Although some people are better at it than others, with practice anyone can become proficient. You can learn a basic technique in Chapter 18, although professional training programs can help you maximize your skill.

Remote viewing allows you to extend your awareness to other places and times by going deeply inside yourself. On a screen in your mind, you can watch events unfold, ask questions, and receive insight into intentions and motivations.

Trusting Your Messages

Whatever method you use, it takes time to develop discernment with the information you get. In general, your first hit on something will be the most accurate. Try to trust your first impression and not overthink your answer. When you start to doubt and think about the "right" result, your outcome will more likely reflect your own bias.

This is true even when receiving a reading from a professional. Everyone deciphers information through their personal filters, and to some degree what they see reflects their belief system. This is especially important if the reader is deciphering glyphs and symbols. Typically, a reader will see the symbols and feel their meaning or hear an interpretation. There's a lot of room for their own bias to be projected onto the information. Always test the information you receive against your own gut reaction. We'll talk more about this in Chapter 19.

Library Links

Colin is an excellent remote viewer. After the Beltway sniper attacks in the Baltimore-Washington-Virginia area in October 2002, Colin remotely viewed the situation. He saw the face of one of the snipers and drew a sketch of the person. Days later, two men were caught. Colin's sketch matched the face of the young teenager, Lee Boyd Malvo, with remarkable detail.

At the Gates

Are you wondering what it's like to arrive at the Hall of Records or how you'll get inside? Although everyone's experience is unique, there are some hallmark descriptions.

First, let's make a distinction between different levels of access. The Record is an imprint on a holographic field. Every time we follow our intuition, we are essentially "reading" the akasha. This level of access is available to everyone all the time. The only thing that's required is that we pay attention to our gut feelings, perceptions, and senses.

Witnessing events from the past, present, or future is an intermediate level of access. Usually, people require some sort of procedure or protocol—although many simply have a talent.

The deepest level of access to the Record allows us to read past lives, soul purpose, and future destiny. You will not be able to access this depth of information unless you are attuned to spiritual principle. Reading the Record at this depth requires training and practice, although you may have natural ability that you have retained from an earlier life. You may also receive guidance in how to do this from ascended masters or spiritual guides. To gain access to the Record at this level requires internal congruency and spiritual integrity.

Attuning to the Gateway

People describe approaching the Record and being met by the Keepers of the Record. You may see them as beings or feel them as a presence. People say they hear a message or simply just know that they can have access to the Record only if they are responsible with the information they receive. This is important. Information we're not ready for can destroy us or others.

> ### Akashic Wisdom
>
> I dreamed I was walking along a path in a dark forest following a tall, radiant being with long white hair and robes. We entered a clearing where 12 other light-beings stood in a circle. They bowed and parted to open the circle, allowing us to pass inside. A podium stood in the center holding a large book opened to a specific page. Light poured out of the book. My guide gestured that I should look inside. The page was covered in glyphs that were scribed in ink made of light. I knew this was my page and each glyph represented an event in my past, and my future, too. I was told I would understand the glyphs when I knew how to use the information.
>
> —Synthia, author

The Keepers of the Record ensure that others do not gain access to your record without your permission. No one can read your private thoughts and intentions except you, unless you ask someone to. Your development is your private journey, and privacy in the Record is respected.

There is a key to entering the library. You must be attuned to the information you seek. Attunement happens through resonance. If you're not in resonance, or alignment, with the information you seek, you won't be able to receive it.

There are two ways someone other than yourself can access your record. First, ask someone whether they can tune in to your frequency and find you in the Record. The level of access they have will depend on their level of spiritual awareness and the questions you're asking. Second, the parts of your life story that are "public record" and interweave with other people's stories can be read as a chain of historical events. These parts will not include your private thoughts and feelings.

Record Keepers

The guardians of the Record are often called the Record Keepers or simply the Guides. They are said to be twelve timeless beings who have taken on the task of guarding the sacred Hall. They not only guide people to their own record and ensure that no one trespasses on another's record, but they also interpret information.

The Keepers are typically described as tall with long flowing robes, hair, and beards. They emanate wisdom and love. They guide, protect, and maintain the Record. Because the Record is essentially cosmic consciousness, or the field of creation, the task is awesome indeed! These beings have been described as the Twelve Pillars that maintain reality.

In addition to guiding you to your part of the record, the Keepers can help you translate the information you receive. Events are imprinted as they happen, and discerning what they mean requires skill. The wisdom and guidance of the Keepers can offer an enlightened understanding of events that were confusing and overwhelming when they occurred.

Open Sesame

There is only one way to enter the Hall of Records, and that is through the vibration of compassion and love. It is only through compassion that we can attune to and understand higher levels of truth.

When we approach the Keepers with humility, the earnest desire for truth, and compassion in the face of all the lessons we have learned, they show us how to obtain the record we seek. The records are reportedly written in a language of light—also called sacred geometry, that also contains a corresponding sound. You may intuitively understand the language of light and sound, or it may be translated for you. Many people see images as if watching a movie. However you receive the information, you will only see that which can be helpful to you at this time. You won't see the entire record of your soul's journey unless it's useful information for you.

Akashic Wisdom

Love and compassion are necessities, not luxuries. Without them, humanity cannot survive.

—His Holiness the 14th Dalai Lama

It's important to understand that your individual soul record is a record of *your* actions, *your* thoughts, *your* emotions, *your* intentions, and *your* perceptions. It does not represent ultimate truth; rather, it represents your experience. Finding the higher meaning is part of your soul journey.

Guiding Soul Evolution

According to the Record, the purpose of life is soul evolution and the purpose of the Record is to guide this process. The Akashic Record creates the playing field of matter. Without matter, we as souls cannot learn and without a record of what we've learned, we cannot grow and evolve. People such as Edgar Cayce and Madame Blavatsky have written volumes on soul evolution in the Akashic Record. What they say is essentially the same as that of every religion and spiritual teaching: we fell from the garden of Eden, and we are spending a lot of time trying to get back!

Edgar Cayce describes individual souls as points of light that separate from their source. Although souls are part of a larger whole, they decide to separate into individual identities in order to gain experience. Complete separation, however, is a fantasy. We are always connected. What souls learn along this path is that power for the sake of power is an illusion. Material gain for the sake of material comfort does not bring joy. Knowledge without love is meaningless. Souls learn that true fulfillment does not come at another's expense because we are, in fact, one.

Library Links
Many religious books, such as parts of the Bible, describe an altered state of consciousness where the writer was shown truths they later reveal in scripture.

Increasing the Capacity for Love

Every teaching from every culture emphasizes love as the most important force in the universe. Love is more than the sentimental attachments we have. It's the energy or force that binds things together. It has been called the glue of the universe. With love, everything has value; without it, nothing matters. It's the one guiding principle in all religious philosophy, often forgotten by today's religious extremists from every tradition.

Experiments done at the Noetic Sciences Institute in San Francisco, California, indicate that the presence of love is the difference between healing prayer that works and healing prayer that doesn't.

Compassion is the key to increasing our capacity to love. Our ability to feel for the well-being of another is paramount to spiritual development. Until we love each other as ourselves—until we see another's pain as our own—we are stuck in the illusion of separation. Reading the Akashic Record offers us the ability to see the connections between us. It allows us to experience what His Holiness the 14th Dalai Lama expresses, that "through compassion we realize that we are all the same."

War, hatred, revenge, and jealousy cannot exist in an environment of love and compassion. We cannot hate and love at the same time. It's a choice, and how we choose determines the development of our soul. By reading our personal record, we can see where we have failed and where we have excelled. We can see where we need to grow.

> **Akashic Wisdom**
>
> I have found the paradox; that if you love until it hurts there can be no more hurt, only more love.
>
> —Mother Teresa, Roman Catholic nun and humanitarian

Accepting Spiritual Identity

Through love and compassion, we arrive at the next great pinnacle: discovering our spiritual identity. The question becomes, "What do you identify with?" Are you a material being seeking a spiritual experience, or are you a spiritual being having a material experience? The next stage in soul evolution is accepting that you are a spiritual being.

The holographic nature of the Record gives a new perspective on what spiritual identity is. As a hologram, each person's experience becomes part of the matrix of the whole. The holographic Record itself evolves as we add our experiences. As we mentioned in Chapter 1, this implies that the universe is an evolving consciousness made up of its individual parts.

This means that our decision to separate from the whole and become individualized was for the growth of the whole. Each of our experiences uses our own unique set of perceptions and becomes our unique contribution. Accepting our spiritual identity is our gift to the evolution of universal consciousness—our gift to the Akashic Record.

Stewards of the Earth

The final step in soul evolution is to become responsible for what we create. It's a three-step process. First we love, then we identify ourselves with spiritual reality, then we create that reality out of love. This is the ultimate goal: to return to the source as a fully awake individual participating in creation.

The Least You Need to Know

- Each of us is designed to read the Akashic Record.

- The Akashic Record became popular with the influx of Eastern mysticism at the turn of the nineteenth century.

- Accessing the Record requires developing your intuition and the ability to quiet and focus the mind.

- No one other than you can read the deeper levels of your record without your permission.

- Compassion and love are prerequisites for opening the Akashic Record.

- Soul evolution consists of developing love, accepting spiritual identity, and responsibly co-creating your own reality.

Written in the Record

In This Chapter

- How the past creates the future
- Investigating reincarnation
- The forces of karma
- Three cases of reliving past lives

The magnitude of the Akashic Record is overwhelming. Many people want to search for information but feel intimidated. How do you make sense of something so vast? Where do you begin to look when every topic has innumerable links to every other topic? Understanding reincarnation and the laws of karma is essential to perceiving the value of the Akashic Record and making sense of its complexity. They help explain the order behind seemingly random acts of fate.

The Journey

Knowing where to start investigating the Akashic Record is challenging due to its size and complexity. You may want to know about past history of Earth or life on other planets. However, the place to start is within yourself. Your soul, at this moment in time and place in history, is your doorway in. The same is true for each of us. The reason is because in a hologram there is no separation between each individual and the whole. Our own unique position is our entryway to the cosmos. If we understand our own journey, we understand something distinct and special about the Record, or consciousness, as a whole.

The Record is clearly more than a database. It not only holds information and provides interconnection, it has self-awareness and self-determination. While it imprints events in the present, it provides direction for the future. Consciousness scientists such as Dean Radin express that consciousness is evolving. The Record evolves with the actions and choices of each of us. As we learn and grow, the Record is learning and growing with us; the whole is evolving as one. The questions now are, "What is the Record evolving toward? And what is directing the process?"

> **Akashic Wisdom**
>
> We see things in their separateness, but we feel them in their connectedness.
>
> —Sanskrit saying

The Path of Consciousness

The evolution of the Akashic Record can be understood by looking at patterns in past history in relation to present conditions. Written in the Record is a compelling drama—one that's still playing itself out today.

Akashic Record readings attest to continual conflict on the planet. Conflict over power and control are pervasive throughout history. Here are some examples:

♦ Atlantis and Lemuria were advanced civilizations that used crystals and subtle energy knowledge to power their empires. According to Akashic Record readings by Edgar Cayce, power struggles developed among those who wanted to control others and those who strived for spiritual wisdom. The civilizations were destroyed in the struggle.

♦ Native Americans lived in harmony with the cycles of nature until Europeans arrived and conflict developed over control of resources and land.

♦ The Mayan shamans retreated before the arrival of the Spaniards and hid their culture and wisdom. The Spanish invaded the lands looking for gold and treasures, massacring the people they found.

♦ There are innumerable instances of the same; the advance of Genghis Khan and the Huns into Europe, the fall of Rome, and the advent of Hitler, to name a few.

The past is full of the struggle between people, or groups of people, striving for control and domination over each other, resources, and territory. It's a battle for power. Throughout history, nothing has changed. Wars are fought; some people suffer and die while others become more dominant. On the flip side, every religion in every culture has given the same way out: through love and forgiveness comes peace. Is this the direction of Akashic Record evolution?

From the evidence, it appears that the collective consciousness within the Akashic Record is engaged in a choice; a choice between material or spiritual values. Each of us is part of this process. The decisions we make promote either spiritual wisdom or material power. Positive evolution, for us and the Record, requires that we choose love as the deeper reality.

The Path of the Soul

Each soul is like a cell in the body of the Record. The direction of the body and the cells within it are the same; they share the same path. The conflict we see in the larger external world is one each of us faces within ourselves. When we overcome our inner conflict, its presence in the outer world is diminished as well.

In our daily lives, we make choices based on creating fulfillment and avoiding pain and suffering. Our choices are personal and reflect our desire for material gain, comfort, spiritual empowerment, peace, and love. We consider how our choices affect our family and friends and often observe that our choices affect our community and possibly even the nation. However, we rarely consider that our actions have more universal consequences—that we are directing something much larger than ourselves.

It may be a new concept, but you're an active element in the Akashic Record. Each of us has daily opportunities to align our choices with our spiritual identity and advance the development of the Record. When we do, we help bring a better future toward ourselves and the world.

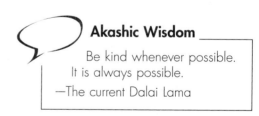

Akashic Wisdom

Be kind whenever possible. It is always possible.
—The current Dalai Lama

Your Unique Purpose, Path, and Destiny

Right about now, you may be wondering who's steering this ship. Is the Record guiding your path, or are *you* determining the course of the Record? Both are the case. The wisdom contained within the Record guides your actions—if you are listening—

and your actions further develop the wisdom of the Record. You have a unique purpose and function to fulfill that can be found within the Record. As you learn to read and understand it, you'll be able to determine your special contribution.

Reincarnation

Reincarnation is the belief that we live more than once. For many people, the idea of reincarnation is impossible—but the concept of reincarnation is central to the Akashic Record. From Akashic Record readings, we understand that the purpose of life is the evolution of awareness—both individual and universal. Yet how can the individual soul evolve in only one lifetime? In one lifetime, we barely learn enough to change the least engrained of our bad habits! The Record reveals that we live multiple lives, or incarnations, and that each life is connected to the ones we've lived before and the ones we will live after.

> ### Library Links
>
> Psychic Edgar Cayce gave more than 14,000 readings in his lifetime; 1,900 dealt with reincarnation.

Reincarnation provides continuity. It explains why people are born into poverty or wealth and into health or illness. It gives meaning to incomprehensible situations. Most importantly, it provides the mechanism of learning and growing from one situation to the next.

Theory and Principles

The key principle of reincarnation is karma; as you sow so shall you reap. In each life, the soul chooses lessons based on the consequences of past actions. Your circumstances, relationships, goals, passions, abilities, and limitations are all a reflection of your past actions and present lessons. If you want to change something in your life, ask yourself, "What is the lesson in this situation?" If you can find the lesson, you can change the circumstance.

It's not important to know who you were in a past life, although it's interesting to do so. What's important is to know how your past life created the circumstances of your present life. With that information, you can gain the perspective you need on what you came to learn and what your path is. How you fulfill your path, and what you offer the world in doing so, is your purpose.

Historical Perspective

The belief in reincarnation has been around for a long time. Many early cultures had religious teachings based on reincarnation such as Hinduism, Buddhism, Taoism, Mayan and Native American teachings, and many Egyptian and African traditions as well. It's also part of the Australian Aborigine tradition. It seems the roots of reincarnation pass through all continents. In addition, many Greek philosophers, such as Pythagoras and Plato, believed in reincarnation, which became part of the philosophical dialogue of Western thought.

The roots of reincarnation pass through Christianity and Judaism as well. It was prevalent among Christian Gnostics as well as Jewish Kabbalists and was central in the early Jewish sect of the Essenes. There are many references to reincarnation in books of the Bible that were removed after the Council of Churches "cursed" the teaching of reincarnation in 553 C.E. Banned from the church, the concept was kept alive by esoteric sects such as the Knights Templar and the Knights of Malta.

The Theosophical perspective of reincarnation is based on the Hindu version, and supported by readings from the Akashic Record. Today, according to the Harris Poll, more than 27 percent of Americans believe in reincarnation.

Misconceptions About Reincarnation

People have some strange ideas about reincarnation. Here are some common fallacies, followed by the truth:

◆ **Reincarnation dispenses punishment.** The circumstances of your life are not punishment. They are opportunities for you to learn and can be changed with changing attitudes.

◆ **If I waste my opportunities or am bad in this life, I'll come back as an animal.** Happily for animals, you're not going to come back in animal form (although many people find animals far superior to people).

◆ **Reincarnation is random—I could end up anywhere.** Reincarnation is not random. It's guided by your own soul to enhance your growth. You pick who, when, where, and how you are reincarnated.

◆ **There's a set amount of time after death before a person can be reborn.** Timelines in the akasha are unclear. It seems you can reincarnate forward or backward in time according to your need. You may also reincarnate sideways and have more than one body in the same time period! When this happens your soul is said to split so that you can live two lives at the same time.

Karma and the Akashic Record

In physics, karma is stated as "every action has an equal and opposite reaction." In other words, we are responsible for the conditions and situations in our lives. They are the result of our previous actions, and in each moment with every thought and deed we are creating the conditions of our future.

Although karma is a teaching tool, it's much more than that: it's a creative mechanism arranging the conditions and circumstances of life. Our past actions show us where we need to grow, and our present circumstances are created to offer the opportunity to do so. Through karma, we learn to be conscious of our effect in the world. Once we've learned what we need to, the circumstances of life can easily be changed.

Creating Karma

According to Hindu thought, we produce karma in four ways:

- Through our thoughts
- Through our words
- Through our actions
- Through the actions others perform under our instructions

Each karmic imprint sets in motion a vibration that is expressed in our life. The vibration may create a life event or health condition, a propensity or talent, a relationship, or any number of life situations. All the vibrations of your past play together in an orchestra that creates the symphony that is your life.

Of course, these thoughts create as many questions as they answer. Does each imprint necessarily have a future effect? Can they be mitigated or erased? Are some more potent than others? Is there ever a zero point of karma?

Karmic Score Card

One of the many misconceptions about karma is that it's a system of retribution—of punishment and reward. The thought goes something like this: you were hurt in this life by a man because you hurt him in a past life and need to learn what it feels like. In addition, because you hurt him then, you owe him something now. The two of you are said to "have karma" together.

This type of thinking implies that there is a big score card of hurts with the maxim "an eye for an eye, a tooth for tooth." It also implies that your being hurt this time somehow makes the other man feel better! The fallacy of this type of thinking is easily seen and aptly refuted by Gandhi with his statement, "An eye for an eye until the whole world is blind." Karma is not a system of retribution. It is actually a system of awakening.

According to the Akashic Record, we're awakening to the realization that we're all interconnected. When you hurt another, you're hurting yourself. Some call this the singularity consciousness—the awareness that there is no separation within the akasha. We are, in fact, all one. In other words, "what goes around comes around."

Library Links

Dannion Brinkley, a well-known transformational speaker, had a near-death experience when he was struck by lightning. While dead, he was taken through an Akashic Record life review. He describes watching his life from a second-person point of view and experiencing every event not only from his own perspective but from that of every person with whom he interacted. He was able to know firsthand the pain or happiness he brought to each person. He also reports watching the wave of his actions ripple outward. Each person he was kind to spread kindness, and each person he was cruel to spread cruelty.

Karma goes beyond punishment and reward. It goes beyond learning and growing. It becomes the mechanism for self-realization. Once you come to full realization of who you are and how you impact the world, you achieve zero-point karma! You are an awakened human.

People Karma

Another misconception about karma is that you have karma with other people; that they owe you or you owe them from past dealings with each other. Actually, people do choose to come together through different lifetimes to help each other grow— but you do not "have karma" with them. Karma exists between you and the Akashic Record. It's a mechanism for your growth, not a score card of debt and punishment.

This is a very different way of looking at karma. It means your links with people are links of love. We come back together for each other's benefit, not for revenge or to settle scores. When you see every person in your life as someone who is there to assist your learning, your relationships change. We'll discuss how and why people come together in Chapter 4.

Transmuting Karma

Because the ultimate goal of karma is to teach, once you've learned the lesson from your situation, you can move on. You don't have to keep learning the same lesson over and over. If you're repeating the same pattern, then either you haven't really learned what you needed to or you haven't demonstrated what you've learned by a change of thought and behavior.

def•i•ni•tion

Transmutation is the conversion of bad karma into good karma. In other words, once you've learned what you needed to, you're no longer tied to the condition you created.

Traditionally, there are four steps to *transmuting*, or shifting, karma:

1. You recognize your wrongdoing.

2. You correct the imbalance.

3. You create new ways of thinking and being in the world.

4. You forgive yourself and others.

You're not required to pay anyone back for the damages you've done. You're simply required to move to a higher level of love. Out of love, however, you may very well choose to reincarnate with those you have harmed and help them in some way.

The law of grace is the law of forgiveness. When someone harms another, they're operating from the illusion that we are separate. Forgiveness is the bridge between the illusion of separation and the knowing that we're all one. We don't forgive because someone deserves it; we forgive because it's inside of ourselves to do so. Deep down, we've learned that one person's pain is everyone's pain. You can transmute immeasurable amounts of karma simply by forgiving those in your life for the pain they inflicted while they learned difficult lessons.

The Karmic Shadow

The karmic shadow is the name for inappropriate judgment. It's the biggest misconception of karma. You cannot judge a person by the circumstances of his or her life. Although we create the circumstances of our life through our own action, circumstances do not reveal a person's soul.

We are more than our circumstances, and we are more than the conditions we have chosen to learn from. You cannot know another person's journey by looking at him or her. For example, some people may be living in poverty because they're learning about the effects of their past greed. Others may have taken a vow of poverty in a past life that they're still bound to. Still other souls may have chosen poverty to bring light into a difficult environment. The quality of the soul cannot be determined by material conditions.

Akashic Wisdom

The hero is the one who kindles a great light in the world, who sets up blazing torches in the dark streets of life for men to see by. The saint is the man who walks through the dark paths of the world, himself a light.

—Felix Adler, philosopher of ethics and morals

Karma has been misused to justify an indifference to human suffering. People will ignore the needs of others because the person's situation is "their karma." In ignoring someone's need, you learn a lot about yourself but very little about the karma of the other person. Who knows? Maybe they were sitting destitute under the bridge as you walked by and refused a helping hand simply for you to see your own indifference. Maybe they were a gift in your path. The truth is, karma is a mirror—and what you see reflected is where you need to grow.

Out of the Mouths of Babes

Scientific study of reincarnation and karma has focused on two areas: past-life memories that are invoked through hypnosis and the past-life memories of children. Memories induced through hypnosis have provided people with needed answers and inspiration but have not been sufficient for scientific study. Information gained through hypnotized subjects is tainted because it can be derived from present-life influences or reflect the subject's desire to please the therapist. Children, however, offer a fresh canvas.

There are a remarkable number of children between the ages of three and five who remember their past lives. Their stories are extraordinary for their specificity. They can provide extensive details of cultures and time periods they have no experience of in this life. They describe foods they ate, clothes they wore, smells, activities, and facts that are entirely unknown to the child they currently are. Some remarkable cases go one step beyond. In these cases, the children recognize people in this life who they knew in their previous life! They correctly identify personal stories, relationships, jewelry, artifacts, and life details. They remember where they lived and can direct their parents to exact locations, identifying still-living neighbors, friends, and relatives.

Other explanations for children's memories include telepathy and the ability of these kids to remotely view other lives and places through the Record. All in all, reincarnation seems more reasonable!

Dr. Ian Stevenson

Dr. Ian Stevenson was the head of the Department of Psychiatry at the University of Virginia until he retired in 2002. He has spent 40 years researching and investigating cases of reincarnation memories in children—documenting cases around the world, including India, Africa, Turkey, Japan, Britain, and the United States.

The children Dr. Stevenson researched not only establish irrefutable details about their previous lives but often also carry the scars of their previous deaths. Birth marks, deformities, and current health issues correlate to wounds they claim killed them in their previous life. Night terrors in young children also seem to have their origin in the trauma of their death in a past life.

Let's take a look at three cases.

Shanti Devi

The story of Shanti Devi is a well-documented and researched story from India. Shanti was born in Delhi in the 1930s. Her case fascinated researchers and drew the attention of Mahatma Gandhi, who encouraged the government to investigate the case.

Shanti's parents reported that she barely spoke until she was four. When she began to talk, she told them that the home she was in wasn't her real home and her parents weren't her real family. She insisted she lived in Mathura, another village, and had to return to care for her son. Shanti revealed that she had died in childbirth and was reborn one year after her death. She provided detailed accounts of her clothing and food as well as personal descriptions of her husband and his business. She suffered a great deal of guilt over leaving her son through her death.

Although her parents explained that this was her current life and she needed to live with them now, she was adamant in her need to return to her husband and son. Eventually, one of Shanti's teachers sent a note to the village of Mathura—and much to her surprise, she received a letter from a man fitting the description of the husband from Shanti's previous life. He verified all the details Shanti had given about her life and family members.

In this extensive—and some say most thorough—modern investigation, Shanti was able to direct researchers to her previous home, identify family members, and provide intimate details of her previous life. She was taken to her former home and identified the layout of the home and changes that had been made since she died. She also revealed where she had hidden money. Her son from that life was now one year older than she.

Library Links

Locating hidden money seems to be a key feature in many reincarnation stories. It's a prominent part of another famous Indian case of a child named Swarnlata. She also went back to her previous home to locate her hidden money. In both cases, the husbands had already retrieved it!

You can read Shanti's story in the book *I Have Lived Before: The True Reincarnation of Shanti Devi* by Sture Lonnerstrand (see Appendix B).

The Story of James Leininger

A remarkable past-life story that has recently been in the news is that of James Leininger. His story begins shortly after his second birthday, when he developed terrible nightmares. While dreaming, he emitted blood-curdling screams—shouting phrases such as, "Plane on fire! Little man can't get out!"

During the next four years, his playtime activities reenacted his nighttime dreams. Playing almost exclusively with airplanes, he knew detailed information such as the difference between a bomb casing and a drop tank under the plane. His nightmares become more frequent, and his parents took him to see past-life psychologist Carol Bowman.

Over time, the youngster told his parents details of his death in a previous life. He described being shot down over Iwo Jima by a Japanese fighter pilot as a Navy pilot during World War II. He claimed his plane had received a direct hit on the engine. He gave details about life on an aircraft carrier and provided the specific carrier he was stationed on—the *Natoma Bay*. He also provided the name of a close friend, Jack Larson. Around this time, he started signing his artwork "James-3."

Researching the historical records, James's father Bruce discovered these were real names. Bruce soon learned that the only pilot from the squadron killed at Iwo Jima was James M. Huston Jr. Locating crewmates from the *Natoma Bay*, Bruce learned that there was an eyewitness to Huston's death—Ralph Clarbour, the rear gunner on an airplane flying alongside Huston's. Clarbour witnessed Huston's plane being struck by anti-aircraft fire and confirmed a direct hit in the middle of the plane's engine.

When it was arranged for young James to meet with surviving WWII *Natoma Bay* veterans, more surprises were in store. He knew the names of the men and significant details of their friendship with Huston.

The Leiningers wrote a letter to Huston's sister Anne, and more remarkable details emerged. The Leiningers absolutely believe their son is the reincarnation of James Huston. They believe he remembered so many details because he has unfinished business to complete. As James has gotten older, details have receded, as is often the case. His favorite objects are still ones Anne sent him that belonged to James M. Huston Jr.

Timeless Tips

Here are some places you can go to read or see more about this remarkable case:

- abcnews.go.com/Primetime/Technology/Story?id=894217&page=1
- lotusborn.wordpress.com/2007/11/02/the-past-life-memories-of-an-ex-pilot-james-leininger-part-i
- Part 1: www.youtube.com/watch?v=_EWwzFwUOxA
- Part 2: www.youtube.com/watch?v=5965wcH2Kx0

Erin's Story

Synthia writes: my daughter Erin is a classic example of how three-year-olds have past-life memories. Her story also illustrates that night terrors and illnesses can relate to the trauma of having died in a previous life.

When Erin was three, she was playing in the living room. I could hear her from the kitchen laughing and talking. She danced into the kitchen and quite joyfully told me, "I remember when you weren't my mother."

"Really," I responded. "Who was your mother?"

"Sue," she said.

"Sue Grandma or Sue our friend?" I asked.

"Neither," she said. "It's someone you don't know."

"Did you like her? Was she a good mom?"

"No!" Erin cried, becoming very upset and running from the room. "Stop, they won't let me tell you any more."

I always believed that Erin was remembering from the Akashic Record and "they" were the Record Keepers. A little more than a year before Erin had this memory, two seemingly unrelated events occurred. First, Erin developed kidney troubles and was prescribed long-term prophylactic antibiotics. Second, she started having night terrors. Her night terrors were very disturbing to her father and me as she did not recognize us and couldn't be woken from her distress.

An Akashic Record reading found that Erin had lived before in England during WWII. She was born to a young mother who had an affair with an American GI. Her father abandoned her pregnant mother when the war was over, and the mother was shunned by the small village she lived in. The mother fell apart, and after the baby was born, she fell into abusive behavior. According to the reading, Erin's previous-life mother accidentally killed her when she was four years old by kicking her in the kidneys. The reader told me Erin's night terrors would stop when Erin reached her fourth birthday, the time of her previous death.

Although there is no way to verify these details, Erin's night terrors did suddenly stop when she reached four. Whether true or not, certainly the story made sense out of Erin's experience and behavior and helped me understand what she needed during this time.

Timeless Tips

If your child is having past-life memories, the best things to do are ask neutral questions, don't push for answers, and accept your child's story. An excellent resource is Carolyn Bowman, who researches children's past-life memories and provides workshops and training. You can learn more at www.childpastlives.com.

Future Journeys

It's said that the Akashic Record holds the history of our future as well as our past. We'll look at this much more closely in Chapter 5. Suffice it to say, however, that the Record is pliable: it lives and grows. The future it holds is a record of probabilities and possibilities. Which possibility becomes our history depends on us.

In every moment, we're in the position of changing our destiny by doing the right thing. This is the gist of many children's stories and movies. Positive action and thought, combined with a dedication to higher ideals, can resolve karma and create entirely new directions. The soul's journey doesn't end with understanding the past. That's only the beginning of creating your future.

The Least You Need to Know

- ◆ The Akashic Record is evolving toward a higher ideal of love and compassion.
- ◆ Personal choice contributes to the evolution or de-evolution of the Record.
- ◆ Reincarnation allows the soul time to grow and provides the continuity to learn.
- ◆ Karma is the mechanism by which the soul chooses its lessons.
- ◆ Children between the ages of three and five often have past-life memories that provide specific details that can be verified.
- ◆ The future that is written in the Record is written in sand. It changes with conditions, decisions, and choices.

Chapter 4

Akashic Contracts

In This Chapter

- ◆ Finding meaning through relationships
- ◆ Examining love relationships
- ◆ Understanding family ties
- ◆ Akashic contracts with a higher force
- ◆ Understanding your karma with strangers

Relationships are the foundation of everything in life. Nothing has meaning in and of itself; it's only in our relationships that we find meaning and purpose in what we do. Consequently, relationships provide a unique opportunity for growth. They reflect our best and worst attributes. Whether easy or not, the Akashic Record reveals that every relationship in your life has been designed for the purpose of your growth—and you participated in choosing the roles.

Akashic Relationships

The moment of death in our last life forms the vibration that sets up the conditions in this life. What we need to learn, where we made mistakes, what we fear, what we love, and the people we are connected with are all established in the matrix of the Akashic Record. Your soul consults the Record before birth and sets in motion the dynamics for your current life.

Consider this vision described by a young woman regarding her family dynamics: "I saw in a trance state my entire family in our spirit bodies before we were born. We sat around a large table located in my grandparents' living room, reading scripts of the new life we were entering. Everyone was debating the script and negotiating for the role that best fit what they needed. Whenever someone chose a character, the script was altered and tailored to them. There was one role nobody wanted. It was the part of the bad guy. We needed someone to take this role; none of us could learn what we needed otherwise. No one wanted it. It was too hard; who wants to be the cause of others' unhappiness? Besides, it was too easy as this character to forget your light and become lost in other people's projection of you. Finally the brightest and clearest and kindest among us stepped forward into the body that would become my father." At this point, it's no surprise that your job as a soul is to grow and develop.

> **Akashic Wisdom**
>
> All the world's a stage and all the men and women merely players.
> —William Shakespeare, playwright

You are a unique expression in the Record, and your job is to be that expression as fully, uniquely, and authentically as possible. People and events challenge you to increase your self-awareness, to develop inner resources, to become more authentic, and—most importantly—to increase your ability to love unconditionally. How people treat you and how you respond reveals your growing edge, or where your current growth is happening.

The Akashic Record holds the memories of all your past encounters forming the connection to the people in your life. What you learn from people is as varied as the people you know. What you learn in relationships is deeper and more personal than what you learn from events. If you consider the people in your life, you know they provoke your greatest enjoyment as well as your greatest frustrations. They can provide support, or they can bring you down. As humans, we seek contact and validation from others. Yet, relationships—even the best ones—are rarely easy!

Prior to this life, you designed the circumstances and made contracts with other souls to construct the life lessons you need. Through your circumstances, you've created the opportunity to correct mistakes of your past and advance the agenda of loving deeply and completely. As you confront the many relationship challenges in life, ask yourself: "What am I being asked to learn through this encounter?" "How can I use this to help others love themselves more fully?"

Whatever you are learning from the people in your life, the most important relationship you have is always with yourself. How you view and treat yourself is reflected in every relationship you have. You are a unique perspective within the Akashic Record, and it is your job to care for the inner light you carry.

Although your relationships provide you with opportunities to grow, whether you do or not is your choice. You can even fail and create more karma rather than less. It's always your choice whether to use your life conditions and relationships to grow or not.

The Purpose of People

People are not only part of our grand performance; they're also mirrors for our self-awareness. How you react to someone tells you about your hidden issues. For example, you may think you have healthy self-regard, yet your anger when someone holds a different opinion shows your deeper insecurity and pain.

According to information from the Akashic Record, relationships are mirrors into our own soul. Whatever you see in the people around you that makes you crazy is part of yourself that you don't want to face. Likewise, whatever you see that you admire and appreciate are parts of yourself you're working to express. Once you start to see relationships as mirrors, it's easier to deal with the reactions we have and stay focused on constructive change.

The key to every interaction is respect. Each person is here to help you see yourself, just as you're here to help them. You may be in competition for the same job, you may be lovers, you may want to impress them or win their favor, or you may be boss and employee. Whatever the relationship or dynamic, it's not accidental. Respect that, and look for the deeper insights and higher ground.

> **Library Links**
>
> When our process with another person stops through his or her death, the unfinished business is felt profoundly and escalates our grief. Consider treating everyone as if this is the last time you'll see them. What thoughts and feelings do you want to leave them with? What work between you do you want to leave for the next time around?

Key Issues

As we seek to be more authentic in our relationships, there are certain obstacles that seem to crop up. The three most common issues are communication, power, and freedom. Each brings a plethora of sub-issues such as self-esteem or ego problems, how we manage anger and other strong emotions, what makes us feel rejected, our desire for admiration, and so on. How you handle these issues reveals your underlying beliefs and attitudes about yourself. Overcoming them allows you to be more fully and completely who you are.

Communicating from the heart requires the genuine expression of your own needs, perspectives, and desires while respecting the needs and opinions of the other person. You may feel vulnerable expressing your needs and not let other people know how you feel. Do you get taken advantage of easily because you don't say what you want? Or maybe you use manipulation or bullying tactics to get what you want.

Communication requires a commitment to honesty, straightforwardness, vulnerability, respect, and a willingness to voice our own convictions.

> **Akashic Wisdom**
>
> The people we are in relationship with are always a mirror, reflecting our own beliefs, and simultaneously we are mirrors, reflecting their beliefs. So … relationship is one of the most powerful tools for growth … If we look honestly at our relationships, we can see so much about how we have created them.
>
> —Shakti Gawain, best-selling author

Power is another difficult arena. Many interactions are power plays of one sort or another. How do you handle power? Do you share it with others and give everyone a chance to express their power, or do you demand to be top dog? What will you do, and how far will you go, in order to fulfill your ambitions? Or are you afraid of power and avoid it, using powerful people to get what you want for you? Being empowered means being in control of your life and at the same time not controlling other people. It forces you to work cooperatively instead of through domination or victimhood.

Freedom issues are about control and the ability to let go. Sometimes you're letting go of other people so they can follow their own path or you can follow yours. You may need to let go of requiring other people to agree with you in order to have a relationship. Too often we feel rejected when people think or act differently than we do. If this is difficult for you, you're being asked to develop your ability to stay connected to people regardless of whether they believe, think, and do what you think they should or not. When freedom is being challenged, you need to examine your expectations and issues of dependency. You need to discover how much you're living your life through other people and expecting them to fulfill your needs—or how much you hold back from being yourself to appease others.

Our relationships are mirrors to our own soul. They tell us about how we perceive ourselves and what our hidden beliefs and attitudes are. The gift of relationships is that they bring issues into the full light of day, even though we would often prefer them to remain hidden. Use every interaction as an opportunity to increase the love and awareness you're encoding into the Akashic Record at each moment.

Moving On

One of the hardest parts of a relationship is being able to let go when it's over. Sometimes it's hard to leave someone we've outgrown; sometimes it's hard to let someone go who we still love. In addition to love relationships, we often have to move on from jobs, friendships, religions, and so on.

In the Akashic Record, we make contracts with people to accomplish certain goals and objectives. The objective may be personal or social. It can be anything—to experience something new, to create something, or to correct a mistake you made in the past. Or you may have contracted to be in a support role to help someone else in their growth. Some contracts last a lifetime, but some are over when the objective is fulfilled.

It's difficult to know whether a contract is finished or whether you're running out on it. Here's the deal: how long you stay connected is a choice. The contract was to show up. What you do after that is free will. Whether you feel things are complete or whether you feel they never will be, it's okay to say, "Time's up!" When a relationship has reached its completion, acknowledge what you've learned, declare the contract fulfilled, and move on.

Love Links

Learning how to genuinely and sincerely love is one of the major pursuits of our spiritual journey. The love roles we play for each other are complicated and intense. The people we draw toward us are people we've had relationships with before. There are many kinds of contracts—some that have spanned lifetimes and some that are relatively new. They can be fulfilling, passionate, and mutually growth oriented or full of pain and unfulfilled promises. Our task in both is the same: to express unconditional love.

While it's difficult to stay focused on the bigger picture, especially when you're over-the-moon in love or trying to end an addictive partnership, it's important to keep your eye on the learning process. The trick is to avoid falling into the same patterns you've repeated again and again. Your job is to find new inner resources, new aspects of who you are, and new solutions to your life issues.

You can certainly assume that whether your relationship is the love of your life, a comfortable companion, or a love disaster, you contracted with this person for a reason. You've been given a role to play; it's up to you how you play it and for how long.

Soul Mates

Soul mates are love partners, two souls who have known each other in many lives. Soul-mate contracts offer a unique opportunity for growth. They are equally beneficial to both people, and provide extraordinary joy. When soul mates meet, they feel as if they've known each other before and connect on deep and immediate levels. They share the same worldview and have the same opinions on life issues. The relationship is deeply fulfilling and enjoyable.

> ### Akashic Wisdom
>
> Soul Mates are brought together for a reason. All their lives they have been preparing for each other. When they look back at different times in their lives they will see a new purpose to actions they have taken. Their lives take on a sense of oneness equaled by no other; oneness of purpose, ambition, and love which can be a beacon to others along their spiritual paths.
>
> —Edgar Cayce, clairvoyant akashic reader

On the other hand, just because you've met your soul mate, don't think there won't be challenges. In some ways, there will be more challenges than in a less-charged relationship. The intensity of soul-mate connections can bring many issues to the surface for healing and growth, as we'll explain in Chapter 12. Soul-mate relationships may last a lifetime or be temporary. The length of time you stay together doesn't determine whether the relationship is with your soul mate or not. Soul mates may contract to be together for one particular purpose. When that purpose has been completed—or if it can't be completed for complicating reasons—the relationship will end. Although heartbreaking, from a higher perspective the love you feel will always be there. No love is ever lost in the universe. And don't forget, you can have more than one soul mate in a lifetime.

Twin Souls

Twin souls, also known as twin flames, are just that: literally, the other half of your soul. It is the strongest type of soul-mate relationship, but unlike soul mates, you have only one twin soul. The idea is that at the time souls were created, they were split into two complete and whole parts. Like human twins, each twin soul is complete in itself, not half of its twin. At the time twin souls are created, the twins separate and go their own way. They typically don't meet again during their various lifetimes as each is involved in gaining independent experience to share with the other in their reunion. When they do meet, it's usually at the end of a karmic cycle, when completion is at hand.

Finding your twin soul is the ultimate love relationship. When you meet your twin, you enter into the most fulfilling connection it's possible to have. You are met on all levels—physical, emotional, mental, and spiritual. These relationships are characterized by huge leaps forward in spiritual understanding and ability to love. When you reunite with your twin, you may find yourself catapulted into a teaching arena as people around you want to understand the growth and upliftment you represent. Your spiritual path will be accelerated.

If you have met your twin soul, you're at the end of your karmic cycle. Each of you has completed your task in becoming more whole and accepting your spiritual identity. It doesn't mean you're perfect; it means you've stopped resisting and are ready to heal. According to the Akashic Record, this is the time of ascension when you return to the source, enlightened and consciously creating conditions on Earth.

Unrequited Love

Perhaps the hardest of all relationships is when the person you love doesn't return your feelings. As hard as it is to understand, you contracted this relationship, too. The best approach is to practice gratitude and use the gift of this experience for learning. There are two ways you can do this. First, notice what you feel and ask yourself the following questions:

- ◆ If you contracted this to learn, what resource is this experience challenging you to develop?

- ◆ Are you being asked to develop your own inner self-love and validation?

- ◆ Are you being asked to develop your self-reliance and resiliency? Or does loving someone who doesn't return your love represent a deep belief that you don't deserve love?

- ◆ Are you meant to heal your own self-love?

If you take the time to examine how you feel and what you need in order to come to terms with your feelings, you can move beyond this situation.

Second, work on the three key issues that relationships bring up: communication, power, and freedom. Challenge yourself to communicate with total honesty and an open heart, even though you're not getting what you want. Don't allow resentment and jealousy to taint your feelings. Be empowered. Stand up for yourself while maintaining respect for the other person's choice. Then finally, let him or her go. It's important to respect the person's right to his or her own path, no matter how hard it is. Don't send letters and phone calls and barrage the person with your desire. It isn't for this lifetime. Respect that and move on to a fulfilling relationship. As long as you hold on to this relationship, a new one can't come.

Etheric Advisory

If you have difficulty letting go of unrequited love, it's because you're still plugged in to this person. You haven't processed the feelings from the experience. Remember, your karma is not with this person, it is with yourself and the Akashic Record. You will continue to draw the same unfulfilling experience over and over with different people until you learn what you set out to learn.

It can be very hard when you truly believe this person is your soul mate and you don't want to let him or her go. Maybe the person *is* your soul mate; it's just that you didn't make a love contract with him or her in this life. Maybe you've been together in a past life and will be again in a future life. What's important to remember is that you have more than one soul mate. You have more than one opportunity to find a wonderful, fulfilling relationship—and after you've learned what you need to with your unrequited love, you may be ready to fulfill your real love contract for this life. With this person, its time to acknowledge what you've learned, declare the contract fulfilled, and move on.

Difficult Relationships

Another type of relationship we may contract is one that's actually harmful. Maybe your partner is abusive or negligent. Perhaps you've tried to leave but are always drawn back. Or maybe you leave one bad relationship only to enter another one just like it. It's easy to lose sight of greater growth when you're immersed in this type of drama.

If you find yourself staying in a bad marriage or attracting the same type of difficult partner, explore your hidden beliefs about yourself and what you deserve. The key is to become more conscious of the dynamics at work. Examine the three prime issues of relationships and how you're doing with each of them. And remember, seeking external love at the price of your own self-love is destructive. This may be what you are trying to learn: self-love.

In order to make a real change, you may need help from friends, counselors, or medical professionals. You may need to cut all ties with the person and clear yourself of all attachments. Remove all pictures, get rid of gifts, change your phone number, change your environment, move the furniture in your house, start over, and shift the energy.

Etheric Advisory

Understanding why an abusive situation came to be doesn't excuse the abuser or the act of abuse. Don't stay with an abuser because you think you have a contract. Just get out, get safe, and get healthy. Your contract with them is over.

The purpose of relationships is clear. They're meant to help us develop our ability to love, and that begins with self-love. Standing up for yourself and leaving may be what you contracted to learn in an abusive relationship. What you can be sure of is that it was not accidental. It was prearranged before you entered this life.

Lack of Relationship

There are many reasons why you may not have found your soul mate in this life. You may be blocking a relationship until you learn to love yourself. You may have issues of self-denial and deserving, or maybe it isn't meant for this life. You may have a different goal to pursue.

If you're seeking a love connection and not finding one, it's hard to consider, but you may not have contracted for one in this life—or at least not until you've experienced certain things. You may have an agenda to complete with yourself before you're ready to put energy into a relationship. The best approach is to grow and find happiness within. Increase your self-validation and self-esteem. Stay focused on what *is* in your life rather than on what's missing. When you've fulfilled your agenda, one day a person you were destined to meet will walk through the door. It won't happen until you're ready.

Of course, you may not want a primary relationship in this lifetime. You may be perfectly happy developing your own skills. Not everyone is learning through partnership; there are many relationships to learn from, and this is only one of them. You may be perfectly happy without a primary partner and can't understand the pain and suffering your friends go through.

Family Ties

The conditions we need to create our life experience are found in our family circumstances. Through our family, we set in motion the major staging for our lives. Family members are people who have been with us through many lifetimes. We switch the type of relationships we have with them and change the roles we have with each other but still share the same commitment to help each other fulfill our karmic directives. The script we enact is recorded in the Akashic Record.

Family is essential in setting up the dynamics we came here to resolve. As children, we assume the attitudes and beliefs that form us. Of course, these attitudes are not new to us; we chose this family because it provided the mindset we needed. In most cases our families are people we have reincarnated with many times. We chose our families for a variety of reasons, as we will see in Chapter 11. Maybe we resonate with the beliefs of our parents, or maybe we need to see these beliefs up close in order to reject their validity. Sometimes we set up conditions that support us as we grow; other times we set up conditions that we must overcome in order to grow. Usually, it's a little of both.

Our family relationships are as important as our love relationships—maybe even more so. How we approach love is learned in childhood. The major issues we're here to confront are established in childhood. We spend the rest of our lives working through, or with, the conditions set in motion in our family interactions.

Parents

We have a very special relationship with our parents that reflects the karma we came here to address. They give us the tools for our partnerships, both good and bad. We watch our parents' interactions and observe how they relate to each other. We learn how men and women communicate and how they treat each other. We learn how to manage power in a relationship and how to get what we want. We learn how much freedom is acceptable. In your life, all of your relationship expectations are set in motion through your parents. Some of what you learn is affirming, and some is not. It's part of your karmic task to sort out the gifts your parents have to teach you from the problems they are sorting out as they strive to grow.

Love connections are not the only type of relationship engrained by your parents. Your response to authority figures and how you behave as an authority figure are established with your parents, too. Do you get unreasonably angry when confronted by authority? Are you afraid of people who have power over you? Do you feel safe and able to communicate with authority figures? It's amazing how often we sabotage our goals by reacting inappropriately to authority. A big part of growth in this life is involved with creating and fulfilling our goals. Changing our karmic patterns with authority can go a long way toward meeting our goals!

What we learn from our parents is what we came to experience—what we needed to set in motion in this life. It's easier to blame our parents for all the things that are wrong than to credit them with giving us what we have. Gratitude for the role they play in our development is more productive and honest than blame. When we come to a place of love and empowerment in our parental relationships, we'll also find better and easier interactions with our primary mates. Authority will take on different meaning to us, and the ability to manifest our goals will be enhanced.

Siblings

Siblings are another of the important connections we chose in the Akashic Record. Our siblings have a strong commitment to our path as we have to theirs. Often, however, it doesn't look like that. Some of our most poignant conflict is with our siblings. Through them, we work out ancient conflicts within ourselves.

In sibling relationships, we learn how to relate to peers. Our professional colleagues, business partners, co-workers, and classmates are reflections of the dynamics we developed with our siblings. Some of what we learned was useful, such as how to share and play together in the sandbox. Some isn't, such as developing competitive patterns and intimidation tactics, and learning how to manipulate. What is certain is that charged peer relationships are reflections of unresolved sibling patterns and remind you to attend to a very specific lesson you came to learn.

Peer relationships take on special meaning when you have no siblings. An only child learns peer interactions in different ways, through cousins, playmates, and sometimes adults. In this case, the emotions generated by having no siblings are reflected in the quality of peer interactions.

Children

Parents have a tremendous role in the growth and development of their children. When you agree to bring a child into the world, you're providing an opportunity for a soul to complete part of its akashic journey. This is a major gift and responsibility. The karmic duty of a parent is greater than in any other relationship. Contracts in this area are not undertaken lightly.

This doesn't mean that if you can't have children or choose not to that you aren't living up to a karmic contract. Everything has its own time and place. If you're missing the parent-child connection in this life and are longing for it, look around. Where can you be a positive influence in the life of a child? The fact that you have the urge to love a child means something. The fact that you don't have your own children means something, too. Follow your instincts and find a way to make a difference in some child's life. You may be the guiding force that changes their direction forever. This may be your contract this time.

Timeless Tips

How we parent our children is more than a personal issue—it's our greatest contribution to society. How we raise and regard our children determines our planetary future.

Spiritual Contracts

The agreements we make before we come into this life go further than individuals. We have agreements with institutions, groups, nations, and religions as well as thought streams and assumptions. We'll talk more about this in Chapter 5. You may not have thought about it, but you have spiritual as well as social contracts.

In our society, we tend to think of spiritual guides and guardians—if they exist at all—as being present to help us. They are our personal support team in the spiritual realms. There is evidence in the Akashic Record that we are also working for the goals and objectives of our spiritual guides. This is not a new idea; religions all teach that people can "do God's work" in the physical.

Yet for many people this is a groundbreaking idea. The Akashic Record confirms that contracts with your guides, guardians, and angels were set in motion long before this life. You may have been working with the same guide for many lifetimes. You may even receive guidance in the form of messages and dreams from deceased loved ones who are committed to helping you achieve a higher good. We'll talk more about this in Chapter 14.

Guidance from Above

There are many different types of spiritual beings—some more prominent in specific cultures than others. They include angels, archangels, saints, ascended masters, guardians, guides, animal totems, and deceased loved ones. Your spiritual helpers are assigned to you before you're born, and the terms of the assignment are agreed upon. They assist you by offering guidance and support, and you represent their spiritual ideals in the physical world. It's an agreement that requires connection and a relationship to carry out.

The relationship is one of mutual respect. Your guides can't assist you unless you connect with them and ask. People do this primarily through meditation and prayer. Asking creates an open door. It allows spiritual energy to flow into the earth realms and shift the dynamics of specific conditions. However, conditions cannot shift unless you have learned something from them and are ready to let them go. At that point, higher forces can help bring positive changes into effect. Until then, your guides will help you change your perspective so you can achieve the learning you set out for.

Working for the Higher Good

Another type of spiritual contract is to support or even represent specific spiritual or social movements. These are movements our souls are in alignment with and to which we have a strong connection. From Madame Blavatsky and Edgar Cayce (see Chapter 2) to the Pope, everyone who is called to a vocation is fulfilling a spiritual contract. This is true whether you hold a high position or not. Any affiliation represents an agreement with the teaching to carry out its goals.

The Dalai Lama, the spiritual leader of Tibet, is a good example. Each person who takes the position as Dalai Lama is chosen as a child by Tibetan monks. Through a series of esoteric tests, they identify him as the reincarnation of his deceased predecessor. This is a 600-year-old system.

Library Links

The 73-year-old current Dalai Lama made an astounding announcement at a meeting in New Delhi, India, in November 2008. He stated that he would break with tradition and choose the next Dalai Lama himself. He further stated his successor would be a girl. The breaking of tradition represents a tremendous paradigm shift for Tibetan Buddhism and was most certainly determined in the Akashic Record prior to his birth.

You may be wondering whether you have a spiritual agreement of this kind. Do you feel such love for a particular way of worship or spiritual path that you want your life to be a witness to its principles? Do you feel so strongly about a social issue, such as animal welfare or civil rights, that you devote your life to it? Then yes, you have this type of spiritual contract. The purpose is to increase the capacity and expression of love in the world on a larger scale.

Clearing Mass Karma

Another type of spiritual contract is to help in transmuting accumulated karma. This concept is a little harder to grasp. Every time a person commits a harmful act, it's stored as a vibration in the Akashic Record. When another person repeats this type of act, the vibration becomes larger. As a harmful vibration becomes stronger, more people are influenced by it. As much as individuals are growing and healing, so is the Record.

Some people agree to be born into specific difficult situations, or to take them on during their lifetimes, for the purpose of healing the vibration in the field of the Akashic Record and transmute the social karma. Just as every harmful act increases the harmful vibration, every healing act reduces it. Here's an example.

Akashic Wisdom

People are like stained-glass windows. They sparkle and shine when the sun is out, but when the darkness sets in their true beauty is revealed only if there is light from within.

—Dr. Elisabeth Kübler-Ross, psychiatrist and author

Anne was abused as a child. Through hard personal work, she was able to process the events she experienced. She was able to shift her internal pain and anger—emotions that fed the harmful vibration—into self-love and forgiveness. In doing so, she reduced the strength of the abuse vibration in the Akashic Record. She then felt called to found an organization to help abused children. Every person whose life was improved helped clear the vibration a little more.

When Anne had a past-life reading, it indicated that she hadn't incarnated to learn the lessons of self-love and forgiveness. She already knew them. In fact, she agreed to be born into the situation in order to fulfill a spiritual contract to heal this vibration. Of course, there are many ways she could have done this without being abused herself—but she agreed to do it this way in order to act as a reflection for the abuser. This doesn't mean she was meant to stay and be abused; in fact, quite the opposite. She was meant to leave and demonstrate self-love.

Strangers and Journeymen

As hard as it is to imagine, even strangers are part of our stage play. Strangers can impact our lives in both profoundly negative and positive ways. Firefighters, police officers, doctors, nurses, and helpful passersby can not only change your life but save your life. On the other hand, the bureaucrat who denies your application to college seems to ruin your life. Somewhere in the middle is the stranger who just lets you see yourself a little better. In all cases, valuable lessons are underway.

Never forget the impact kind strangers have had on your own life. Many people can relate to the teacher or neighbor who showed interest in their path and offered assistance through kind words and support. We all have been in high-stress situations where one person we didn't even know made the difference between us falling apart or making it through. Be resolved within yourself to be that kind of stranger, rather than the one who purposefully obstructs simply for the enjoyment of feeling powerful.

Timeless Tips

An excellent source for information on relationship contracts is the book *Sacred Contracts* by Caroline Myss (see Appendix B). She explains the types of relationships we have and the archetypical roles we play for each other. You can learn more at www.myss.com.

Interactions with strangers are orchestrated to show us specific patterns of behavior. We can use these interactions to find nuggets of gold. With strangers, we often let down the masks we wear with those whose good opinion we seek. We may not hold strangers with the same regard that we do people we have a relationship with. This provides an opportunity to see our true behaviors and our deeper patterns. On the other hand, we might put on our public face with strangers and hide our true selves. Either way, they are mirrors for our learning.

Although there are many types of stranger relationships in life, here are two we have a lot to learn from.

Boss and Employee

Our work relationships are very significant and reflect all of our family patterns. We have strong past-life bonds with some co-workers with whom we are fulfilling goals and agreements. Others are more casual, but both are excellent reflections for how well we have integrated our childhood dynamics.

In the workplace, our authority issues and sibling rivalries are fully reflected. If you have any doubts about whether you've gotten over your family issues, just look at how you relate to co-workers and bosses. You may find it easier to shift dynamics in the workplace than in your family; however, once you've seen a pattern, it's not going away until you address it at its origin.

You can't change another person, and your desire to shift a problem may not be sufficient to change it. If you've done your part, it's fair enough to acknowledge the learning, call the contract complete, and move to a more distant relationship with this person.

Petty Tyrants

Petty tyrants run rampant in the world. Having no true power, they use what little power they do have obstructing others. They may appear in your life as the planning and zoning commissioner who stands in the way of your architectural genius. You may meet them at the Department of Motor Vehicles, where your desire to register your car takes eight hours of line changing. You may find them in the bank, the grocery store, or the school nurse's office. Wherever you find them, you can be sure of one thing: you will feel frustrated.

Petty tyrants are great at showing us how we waste our energy. They show us where our emotional triggers are and how much it takes to get us angry. They teach us how well we manage obstruction and how we sabotage our results through temper or manipulation.

The next time you meet a petty tyrant, observe how you react. Move the focus away from what you're trying to do, such as get through customs or apply for a loan, and find out what you're trying to learn. You'll be surprised by how much petty tyrants can teach us. Also, don't forget to ask yourself how and when you behave as a petty tyrant and why.

The Least You Need to Know

◆ The conditions we need to grow are established from the acts in our previous lives.

◆ We contract the relationships in this life before birth; their purpose is to learn unconditional love.

◆ The contracts we have with people are mirrors for our growth.

◆ Love relationships allow for the deepest growth and healing.

◆ We have spiritual contracts with our guides, guardians, and spiritual institutions.

◆ All types of relationships are contracted, including families, employers, and strangers.

Chapter 5

Destiny, Fate, and Free Will

In This Chapter

♦ Discovering group connections

♦ Getting the most from the time you're in

♦ Understanding today's growth challenges

♦ Is the future predestined?

♦ Deciding your future through free will

We choose the circumstances, time periods, nations, conditions, and people in our life before birth—but we don't choose our lives ahead of time. We create them in each moment. How we respond to and change the circumstances and relationships we're born with is our choice. It's not destined. The future is mutable. It shifts and changes as new potentials arise, and it doesn't solidify until it becomes the present. The point of power is always in the present moment.

Group Karma

People who live through significant events together and share pivotal times in history have a special bond with each other. The events you've lived through in the past create particular conditions and karmic agreements.

Although you don't owe other people, your actions have created bonds and consequences. We need each other to fulfill our karmic goals, and we help each other dissipate our karma through the contracts we engage.

Remember from Chapter 3 that karma is not a cosmic debt and reward card. When we cause harm, we set in motion a chain of events to teach us the consequences of our actions. As soon as we recognize our error and realign our actions, the karma is transmuted. "Bad karma" is between us and our higher selves, not between us and other people.

You can imagine that men who died together in a foxhole in World War I, or people who went through the Civil Rights movement of the 1960s, will share a bond and desire to meet again and help each other in future lives. The activities, institutions, associations, jobs, religions, and hobbies you're attracted to reflect your past experiences. You can expect that the people you meet and connect with in these arenas are likely those you were with in the past.

People are drawn together to complete episodes and dramas they didn't finish. They relive events, perspectives, loyalties, and betrayals and come together because they're linked through history. Look around. The people you see are people you've known before. In all likelihood, none of them are actual strangers.

Soul Groups

Quite often, the people we become close to are members of our *soul group*. In Chapter 4, we talked about soul mates—our love partners with whom we reincarnate for our mutual benefit. Soul mates are part of this larger soul group that we repeatedly reincarnate with in order to assist each other's goals.

def•i•ni•tion

A **soul group** is a group of souls who come into being at the same time and share many reincarnations together. They are like a soul family and are dedicated to helping each other grow. Soul mates are derived from members of your soul group.

The members of our soul group are found among our families, best friends, colleagues, church groups, and so on. Typically, there are between 3 and 25 members. Obviously, you know more than 25 people and have likely gone through significant events with hundreds of people. The members of your soul group are the ones you feel a strong and immediate connection with. These are people you've explored many lives with and with whom you've completed many missions of growth and discovery.

The connections you feel with soul group members are not always positive. They're direct and deep, but that doesn't always mean happy. You may meet someone you immediately and intensely dislike. You may feel you know them, understand their deeper intentions, and distrust them. This may be someone from your soul group with whom you are intimately linked. Every strong emotion is a connection. Alternately, you may live in a family where none of the people are from your soul group. How lonely a feeling is that?

Friends and Company

Typically, we reincarnate with our soul group not only to fulfill personal missions but also to fulfill larger social missions. Each of us has personal objectives to meet; however, they're not independent of the society and times in which we live. The people we associate with in groups are those with whom we have agreed to work on larger issues and with whom we share common ideals.

If you feel yourself pulled toward specific causes, churches, or political movements, these are clues to what you've done in your past. The more passionately you feel, the more likely it's a continuation of a past situation. You may want to consider whether this ideal is still active for you or whether your continued involvement is due to a past-life pact.

Pacts

Pacts are agreements we make with two or more people and are held in the Akashic Record. Usually, they involve groups of people and are made during emotionally intense situations. They always involve larger ideals that we feel are worth dying for, such as patriotism, loyalty, religion, honor, freedom, justice, discrimination, revenge, and of course, love.

The pacts we make with others in previous lives can have dramatic impacts on the choices and directions we make in this life. Pacts made out of love and a desire for higher ideals can be uplifting and growth enhancing. Pacts to uphold social justice, for instance, may compel you to a career as a county prosecutor. Don't be surprised if the judge, defense attorney, and court stenographer are all part of the same pact and maybe even the same soul group.

Pacts made from lower impulses, such as the desire for revenge, can seriously retard your growth. There are reports of souls who spend lifetimes seeking revenge for a past betrayal. You can waste lives going backward in your development until you realize everyone is trying to grow and everyone makes mistakes.

Lower-level pacts will fill your path with obstacles and obstructions. If you allow conditions to continually throw you into cycles of negativity and vengeful thoughts and/or actions, you will continue to be plagued. However, when you are able to meet obstacles with an enlightened perspective of seeking the highest good for all, you will begin to free yourself of the effects of this old agreement.

Breaking free of lower-level agreements requires two actions. First, you need to be able to forgive those against whom you have created the pact. Second, you need to break ties with the people with whom you made the pact. This can be very hard as the forces that brought you together are strong ones. However, lower-level pacts are often responsible for disabling behavior that destroys people. For example, alcoholics are frequently people who are unable to break free of a past pact and seek obliteration over disappointing or abandoning their fellow pact-mates. They may spend a lifetime trying to get their mates to change, to no avail. Breaking ties may be the only way forward. Higher-level pacts are often made between people who want to represent an ideal and bring it forth in the world. These are sacred agreements that can't be ignored. It would be nice if higher-level pacts were free from obstacles; however, bringing something new into the world requires replacing something old, and this is not easily done. People are attached to the old, either because it profits them or because it's safe. A group of people with a higher-level pact of this type may meet as many obstacles as those with lower-level pacts. However, they will always have spiritual support and feel uplifted by the battle they're engaged in—no matter how difficult it is.

Library Links

If you're having trouble releasing a pact from a past life, flower essences can be helpful in shifting the vibrational patterns. Here are a few Perelandra flower essences you might try:

- ◆ Comfrey: repairs soul damage from past lives
- ◆ Dill: releases victimization
- ◆ Okra: restores the ability to see the positive in one's life and environment
- ◆ Sweet bell pepper: restores inner peace and clarity

You can obtain these essences at www.perelandra.com.

Vows

Vows are promises we make to ourselves. Although not necessarily involving a group, they are played out within group dynamics. People often make vows of love and may hold themselves to these vows through lifetimes. Soul mates make vows of love that are mutual and fulfilling. If you suffer from unrequited love, you may have made a love vow in a past life when your partner didn't. It may be perfectly obvious to you that this relationship won't work, but because of your vow you're unable to let go and move on.

Other types of vows people make are vows of poverty, chastity, loyalty, service, and of course, revenge. As with pacts, vows can enhance your growth or retard it. This depends on the ideals behind the vow and whether it still serves you or not.

For example, a man who was a monk in his past life made a vow of poverty. In his current life, everything he owns fits in one suitcase and he can move out of his house easily, leaving no trace he was ever there, within 15 minutes. As a monk, this vow demonstrated a spiritual commitment—but now, it's keeping him from making a spiritual commitment to his family and being able to provide for their needs.

It's easier to break a vow than it is to break a pact. It requires that you acknowledge the vow and its original intent. Honor it and declare it complete. Then orient yourself to new values and ideals.

Nations

Nations, just as every other group, share a collective karma. Remember from Chapter 2 that karma is the law of cause and effect. It's not punishment; it's a mechanism of growth. Nations have a destiny and purpose and a referendum to grow socially, and as with individuals, their histories are held in the Record.

It has been said that the destiny of the United States is to be the world's experiment in citizen-controlled democracy. Manly P. Hall, a famous mystic, author, and reader of the Akashic Record, declared that the entire American continent was destined for a "world-shaking experiment in enlightened self-government and religious liberty." To that end, every citizen as well as every leader is entrusted with the failure or success of this experiment.

Manly Hall believed the karma that prepared the way for the inception of the United States was established before the Christian era. Many recognize the United States as a continuation of the Roman Empire, and many people living in the United States were present during the fall of Rome. The issues that brought down the empire—corruption among the government and people—are said to be the forces at work today.

Timing Is Everything

What you're here to learn, experience, and contribute is intricately linked to the place and groups into which you're born. It's not surprising that the time you're born in is also important to the contribution and challenges of your soul growth.

Certain times in history are pivotal and more highly charged than others. We can look through history and see that centuries can go by with very little change and opportunity for growth. Then all of the sudden, there's massive change. Society is hurled into unrest, and huge opportunities are available. The Industrial Revolution, the technological revolution, the Space Age, and the computer age are a few examples of fast and revolutionary changes. Wars, famines, and Earth changes also provoke huge change. In terms of growth, prosperity may be comfortable but not always growth promoting!

Pivotal times offer a heightened opportunity to redeem your karma. In extreme times, we can rise to our highest selves or fall to our lowest selves. The stakes are high, and people born in such times are here on a mission—willing to risk everything for major advancement. Whether you advance or fall will be determined by how well you can hold your alignment with higher ideals and maintain your soul's mission.

The Challenges of Today

This is an exceptional time in history. The challenges we face today represent the collective karma of our nation (and, in fact, the world). What the times are calling for is the reevaluation of the core values of humanity. Readers of the Akashic Record indicate that this is one of the most significant, pivotal times in the history of the planet simply by virtue of the magnitude of damage or good that can come from it.

The Mayans predicted this time period with the end of their Long count calendar. They predicted a time of social unrest, famine, and economic collapse as the old is transformed into a new and magnificent era. We are creating the new era in the choices we make while facing the peril of today. Present-day Akashic Record readers suggest this period is a cleansing of the inhumanities of man against each other

and the planet. The more society resists
the adjustments that need to be made, the
harder conditions will become until either
we grow or we collapse. The thing to
remember is that it is a choice. It's time to
reassess the basic assumptions we have about
the world and shift our *paradigm*. If we can
do this—if we can expand our compassion—
we have an opportunity for a great and
wonderful advancement.

def•i•ni•tion

A **paradigm** is a set of assumptions, concepts, values, and practices that constitutes a way of viewing reality for the community that shares them, especially in an intellectual discipline.

Some readers of the Akashic Record believe humanity will have spiritual help transmuting the karma held within the Record. Help is underway in the form of higher frequencies entering the earth, providing people with the necessary wisdom and upliftment to shift the current paradigm.

It's important to remember that the readers of the Akashic Record are not final authorities. In Chapter 2, we explained that what is received from the Record is tainted to varying degrees by the reader's own bias and limitations of perspective. The extent to which the reader can be neutral determines the depth of truth in his or her reading. Never trust anything anyone says if your gut says it's not right.

Being born in this time with these challenges provides you with a unique arena of opportunity. How do you want to use this opportunity, and what do you need to adjust to deal with the times to come?

World Economy

It's no secret that we're in the midst of a world economic crisis. Many think it was an inevitable reconciliation as spending and credit went out of control. Although there are many factors in any situation, especially one as complicated as this, it's also clear that an element of greed and entitlement entered the social climate—an element that requires rebalancing.

Economists have sought to understand the money needs of today through computer models, past investment theories, and most importantly their gut feelings. Computer models are based on the best past records, but unlike the Akashic Record, they don't hold all the dynamics that are at work.

Channeled messages from the Akashic Record predicted the current trends. They declare the economic crisis to be an opportunity to "eliminate dynamics that no longer serve the nation and humanity as a whole." It's a cleansing process meant to eliminate wastefulness, dishonesty, and greed. Readings suggest our economic practices have increased pain and suffering in the world and have caused damage to the planet. What we produced is returning as an opportunity to grow and change.

Library Links

On July 19, 2008, President George W. Bush informed Congress and the American people that the economy was sound. On September 16, 2008, the United States Treasury secretary asked for 85 billion dollars to inject into failing banks. Messages from the Akashic Record had been predicting the economic collapse, including the Mayan prophecies.

Ecological Challenges

The Akashic Record is clear that all life is part of its quantum hologram and is sacred. This includes the consciousness of humans, animals, the planet itself, and spiritual energies. Ecological harm causes diminished vibrations within the akasha and like everything else incurs consequences according to the law of cause and effect. The term "carbon footprint" is a useful metaphor speaking to the fact that every one of our actions, good and bad, leaves an imprint in the akasha and affects the ecology of the planet.

Akashic Wisdom

Non-violence leads to the highest ethics, which is the goal of all evolution. Until we stop harming all other living beings, we are still savages.
—Thomas Edison, inventor

Being unaware of a consequence doesn't mitigate its impact. We didn't know the full extent of the harm of smoking cigarettes in the past, but people still died of lung cancer. Trees are the lungs of the planet, and as corporations cut down the rain forests, the earth's ability to restore the atmosphere is being destroyed. We rarely consider the importance of individual trees, plants, and animals in the ecology of a park or neighborhood—but they are part of the conscious whole and are important.

According to information channeled from the Record, it's time for humanity to think in terms of sustainable and humane lifestyles. The adage "what goes around comes around" is true. When we pollute our rivers and streams, more than the animals are poisoned: we are, too. When we torture people or animals, it brings the vibration of the entire Akashic Record down. We're being asked to live the truth that the health of the planet is our health, too.

Changing Paradigms

Throughout history, major social and technological changes have been preceded by changes in paradigms, or sets of assumptions. For example, people once thought Earth was the center of the universe. Those who disagreed, such as Copernicus and Galileo, were imprisoned or killed. When science proved that Earth revolved around the sun, the paradigm shifted. This opened the door for new scientific observations and changed how we thought. There was a similar shift when Albert Einstein established the theory of relativity and the continuity of energy and matter, breaking free from Sir Isaac Newton's physics of causation.

We're currently in the process of shifting from the paradigm of duality to the paradigm of quantum holography. Quantum physics has demonstrated that our ideas of time, space, and the separation of energy and matter are illusions. Experiments in the 1980s established the ability of particles to communicate with each other simultaneously from the other side of the world. Quantum science has revealed what the Akashic Record has said: that we're all part of the same whole. In addition, each part has access to the information contained in the whole.

Also known as consciousness singularity, this new paradigm changes everything. If you really believed that what you do to another you do to yourself, how would your actions change? For example, if someone asks for a favor, do you immediately wonder how it will benefit you to help him or her? In this paradigm shift, you will know that doing something for someone else benefits you, too.

Living in the Quantum Paradigm

The paradigm we're entering suggests a more humane society. Akashic Record readings say that how we relate to money, science, governments, people, and religion is changing. We're learning our place as citizens of the universe and each of us is contributing to raising the planet to higher levels of awareness. As we embrace this paradigm, we can transmute old karma and rise to greater understanding and responsibility in our actions and relationships.

Timeless Tips

For more information on quantum holography, check out *The Holographic Universe* by Michael Talbot (HarperCollins, 1992). To understand the implications for expanding the abilities of the human mind, read *Conscious Universe* (HarpersEdge, 1997) and *Entangled Minds* (Paraview Books, 2006), both by Dean Radin.

Another aspect of the changing paradigm is the expansion of human abilities. The experiments of quantum physics break down the separation between mind and matter. Unexplained phenomenon such as bending spoons and mental telepathy are understandable abilities in the world of quantum physics. As the new paradigm unfolds, telepathy, extra-sensory perception (ESP), and other forms of expanded awareness will be commonplace. The ramifications are astonishing and herald a time of increased honesty and transparency between people, nations, and governments.

Possibility and Probability: Looking at the Future

The fact that the Akashic Record stores the impressions of the future as well as the past suggests we're living in a predestined universe. This rubs against all our beliefs about free will and the ability to choose our path and actions. According to the Akashic Record, is the future really fixed in advance? Actually … no.

Akashic Record readings say the Record holds the past and present along with all the possibilities of every conceivable future. In every present moment, you have multiple possible actions, thoughts, feelings, and intentions. The Record holds each one as a vibration. The strength of each vibration increases as the likelihood of you doing, thinking, or saying something gets stronger. When you choose your actions and words, all the other possible things you could have chosen disappear. The choice you made is fixed in the Record and becomes your past.

> **Etheric Advisory**
>
> It's important to remember that when we focus on future predictions, we're sending energy toward that outcome. Prophecy is often self-fulfilling, so submerging yourself in negative outcomes is never wise!

Akashic Record readings that tell of future events are not reading the future. They're reading the future possibility that has the most energy going toward it in that moment. It's the most probable of the future possibilities and the one that will happen if nothing in the present is changed. We'll talk more about this and what it means in Chapter 16.

Dean Radin

Dean Radin is one of the main scientists studying presentiment, or the ability to sense that something is going to happen. In double-blind controlled studies, he can demonstrate that a person's physiology changes seconds before he or she is confronted with different types of stimuli. He has found that there is typically an increase in physical reaction about three to eight seconds prior to an event happening. This explains things such as knowing who is calling before you pick up the phone or having a sense that something is going to occur before it does.

The three- to eight-second interval is described as the "bow wave" of an event approaching. The higher degree of emotion in the event, the better able we are to feel it. This implies that while each of us affects the Record, the Record may also affect us. For example, as you approach a decision, you're putting energy into the choice you're going to make. More of your energy is going in one direction than another. At some point, the energy going in that direction is great enough that it begins bouncing back toward you as the bow wave of the decision you are about to make—thus influencing the decision!

Web Bot Project

The Web Bot Project is a computer program that detects the bow wave of coming events. The project was developed in the late 1990s to assist stock market predictions. If you're a computer geek, you'll get how this is done. For the rest of us, it's new language!

The Web Bot uses a system of "spiders" to crawl the Internet and search for key words, much the same way a search engine does. Web Bot is different, however, in that when it locates a key word, it takes a snapshot of the text before and after the key word—thus putting it into some type of context. Sent back to a central computer, the project aims at tapping into the collective unconscious. What the project has discovered is that when enough buzz happens around a key word, there's a tipping point where probabilities become reality.

Library Links

It's interesting to note that the Web Bot has picked up trends in the collective computer unconscious that agree with Akashic Record readings and are published on several websites, including www.urbansurvival.com/simplebots.htm. Here are a few common trends:

- The collapse of the dollar
- Pandemic or other catastrophe
- Spiritual assistance in the form of alien intelligence
- The engagement of sustainable living practices

In this way, the Web Bot predicted that an event would happen on September 11, 2001. In June 2001, the program detected a "life-altering event" taking place within the next 60 to 90 days that would be of "such proportions that its effect would be felt worldwide." This conclusion was arrived at after analyzing the text before and after the key words. It represents the expression of the collective unconscious, or Akashic Record, through our subconscious minds.

Princeton Global Consciousness Project

This project, initiated at Princeton University, is an "international, multidisciplinary collaboration of scientists, engineers, artists and others." Based on the use of random generators, the 10-year-old program seeks to examine correlations between events and random generator activity that indicate the presence and influence of consciousness. Random generators are devices that throw balls into the air, allowing them to randomly fall into different slots—similar to a lottery machine. The project maintains 65 generating sites around the world.

The theory is that events with high emotional content and significant human impact will affect the randomness of the data and the balls will fall into slots in systematic patterns. The project has demonstrated that seconds before a significant event happens, the generators become less random.

Free Will vs. Fate

If the Akashic Record holds all the thoughts, feelings, intentions, actions, and events of the past and future, the question has to be asked: What is the role of free will, and how does it operate? We tend to assume that we have unlimited ability to exercise free will as if there are no limitations.

Actually, free will does have limitations. It's defined by the time and place we're born, the conditions we're born into, and the cultural values we hold. All of these conditions are influences from the impressions of our past karma. We could say that we have free will within the constraints we have created from the past.

This doesn't mean we can't overcome our conditioning with free will; it just means it will take effort and dedication to break from the past. You can look at obstacles in your path in two ways. Either they're messages to tell you you're off track, or they're messages to tell you that you have to reconcile your past before you can go forward. Obstacles are then simply indicators that you're working against past patterns.

Instead of signaling that you should give up, it may be a message to put in more effort or face and account for your past deeds. In this way, obstacles can guide your present actions and help direct your choices.

What we know from the Akashic Record is that fate is not outside ourselves. It is the sum total of our past actions. Fate represents our past choices while free will represents our current choices.

Areas of Control

If we are to change our fates, we must act in the arenas that can be changed. There are areas we have no control over, and trying to change them would be a waste of time and energy. Areas we obviously can't change are things such as our genetic material and families, times we're born into, and certain health conditions. What we have control over are our thoughts, attitudes, beliefs, levels of awareness, moral standards, character, and where we apply ourselves in life. Changing these elements changes the vibration of our karma. It allows us to shift the views we held when we created the conditions we're living in. By acknowledging our lessons and reorienting ourselves and our actions, we can redeem our past and change our future.

Power of Choice

Power exists in the present moment. The power to create our future exists in the decisions we make in each moment. The experiments of Radin, the Web Bot Project, and the Princeton Consciousness Project imply that the future fixes slightly ahead of the present. This means that in every thought, we're building the energy for the next thought until the weight of our direction becomes so heavy it begins to steer us. The thoughts you are thinking are steering your ship. Train yourself to think with an open mind and a generous heart. Look for what benefits the many, and act upon that. Demonstrate the world you want to live in.

The Least You Need to Know

- ◆ You reincarnate with groups of people in the same time period to fulfill past ideals.

- ◆ Pacts and vows from the past can help or hinder your current path and may need to be dissolved.

- Nations have karma that involves the combined action of individuals within the nations.

- Future predictions are not written in the Akashic Record as fact; rather, they are probabilities based on the current situation.

- Fate created the conditions of your life; free will creates your future.

2

Pieces of the Akashic Puzzle

The mysteries of the past hold special intrigue. Have you ever wondered about the claims of lost civilizations such as Shambala and Lemuria? Have you been told you once lived in Atlantis? Maybe you wonder how the pyramids were built and where the knowledge of the Mayans originated. All this and more is stored in the Akashic Record, but can we retrieve it accurately?

Many say the Akashic Record influences history, inspiring inventions, science, and politics. We'll look at a few examples of those whose inspiration has changed the course of history. You'll also find how the akasha can influence and inspire your own life as you uncover information from your past lives and explore the potential to heal your past through the Akashic Record.

"If these 'archaeologists' would just consult the Record, they'd know our origins."

2ND LAW – Create an i[n]
tention to attain your goal
morning and evening, by using meditation and visualization.

3RD LAW
verse

Chapter 6

The Unknown Past

In This Chapter

- ◆ Akashic Record insight into lost lands
- ◆ Missing wisdom from ancient civilizations
- ◆ The presence of spiritual beings
- ◆ Elemental beings in the Record

Since the dawn of written history, humans have been enthralled with the remnants of lost and powerful civilizations. Huge and majestic ruins grace the landscape, such as the pyramids of Egypt and Central America or the massive, imposing heads of Easter Island. Past-life readings from the Akashic Record provide insight into these cultures—and equally important, provide insight into soul groups reincarnating today.

Legendary Lands

Myths and legends from around the world speak of advanced civilizations lost in history, leaving remnants from their culture in the form of buildings, pyramids, and monuments. Mayan codices reveal the technology used to calculate their phenomenally accurate calendars and to build their pyramids came from their ancient homeland of Atzlan. What were these ancient cultures, and what do they have to teach us? Not surprisingly, the Akashic Record provides insight.

Our interest in these civilizations is fueled by more than curiosity alone. According to Edgar Cayce and others, soul groups from Atlantis are reincarnating in large numbers at this time in history. What do they bring to the challenges of today? Are you one of them?

Akashic Record readers such as Cayce, Madame Blavatsky, Dion Fortune, Manly Hall, and Rudolf Steiner provide extensive information about the history and wisdom of ancient lost societies. Akashic Record readers of today, such as Douglas Cottrell and Lyssa Royal, also provide information about these lost lands. According to the readings, Atlantis and Lemuria were the first civilizations in which spiritual beings took physical form. They were the original Earth colonies. While some members maintained their spiritual connection and insight, some were overcome with the lower impulses of being in a physical body. Conflict developed between the two groups. The cultures ascended to great technological heights but destroyed themselves in their conflict. The destruction was initiated by Earth changes culminating in the great flood recorded in the Bible.

Large numbers of soul groups from the last days of Atlantis and Lemuria are said to be reincarnating in this century because of the pivotal nature of these times. We're poised on the same brink of destruction or enlightenment that existed in these past cultures and today's conditions provide an opportunity to complete the karmic cycle. Souls reincarnating from Atlantis or Lemuria are working to usher in the paradigm shift underway.

Many individuals today report dreams, visions, and flitting memories of past lives in these ancient cultures. If this has happened to you, you may be here to complete a mission started a long time ago.

Atlantis

The legend of Atlantis is one of the oldest on the planet and has roots in many cultures. Although attributed to Plato, the legend began with Plato's hero, the Greek scholar and philosopher Solon. In the life readings of Edgar Cayce, Atlantis is described as a technologically and spiritually advanced nation. It's claimed the culture flourished between 20,000 and 10,000 years ago, before the continent was destroyed by the misuse of technology.

Some of the advanced technologies in Atlantis included:

♦ The use of "unknown metals" to create vehicles that traveled in both air and water

♦ The use of gas, electricity, and "energy rays" to power their vehicles

♦ Forces from the sun's rays caught and reflected by crystals as an energy source

♦ The use of an unknown death-ray

The readings describe the cities of Atlantis as made of highly polished semi-precious and precious gemstones inlaid in marble, granite, and other rock. They used a sophisticated water delivery system, created tiered gardens and beautiful palaces, and powered everything with their advanced crystal energy system.

The downfall of Atlantis, as revealed in Akashic Record life readings, was due to a conflict between the advanced members of the culture and those beings who couldn't handle the animal impulses inherent in a physical body. It is said that during the conflict, energy produced by the powerful crystals was misdirected, causing massive Earth changes. The destruction took place in three upheavals resulting in mass migrations around the globe. These migrations became the seeds of ancient civilizations and produced the ancient ruins and monuments we see around the world, such as the heads of Easter Island and the pyramids of Egypt.

Lemuria

While accounts of Atlantis are pretty consistent, accounts of Lemuria, also known as Mu, are varied and often at odds with each other. Here's an amalgamation taken from several sources, including Cayce, Blavatsky, and Lyssa Royal channeling an entity named Germane.

The majority of readers agree that Lemuria existed in the Pacific Ocean 14,000 years ago, concurrently with Atlantis. It was an advanced race that some readers say preceded and seeded the Atlantean culture. They communicated through telepathy and were deeply connected to Earth energy and the sacred power sites on the planet. (Knowledge stored in the earth by the Lemurians is said to be retrievable at sacred sites around the world. The sites raise people's vibrations, giving them access to the knowledge entrained within.)

The Earth changes initiated by the destruction of Atlantis are said to have caused the great flood mentioned in the Bible. Lemurians telepathically knew destruction was coming and sought to preserve their knowledge by spreading their history to all the people of the world. This is the reason for the prevalence of legends about lost advanced civilizations. The Lemurians survived the flood in underground tunnels and emerged as the first Native Americans after the flood receded.

Timeless Tips

If you're interested in the technology of past civilizations, you may want to read *Technology of the Gods: The Incredible Sciences of the Ancients* by David Childress (Adventure Unlimited Press, 2000).

Madame Blavatsky's description of Lemuria is different from the majority. She claims Lemuria is much older and was not present at the same time as Atlantis. Blavatsky claims there have been five "root races" in the creation of humans, with each previous race being destroyed prior to the advent of the next.

The Mayans also relate five worlds or ages in the evolution of creation. Each age was a progression of human evolution that ended in destruction of the humans at that time. The last age ended through destruction by water; this one will end through destruction by fire. With the ending of the current age in 2012, we will enter the fifth and golden age. To learn more, read *The Complete Idiot's Guide to 2012* (see Appendix B).

Reconciling Past History

Many of the descriptions of these lost worlds are similar, but many are not. This may be due to the fact that much of the information was obtained through past-life readings. As we discussed in Chapter 2, the personal information imprinted in the Record is based on the perspective of the person being imprinted. Since people don't share identical experiences and memories, imprints from the same place can give very different information. For example, an Akashic Record reading today of a person living in a Mexican mountain village versus that of someone living in Hollywood, California, would give much different accounts of life and technology. In addition, different time periods in the same place will provide different accounts of life. Just look at the changes in our culture during the course of the twentieth century and into the twenty-first!

It's difficult to imagine something we've never seen, and many details about these ancient cultures seem outright fanciful. On the other hand, there are often no words to describe something we can't conceptualize. For example, how would someone from the 1800s describe titanium? (Probably as an unknown metal.) How would those same people describe a laser beam? (Perhaps as an energy ray.) The bottom line is that we can't adequately describe what's outside our own frame of reference. It's possible that the distant past and the far future are both shrouded in the Record and difficult to retrieve.

However, if you're fascinated with the subject, you may have come from one of these ancient times. Do you have dreams of living in stone cities with massive crystals? Do you feel a connection to deeper spiritual knowledge that you believe we're on the verge of understanding? Do you have images of inventions you feel compelled to make? You may have lived in one of these lost lands and have your own contribution to make toward solving the challenges we're encountering today.

Ancient Monuments and Societies

Ancient civilizations have always held a fascination and mystery for us. The huge monuments left behind seem incongruous with the primitive societies we imagine lived there. The technology used to move massive stones and the precision of their alignments boggle our minds. Not surprisingly, the Akashic Record has light to shed.

The Edgar Cayce readings reveal that records of the lost civilization of Atlantis are hidden in, or beneath, the monuments of the Egyptians, Mayans, and in underwater temples at Bimini. He predicts that technology will eventually uncover them, at which point many of the mysteries of the planet's history will be explained.

According to Cayce, the hidden records document the various destructions of Atlantis and the exodus of its people to other lands. The records supposedly describe the building of the great pyramids as well. Cayce claims that due to the importance of this information to current times, spiritual beings are in line to assist with finding and opening these records. There are many readers in addition to Cayce who predict spiritual help through the paradigm shift underway.

Library Links

Modern science is confirming some of the Atlantean mythology. Researcher Robert Sarmast directed a project to locate Atlantis in the ocean off the shores of Cyprus. The Cyprus-Atlantis Project was conducted in 2003 and created three-dimensional mapping images of the eastern Mediterranean sea floor. He made headlines around the world when his project detected evidence of Plato's Atlantis. His images reveal that Cyprus is the mountaintop of a larger island with a valley (currently underwater) stretching between Cyprus and Syria. He calls this valley the "great plain" of Atlantis and shows details that conform to Plato's description of the ancient city, including the Acropolis Hill. You can read about this at www.discoveryofatlantis.com.

Egyptian Pyramids

The Pyramids of Giza have the power to awe and inspire the millions of people who visit them each year. They're extraordinary in their precision and magnitude. There are more than 2.3 million stones that make up the Great Pyramid, some of them weighing many tons. Theories on how they were built are controversial.

Conventional wisdom holds that the pyramids were constructed using ramps, a mix of skilled workers and slave labor, and various combinations of boats, oiled animal skins, leveraging equipment, and planks. Many feel the theories don't match the evidence and are not adequate explanations for the mystery. Egyptologists believe the Great Pyramid was built as a tomb for King Khufu around 2,600 B.C.E.

Edgar Cayce readings place the date of the building of the Great Pyramid at 12,000 years ago and the builders as the emigrants from Atlantis. He claims the pyramids are not tombs but advanced harmonic structures that help align consciousness with spiritual realms. The Akashic Record readings describe how the pyramids were built using Atlantean technology: "By the use of those forces in nature as make for iron to swim. Stone floats in the air in the same manner." Although this reading makes no sense to our science of today, some researchers such as Professor James Hurtak, author of *The Book of Wisdom: Keys of Enoch*, believe that sound was used to levitate the stones and place them in position.

Egyptian Sphinx

More perplexing than the Pyramids of Giza is the giant Sphinx that sits gazing over the Egyptian plains. The Sphinx is believed by archeologists to be contemporary with the Great Pyramid, therefore 2,600 years old; however, research indicates it's actually much older. An inventory *stele* from 678–525 B.C.E. tells the story of how King Khufu discovered the Sphinx already buried in the sand.

Cayce also places the building of the Sphinx with that of the Great Pyramid, but places them both 12,000 years ago. He claims the Sphinx guards a Hall of Records from Atlantis (not to be confused with the Akashic Record) in a room under its right paw. He claims this is where we will find the physical documents of the history of the earth.

Expeditions led by researcher and author John Anthony West in 1991 and 1993 reveal two important breaks with modern Egyptologists. Studying the weathering and water patterns of the Sphinx, his team determined the age of the Sphinx to be the same as Cayce claimed, about 12,000 years old. Seismic surveys of the ground around the Sphinx uncovered a series of tunnels and caverns in the bedrock, including a chamber 25 feet beneath the right paw. Unfortunately, the Egyptian government is not approving further study and excavation, so the mystery remains intact.

Mayans

The ancient Mayans are even more enigmatic than their Egyptian counterparts. Also revealed by Cayce as an offspring of Atlantean emigration, their culture and legends reflect their Atlantean influence.

The Mayan culture is thought to have started on the Yucatan Peninsula 10,000 years ago. Much like the Egyptians, the Mayans were master historians. They kept meticulous records in scrolls called codices. The majority of scrolls were destroyed in the 1500s by the invading Spanish; however, five codices survived. In them was a reference to the astonishing origin of the Mayas.

The Mayan codices say that their ancestors came from the stars, some say the Pleiades, to live on a continent called Atzlan. Atzlan was destroyed by a flood, and the survivors fled in boats to the Yucatan. The description of the destruction of Atzlan and the emigration to the Yucatan is depicted in carvings on temple walls as well as in the codices. This is a remarkable confirmation of Cayce's readings taken in 1933 prior to the discovery of the Mayan ruins.

The Mayans were a truly remarkable culture. They created the world's most accurate calendar, even to this day. Their astronomical and mathematical understanding and abilities exceeded anything seen before. Without the advanced technology of computers and telescopes, they knew more about the planets, galaxy, and universe than we did until Edwin Hubble and the advent of the Hubble telescope. Their advanced knowledge of the galaxy seems to support their belief of having come from the stars.

Additional Mysteries

There are many magnificent and mysterious places on Earth. Easter Island is one of them. The island is part of the Ring of Fire, or volcanic ring, in the southeastern Pacific Ocean. It's made from volcanic rock, and what makes it mysterious is not just the remote barrenness. It's the massive head statues that stand as sentinels facing the sea. Explanations of how they came to be are unconvincing. An Akashic Record reading by Douglas Cottrell reveals that the island was inhabited by the Lemurians who had escaped the destruction of their land. He claims the monuments were built in respect to those who had died.

Timeless Tips

You can learn more about Douglas Cottrell and his Akashic Record readings at www.douglascottrell.com.

Another of the ancient mysteries are the Lines of Nazca. The Nazca lines are located in the Nazca Desert, a high plateau in Peru. The lines are believed to have been constructed around 2,200 years ago. When viewed from high above, the Lines of Nazca reveal themselves to be hundreds of individual images. Some are geometric forms; others are stylized human and animal figures such as hummingbirds, spiders, monkeys, fish, and lizards. The largest is more than 660 feet. Conventional thought is that they have religious significance. Douglas Cottrell readings from the Akashic Record indicate the lines are a star map, measuring time through the passing of the constellations across different designs.

Spiritual Beings in the Record

Every religion, spiritual teaching, and culture in all time periods makes reference to spiritual beings. Their presence is established in the Akashic Record as well. Called angels, guides, guardians, totems, wayebs, and ascended masters, their place in our history is incontrovertible.

Many people experience interactions with spiritual beings. At pivotal times in people's lives, they often feel the presence of spiritual help. During mass tragedies, large numbers of people witness sightings of angels or other helpers. People who have had near-death experiences report interactions with spiritual beings while being dead. The Akashic Record itself is protected and maintained by the Guardians of the Record, or Record Keepers. You probably have your own personal story that confirms the presence of spiritual guidance and protection and are not surprised that the Akashic Record speaks of these beings as well.

According to Akashic Record readings, there are many levels of existence beyond the purely physical one we inhabit. These other realms co-exist with us in the universe and are involved in the direction and evolution of the Record. We are intricately linked together, and our progress is important to these beings both through purely altruistic love and because what we do affects the rest of the universe, in all dimensions.

There are many different types of spiritual beings that essentially can be described in four main groups: angels and guardians, guides, ascended masters, and demons. We would be remiss to talk about spiritual beings and not acknowledge the presence of evil spirits, or demons. As with angels, they exist in all cultures and teachings. However, the Akashic Record puts a slightly different slant on their purpose than you might otherwise think.

Angels, Archangels, and Guardian Angels

Angels are often described as beings of light. Like all spiritual beings, they inhabit the same world we do but vibrate at a much higher level, inhabiting a higher-frequency dimension. Although they are here with us, we usually can't see them without raising our level of consciousness. It's said that spiritual beings can slow their own rate of vibration in order to interact with us if they choose. Angels work directly with people and all other sentient beings on the planet as well. Its said that angels can incarnate if necessary and do so when extreme conditions on Earth call for higher levels of help. Archangels are higher-frequency beings than the angels and oversee angelic affairs. Although they work with humans, they don't incarnate.

> **Timeless Tips**
>
> Doreen Virtue is a clairvoyant and psychotherapist who uses communication with angels as part of psychotherapeutic treatment. She has created sets of oracle cards based on angels and archangels. Drawing a daily card is one way to connect to angels. You can find out more at www.angeltherapy.com.

Each of us is said to have a guardian angel that works directly with us to protect our path and purpose. Although the soul can never be actually harmed, it can be impeded in its progress.

Angels speak to us in "streams of light" that connect to our thoughts, feelings, and sensations. Pay attention to recurring thoughts or thoughts that seem to arrive from nowhere and significantly change your direction. Notice sudden strong feelings or inclinations and listen to them. Observe your emotions and how they draw you to or away from people and situations. All of these are tools your guardian angels use to protect you.

Guides

Guides come in many forms depending on your culture or beliefs. Your guide may be an angel, an animal totem, an ascended master, or even a loved one who has passed away and made a commitment to your growth and well-being. You may have more than one guide, and they may work together as a team. For example, a man named James worked with a Native American guide who was himself guided by both a wolf and an owl totem. Working as a team, they provided James with spiritual guidance. He reported seeing them individually and together in lucid dreams, visions, and meditations.

Our guides, like our guardian angels, are always sending guidance to us. You're probably more connected to your guides than you realize. Flashes of insight, sudden revelations, lucid dreams, and gut instinct are all ways in which your guides interact. You can connect with them in the same simple ways described for your guardian angels.

You may want to consider keeping a journal and writing down your thoughts and inspirations. Keep a log of your dreams and notice repeating patterns. Once you set in motion a mechanism to pay attention to your guide, you can be sure your guides will start using it to speak with you on a regular basis.

Ascended Masters

Ascended masters are former humans that have transcended their karma. They work on the etheric plane to guide the evolution of humanity, and because they are former humans, they have a strong commitment and connection to us. They choose to incarnate as a service to humanity, bringing new directions and paradigm-shifting concepts to Earth. The following people are said to be ascended masters: St. Germain, Buddha, Melchizedek, and Jesus, to name a few.

Library Links

Many readings from the Akashic Record speak to the return of ascended masters. Different spiritual traditions also talk of masters returning to help humanity. The Mayan codex, *The Chilam Balam,* tells us that during the end times, the ancient Mayans predicted the return of the masters who promised to awaken each person's inner wisdom and spiritual memory.

According to the Akashic Record, there are many ascended masters on the planet to help as we shift into the new paradigm. They are here to help humanity reach for greater spiritual expression and connection. Akashic Record readings assert that humans originally descended from beings of light and that we already know spiritual truth. Our job is to reconnect with this knowledge and bring it into expression.

Demons

Demons are equal to angels in their mention in all spiritual traditions and holy books. Often thought of as evil spirits who seek to lead humanity astray and destroy humankind, the Akashic Record sheds new light. According to the Record, demons are beings whose mission is to test humans. When people begin a rise in stature and influence, especially in spiritual realms, they need to undergo testing. This is described as similar to metals being tempered in the fires to rid them of impurities. Demons attach to the undeveloped parts of the psyche and bring these parts of self into awareness for healing. Rather than being evil, they are a necessary part of growth.

Overcoming demonic influence requires aligning to the light within and strengthening your commitment and connection to your spiritual wisdom. It requires healing the undeveloped places inside that leave you open to being manipulated and undermined in your spiritual pursuits. If you feel you are being harassed by a demon, look at the areas within yourself that are being challenged. Write them down. Then thank the entity for the awareness you have gained and declare the demon's mission complete. Align yourself to your spiritual ideal, and ask what you need to do to heal.

Myths and Elemental Beings

Persistent cultural myths revolve around more than angels and demons. Fairies, gnomes, and elves all have their place in the Record as well. Considered fanciful imaginings by modern man, these entities had the ability to influence individuals and communities throughout history. If they are purely imagination, why did so many different cultures with no communication between them develop the same images and story types?

Consciousness researcher Graham Hancock, author of *Supernatural* (2005), believes these myths are evidence that we are not alone in the universe. According to Rudolph Steiner, one of the early readers of the Akashic Record, fairies, elves, and gnomes are elemental spirits from the nature kingdom. They are also called devas, a Hindu word for celestial being. While humans are represented in the spiritual world through their soul-body, or astral body, the plant and mineral kingdom is represented by devas, or their spiritual essence. Like angels and guides, devas inhabit the same space as humans but vibrate at different levels of frequency.

Modern-day communities such as Findhorn in Scotland (www.findhorn.org) and Perelandra in Virginia (www.perelandra.com) have developed massive gardens using guidance from the devic realms to produce energy-enhanced food. They boast cabbages that grow to 40 or more pounds and other gardening feats. In addition to growing food, healing flower essences are extracted from the plants grown in these gardens.

The Least You Need to Know

- ◆ The Akashic Record reveals the existence of pre-historical, highly advanced civilizations.

- ◆ Remnants of these civilizations can be seen in the accomplishments of ancient cultures such as the Egyptian and Mayan civilizations and through the ancient and massive monuments scattered across the planet.

- ◆ The presence of guides, angels, ascended masters, and other spiritual beings are confirmed in the Akashic Record.

- ◆ Elemental beings are the spiritual essence of plants and minerals. Some communities interact with elementals to enhance the growth of their gardens and make healing flower essences from the plants.

Chapter 7

Akashic Inspiration

In This Chapter

- ◆ The Hall of Learning
- ◆ Akashic inventions
- ◆ Scientific and medical breakthroughs from the Record
- ◆ A spark of creativity from the Record
- ◆ Individuals who changed soul evolution
- ◆ Who are the evolved souls?

The Akashic Record is the birthplace of ideas, the mixing pot of disparate tidbits commingling to create something never seen before. Within the Record is a great Hall of Learning that contains all the breakthroughs of science, the achievements of humanity, and the future technology we will uncover. On some level, everyone is familiar with the Hall of Learning because we all access it, knowingly or unknowingly. In our quiet moments when we're open to receive, in our dreams, and through creative insight, each of us contacts the inspiration of the Record.

The Place of Visions

Have you ever been stuck trying to figure out a problem or find a solution to a personal dilemma, then out of the blue you're struck with a lightning bolt of inspiration? After you've seen the answer, it seems so obvious you can't believe you missed it! These are the moments when we visit the Akashic Record, or more specifically, the Hall of Learning within the Akashic Record.

According to Madame Blavatsky, Edgar Cayce, and psychic Sylvia Browne, the Akashic Record contains subsections, or halls. They claim there are three main halls: the Hall of Learning, the Hall of Wisdom, and the Hall of Records. Each one is further subdivided into its own categories of mini-halls. Many people report visiting these distinct halls in dreams and altered trance states.

The idea that there's a place we're connected with where we have access to knowledge might seem strange, but it has been referred to in many cultures and myths. People who have undergone near-death experiences (NDRs), for example, describe being in a place where they "know all things." Some people describe this place as a giant computer while others describe visiting a temple complex. How a person describes the Halls is his or her own reflection—the person's metaphor to describe a dimension we have no words for.

The Hall of Learning is the inner search for the truth of our being—the truth that one is always connected with the source. To know any of these places, we simply need to know ourselves. Accessing the Hall of Learning is not a change of place; it's a change of consciousness. It's not about going outside yourself; instead, it's about going more deeply *inside* yourself.

Accessing Inspiration

The Akashic Record is another name for universal consciousness where everything is connected and accessible to all. Gaining entrance requires an initial shift in awareness, or an altered state of mind. The experience of being in the Record might be familiar to you. Many people access the Record in their dreams, receiving guidance and insight to problems with which they struggle. Some access it through deep concentration.

Have you ever had the experience of becoming so deeply engrossed in solving a problem that hours can go by with no awareness of time passing? You may have been so focused you lost track of needing to eat or sleep or even go to the bathroom.

Awakening from this deep place of concentration can be disorienting. This type of focus is a type of altered state where ideas and solutions present themselves.

Chapter 2 discussed different ways of shifting awareness to gain entrance to the Record. This shift can be accidental, as in the moments before you fall asleep when your brain is alert but relaxed. It can also be induced, as it is with meditation. When your mind is free of distractions, great ideas can be transferred from the realm of possibility within the Record to the realm of physical reality.

Morphic Resonance

Have you ever wondered why an idea whose time has come erupts across the planet at the same moment? Biologist Rupert Sheldrake was unknowingly describing the Akashic Record with his theory of a morphic-resonant field (see Chapter 1). In case you've forgotten, his theory states that members of a species are connected through a field of energy. The morphic field of humans holds a record of everything learned from each person and is available to all people through resonance.

Sheldrake describes information increasing in vibration within the morphic field each time someone connects with it. When enough people are thinking in a certain direction, the vibration becomes so pronounced that suddenly everyone "gets it." It's no accident that scientific breakthroughs and inventions occur in labs across the world simultaneously. In fact, everyone's subconscious may be working together in the Akashic Record on the problems of humanity!

Inspired Inventions

Inventors consistently tap into the Record to find inspiration for their ideas. Some, such as Thomas Edison, Nikola Tesla, and Albert Einstein, consciously shifted their awareness to receive ideas. For others, it happens in their dreams.

Thomas Edison (1847–1931), inventor of the incandescent light bulb, is a good example of an inventor who made time each day to connect with the Record. Edison demonstrated extraordinary

Akashic Wisdom

I know this world is ruled by infinite intelligence. Everything that surrounds us—everything that exists—proves that there are infinite laws behind it. There can be no denying this fact. It is mathematical in its precision.

—Thomas Edison, inventor

qualities of determination and inspiration. In addition, he adhered to a practice of "waiting on inspiration." He discovered this practice during his famous "power naps."

def•i•ni•tion

The **hypnagogic** state refers to the time between full wakefulness and sleep when the mind is in an altered state of awareness characterized by alpha and theta brainwaves. It's a time of elevated insight and inspiration.

Edison didn't spend much time sleeping and refreshed himself every afternoon by lying down on his workbench for a short 20-minute nap. In the moments between being fully awake and asleep, called the *hypnagogic* state, he received great flashes of inspiration for the projects he was working on. With practice, he found he could maintain the hypnagogic state for longer periods and receive greater insight. Using journaling, he wrote down all his thoughts, ideas, and inspirations—filling more than 3,500 notebooks over the course of his life.

Inventions usually come about from a need to make a process more efficient or create a new way of doing things. If you see the need for a new device, use the three-step example of Thomas Edison: spend time each day focusing your mind exclusively on the problem, spend time each day in relaxed free flow, and write everything down!

Simultaneous Inventions

It seems odd to many that ideas and inventions pop up at the same time around the world, but researchers into the history of science say it's the norm. Researchers William Ogburn and Dorothy Thomas wrote as early as 1922 about simultaneous inventions. In their investigations they found 148 historical examples of simultaneous discoveries. Here are some that were reported in a *New Yorker* article, "In the Air," written by Malcolm Gladwell:

♦ Calculus was discovered by two people, Sir Issac Newton, who published his findings in 1687; and Gottfried Wilhelm von Leibniz, who published his findings in Paris in 1684 and 1686. Although the years of publication are different, their notes indicate simultaneous discovery and both have been given credit for it.

♦ Charles Darwin and Alfred Russel Wallace both developed the idea of evolution. Rather than compete with each other, in 1858 they presented their idea in a joint 18-page paper at the Linnaean Society of London.

♦ Three people lay claim to the discovery of oxygen: Swedish chemist Carl Wilhelm Scheele in 1772, English chemist Joseph Priestly in 1774, and French chemist Antoine Lavoisier in 1775. Lavoisier coined the term "oxygen."

◆ The introduction of the telescope allowed close observation of the sun, and in 1611 astronomer Johannes Fabricius published a book on sunspots. Later the same year, Jesuit astronomer Christopher Scheiner published his discovery of sunspots under the name of Appelles. Galileo Galilei claimed to have an earlier unpublished discovery witnessed by friends, and a bitter dispute broke out as to who was the discoverer.

Other synchronistic inventions include six people inventing the thermometer, nine people inventing the telescope, and multiple inventions of the typewriter, steamboat, bicycle, and radar.

Akashic Wisdom

My method is different. I do not rush into actual work. When I get a new idea, I start at once building it up in my imagination, and make improvements and operate the device in my mind. When I have gone so far as to embody everything in my invention, every possible improvement I can think of, and when I see no fault anywhere, I put into concrete form the final product of my brain.

—Nikola Tesla, inventor

Researchers conclude that inventions come into being as a function of timing and intellectual climate. Although both are important, could there be more to it? Hundreds of people can work on the same problem while only handfuls are inspired with the answer. What if timing and climate are combined with Akashic Record inspiration for those who free their minds to receive it?

Dream It, Create It

Dreams are another powerful way to connect to the Akashic Record. In dreams, the subconscious mind is free from the limits of our perceptions and beliefs. Inventors often cite dreams as the source of brilliant inspiration, allowing them to see a problem from a different angle. Elias Howe (1819–1867) is one such inventor. Howe was trying to make an automated sewing machine. The mechanism was easy; the needle, however, was not.

Needles of the day were all handheld with the point at one end and the hole for threading at the other. Machines could not manipulate this type of needle efficiently. One night, Howe dreamed he was captured by natives who ordered him to invent a sewing machine by morning. When the sun rose, he had no machine. The natives attacked him, jabbing spears at his body. As they came menacingly closer, Howe noticed that the spears had holes in the spear points. He watched as the spears were thrust at him, moving backward and forward, backward and forward.

He woke and rushed to the shop. The imagery of the dream brought to the surface of his mind an idea that had probably been lurking there unable to break through. He moved the position of the needle's threading hole, an idea that broke through the constraints of logic. This breakthrough made his sewing machine possible.

Scientific and Medical Breakthroughs

The pragmatic, mathematical world of science is difficult to envision as the place of Akashic Record inspiration. Scientists would seem to be the last candidate for altered states of awareness. However, this statement is wrong.

Scientists are some of the most creative thinkers on the planet. Partly because of the extreme focus on a single idea and partly because of the long hours lost in thought, scientists are often in altered states of consciousness. While the rest of us are busy with the activities of life, reserving the shower for our thinking time, scientists live in a world of thought.

Thought Experiments

Albert Einstein (1879–1955) is a classic example of someone who entered altered states when developing his scientific theories. He may not have named the Akashic Record as the source of his insight, but the likelihood that he was connecting to universal consciousness is absolute. Einstein spent 14 or more hours a day in deep thought. He allowed himself the time to think outside the box, use his imagination, and be free from the constraints of the physical world.

def•i•ni•tion

> **Thought experiments** are experiments that cannot be conducted in the physical world and can only be demonstrated through the process of thinking.

His theories were not provable by physical experiments. They dealt in the realm of the impossible. To develop and prove his theories, Einstein used *thought experiments*, or experiments that you perform in your head. Einstein developed the Theory of Relativity by imagining what it would be like to ride on a light beam. Traveling through space on a beam of light showed Einstein the relationships between light and time and energy and matter.

Dreaming the Nobel Prize

In 1936, Dr. Otto Loewi, a German pharmacologist and physiologist, won the Nobel Prize for medicine. He discovered a way to prove the missing link in nerve transmission through a dream. At the time, only the electrical component of the nervous system was known. The idea that there was a chemical transmission as well had occurred to Loewi in 1903, but had slipped into the back of his mind. Seventeen years later, he had the following experience (from "An Autobiographical Sketch," *Perspectives in Biology and Medicine*, 1960, by Otto Loewi):

> The night before Easter Sunday of that year I awoke, turned on the light, and jotted down a few notes on a tiny slip of paper. Then I fell asleep again. It occurred to me at 6 o'clock in the morning that during the night I had written down something most important, but I was unable to decipher the scrawl. The next night, at 3 o'clock, the idea returned. It was the design of an experiment to determine whether or not the hypothesis of chemical transmission that I had uttered 17 years ago was correct. I got up immediately, went to the laboratory, and performed a single experiment on a frog's heart according to the nocturnal design.

It took 14 years before his theory was accepted—a feat that earned him the Nobel Prize in 1936, which he shared with British scientist Henry Dale. In 1938 Loewi and his wife were arrested in Austria by the Nazis. Losing all their possessions, they bribed their way out of jail and the country using the money from the Nobel Prize. His dream inspiration certainly helped him in more ways than one.

You may want to take note of two things for your own dream inspiration: he kept pen and paper by the bed to write things down and he was willing to act on his inspiration.

Developing Your Mind

You can wait on serendipity to bring the eureka moment, or you can find ways to expand your consciousness, like Edison and Einstein, and create your moment of inspiration. There are many training courses available; one of the best known is the Silva UltraMind System. According to Ken Obermeyer, a director at Silva, people who come to the trainings receive insight into medical, scientific, industrial, and technological problems. A research director at New Dimensions Medicine in Ohio is said to have received the solution to the creation of artificial arteries at the Silva training. As with other cases, the scientist reported that the solution was not one his logical mind would have considered.

Timeless Tips _____

If you're interested in taking the Silva UltraMind training, you can get more information at www.ultramind.ws/invention_in_a_dream.htm. For more information on inspirations in thinking, visit www.creativethinkingwith.com.

Inspiration and the Arts

Artists, musicians, and writers are often thought to live in a different world than the rest of us. They seem to have an easier time accessing the altered states that shift awareness and invite insight. Devoting their lives to creative expression, they provide the world with reminders of our connection to something bigger than ourselves.

Spiritualist Harry Edwards describes special rooms in the Hall of Learning for music, art, and literature. Connecting with these rooms sparks the excitement of creativity. Although the arts are being lost in today's educational process, they are an essential part of culture. Societies' values are reflected through art and help us see underlying truth.

Music, literature, and art connect people through a shared appreciation. More importantly, they stimulate the knowledge within that we are more than our physical bodies. Artistic expression inspires us, uplifts us, and lets us explore other domains. It reminds us of our spiritual identity.

Music of the Muses

Harry Edwards (1893–1976), a British spiritual healer, described music as being telepathically transmitted from the music room in the Hall of Learning directly into the minds of different musicians. Child prodigies bring their aptitude for playing music from past-life development; their compositional inspiration is said to come directly from the Record.

Reg Presley, lead singer and songwriter for the 1960s group The Troggs, described to Colin his experience writing the band's biggest hit, *Love Is All Around.* The song was inspired when Reg was watching a Sunday evening television broadcast of the Joy Strings Salvation Army band in England. Not being a particularly religious person, he was nonetheless overcome with emotion. In a matter of minutes, the words and tune to *Love Is All Around* flowed through his pen as if channeled from somewhere else. The song made it into the Top Ten charts around the world and sold millions. It held the number one spot in Great Britain for 15 weeks.

Paul McCartney reported the tune to his 1965 Beatles hit *Yesterday* was the result of a dream. The song was performed more than seven million times in the twentieth century, according to the BMI record label. In *McCartney—Many Years From Now* by Barry Miles (Henry Holt, 1997), McCartney is quoted as saying:

> I woke up with a lovely tune in my head. I thought, "That's great, I wonder what that is?" There was an upright piano next to me, to the right of the bed by the window. I got out of bed, sat at the piano, found G, found F sharp minor 7th—and that leads you through then to B to E minor, and finally back to E. It all leads forward logically. I liked the melody a lot, but because I'd dreamed it, I couldn't believe I'd written it. I thought, "No, I've never written anything like this before." But I had the tune, which was the most magic thing!

Akashic Art

Have you ever looked at a piece of artwork and felt overcome with emotion, even if the scene was not especially emotional? Theosophists claim there is a special section called the Hall of Artistic Inspiration meant to uplift society through art. Inspired artwork is said to have the ability to translate emotions into expression of color and shape—and when viewed, to transform people's inner selves.

Nicholas Roerich (1884–1947), a Russian artist, connected with this hall in his work. He believed that art and knowledge could restore the world. Roerich created more than 7,000 pieces of visionary artwork, stating that beauty reminds people of their spiritual identities. He promoted the beautification of buildings, institutions, and cities to keep people connected with their higher impulses.

Roerich and his wife, Helene, created the Banner of Peace during World War I. This symbol, like the red cross, was utilized as a "no bombing" sign. The red cross, placed on hospitals, was universally recognized as a bomb-free zone. The Banner of Peace, consisting of a white flag with a red ring containing three red circles, was flown

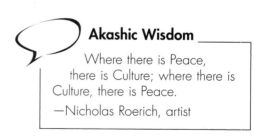

Akashic Wisdom

Where there is Peace, there is Culture; where there is Culture, there is Peace.

—Nicholas Roerich, artist

over buildings of cultural significance that were important to preserve for humankind. Roerich's Peace Pact was ratified by 33 countries, all agreeing not to bomb buildings of cultural significance. The United States was among the first to sign the pact in 1935—something we forgot when the museums of Iraq were ransacked during the Iraqi War, destroying centuries of relics.

Timeless Tips _____

You can read more about dream-inspired ideas at www.brilliantdreams.com/product/famous-dreams.htm.

Leonardo da Vinci was another artist who connected with the Hall of Artistic Inspiration. He is famous for searching for connections between unrelated items. His trick for altering consciousness was to look for patterns in random elements, such as ashes in a fireplace, clouds, and shadows. He was able to use whatever was before him to create perceptual shifts.

Library Literature

Spiritualists claim there is a separate language in the Hall of Learning—one that conveys meaning and emotion through shape. It is gifted to those who write the inspirations that come through the Record.

Mary Wollstonecraft Shelley, creator of *Frankenstein*, reports in the introduction to her book that the inspiration came from an "acute mental vision" that haunted her until she allowed her mind to create the vision as the story that terrified her readers!

Robert Louis Stevenson also is reported to have created *Dr. Jekyll and Mr. Hyde* from a dream. In fact, Stevenson has described how his passion for writing originated with his dreams, which from childhood were more entertaining to him than books. He claims to have dreamed complete stories that he could return to on different nights. He trained himself to remember his dreams, from which he created his story lines. Clearly, Stevenson was receiving information from somewhere!

People Who Changed History

Throughout time, there have been unique individuals who have, through the force of their visions, changed the course of history. The Wright brothers, for example, changed the world when they invented the airplane. Buckminster Fuller changed architecture with his idea of tensegrity and changed our global vision with his concept of Spaceship Earth. Just as visionary people have expressed their inspiration through art, science, and technology, they have done so in social issues.

Some individuals have been motivated by the highest of ideals—and some for the worst. In either case, the Akashic Record (our collective consciousness) has grown and evolved. What is it about such an individual that creates this dynamic purpose? According to Cayce and Blavatsky, souls respond to the collective need expressed in the Akashic Record and come forward to serve the goals of humanity. In doing so, they also serve their own evolutions.

Gandhi

Mohandas (Mahatma) Gandhi (1869–1948) inspired millions. His belief in dignity, non-cooperation with injustice, and self-reliance moved his country to non-violent reform and eventually to independence. He inspired Martin Luther King Jr. in the advance of civil rights and the current Dalai Lama in the advance of Tibetan freedom. Many feel he showed the world a way out of the conflict our exploitive behaviors perpetuated.

Many feel that Gandhi's real impact was demonstrating the power of an individual to make a profound difference. He showed that a single person can stand against an empire. Others, however, believe his greatest gift was revealing the dignity of the human spirit. Through his words and actions, he demonstrated that personal dignity, which he defined as respect for all life and alignment with inner values, was the single most important thing in life. He showed that dignity is more important than physical well-being and not something that can be taken away by another's violence, suppression, or coercion. Only you can bestow dignity on yourself or give it to others.

> **Akashic Wisdom**
>
> If we were to drive out the English with the weapons with which they enslaved us, our slavery would still be with us even when they have gone.
> —Mahatma Gandhi

Gandhi was a champion of non-violence and changed the world. His true gift to the Akashic Record, however, was the imprint of a vibration of the power of our inner truth. Simply by meditating on Gandhi's life, you can connect to this vibration in the Record and strengthen it within yourself.

The Hitler Factor

Many people will not like being reminded of the horror that Adolf Hitler (1889–1945) unleashed on the world during World War II. More than any person in history, he demonstrates the perversion of spiritual ideals. Taking the teachings of Blavatsky and other spiritual writings, Hitler declared himself the savior of Germany. He justified horrific acts through his beliefs, yet he was part of the collective akashic field. How does this reconcile?

In a strange way, Hitler and Gandhi represented the opposite sides of the same truth. The atrocities committed by the Third Reich devastated our senses and destroyed our belief in the higher truth of humanity. Gandhi's actions restored our senses.

If we pause for a minute, we see something else—that Hitler unwittingly caused needed and necessary reform. In the aftermath of the carnage and mayhem he unleashed, the world responded with enlightened change. International laws governing the treatment of prisoners, torture, and rules of engagement were agreed upon. Hitler showed us the very worst of what humans can do. While he made an imprint in the Akashic Record that will take ages to undo, he also advanced the evolution of the Record through reverse inspiration.

Akashic Wisdom

There will one day spring from the brain of science a machine or force so fearful in its potentialities, so absolutely terrifying, that even man, the fighter, who will dare torture and death in order to inflict torture and death, will be appalled, and so abandon war forever.

—Thomas Edison, inventor

Evolutionary Advancement

The world faces many challenges today that are unique to any other time in history. We face environmental, social, economic, and political challenges. The polarization within society is creating a dividing line that's escalating tension. Even families are losing sight of respect for each other.

In the past, social challenge has pulled people together—but that doesn't seem true at the moment. According to Cayce, due to the severity of issues and the ability we have to annihilate the planet, advanced souls are returning to Earth in large numbers to avert disaster. By all accounts, their return is reproducing the tension that existed at the time of the fall of Atlantis, when the two factions were so polarized that they destroyed a continent.

Cayce targeted the years between 1998 and 2010 as the period when our advancement to the next root race would be fully underway. Mystics go further. They refer to an alteration in the "life stream" that is bringing new waves of souls from other planets and dimensions. Even beings from the future are said to be arriving for incarnation at this time.

Advanced Souls

Blavatsky claims that there have always been a scattering of advanced souls who act like sparks for new ideas and directions. A good example is that of the revolutionary inventor, Nikola Tesla (1856–1943). Tesla, the inventor of the alternating-current electric power systems and AC motor, was able to visualize with uncanny precision and intensity. In his autobiography, he describes the process of creating a complete machine in his mind, running it to find its errors, correcting the errors, then disassembling it to look for places of wear and tear. After his thought experiments, he was able to build a perfectly running machine without blueprints. Cayce called the advanced souls that are arriving in this time period the Indigo children. The Indigo children are, he claims, preparing the way for the Psychic, Crystal, and Rainbow children.

Indigo, Crystal, and Rainbow Kids

Indigo, Crystal, and Rainbow kids sounds something like a children's TV program! According to Cayce, the names are descriptive of the colors of their auras. Each is a unique type of advanced soul who has come to bring a specific level of enlightenment to the planet.

All kids are special, and everyone is born in a particular time and place to fulfill a particular purpose. What's different at this time is the number of advanced souls arriving to fulfill the same purpose. The children arriving now are the bridge to the new advancement of humanity. Although uniquely individual, they all share some identifying qualities.

Indigo, Crystal, Rainbow, and the other children of this time are psychic, intuitive, telepathic, and sensitive to emotions. They are highly reactive to toxic thoughts and environmental toxins. They are intelligent, non-conformists, and intolerant of high-handed authority and dishonesty. They are highly attuned to animals and nature. They are often diagnosed with attention deficit disorder (ADD) or attention deficit hyper-activity disorder (ADHD), and their parents can be overwhelmed with the difficulties they present in raising them. Indigo children are said to represent the evolutionary direction of the human soul.

Etheric Advisory

Giving kids labels does more to separate them than acknowledge their specialness. Every kid on the planet is here at this time with a mission and a purpose. Don't let labels cause you to separate and diminish some while elevating and extolling others.

The Least You Need to Know

- Past civilizations are part of the returning soul group of today.

- Atlantis and Lemuria were destroyed by conflict between advanced souls and souls unable to handle physical bodies.

- Inspiration from the Akashic Record can spark inventions, breakthroughs, and cultural accomplishments.

- Individuals inspired by the Record can profoundly affect history, both good and bad.

- There are many advanced souls entering Earth at this time. They are often referred to as Indigo, Crystal, and Rainbow children.

Chapter 8

Clues to Your Akashic Past

In This Chapter

- The benefits and consequences of knowing your past life
- Unraveling preferences and inclinations
- Understanding emotional responses
- What repeating patterns tell us
- Putting the pieces together to find your past

Your past lives live in the Akashic Record. Clues to who you once were and how you lived exist all around you and learning to read them is easy and fun. All your likes and dislikes, fears and phobias, the trends of your life, what you gravitate toward, your dreams, and even your fashion sense are influenced by your past lives. Discovering the many signs and signals is just a matter of paying attention. The benefit is gaining more understanding of who you are and where you're going, but remember, you may not like all the information you find about your past.

The Living Past

People want to know about their past lives for many different reasons. Maybe you feel strong, underlying forces in your personality that influence your relationships. You may want to take a job in another part of the country but for some reason don't feel comfortable leaving the area where you live. Strong influences on the decisions you make are good reasons to research your past lives.

Often, people are drawn to find out about their past lives to explain deep inner feelings. You may feel the need to complete something but don't know what it is. Many people feel they have a mission in this life and seek to find it. Others are drawn to the past because they feel unfulfilled in this life and don't know what's missing. Whatever your reason, there is growth to be gained from seeking your past.

> **Akashic Wisdom**
>
> If you want to know the past, look at your present. If you want to know the future, look at your present.
>
> —Gautama Buddha, spiritual teacher and founder of Buddhism

Although all your previous lives are written in the Akashic Record and you have access to your record inside yourself, the Guardians of the Record decide how much information is useful for you. There's a reason we're born with a veil to our past-life information—it's easy to get caught up living in the past. The challenges of our soul's growth are for today. Although past-life information can be very helpful in setting your direction and answering questions, it can also cause problems.

Benefits

The benefits from past-life information depend on your reasons for seeking it. If you're just satisfying an idle curiosity, which is fine, past-life research may simply be entertainment. On the other hand, what started as idle curiosity may change your life.

Many people find their past life holds the resolution to long-held challenges. Finding the past-life cause of a persistent fear or phobia can completely eliminate it. For example, a young man who was terrified of lightning went through a past-life regression. He relived his death in a petrifying battle in the American Revolutionary War. In his regression, he was shot and died a slow, agonizing death, watching the flashes of bombs overhead and hearing the sounds of battle and pain all around him. Reliving this experience allowed him to come to terms with his fear. Once he understood where his strong feelings came from, lightning stopped frightening him.

Many people report feeling deep peace, contentment, and completion after discovering one or more of their past lives. The information helps them determine their path and purpose or understand their hidden talents. It sets them on a new course of growth and development. Most importantly, after learning firsthand that there is life after death, many people lose their fear of dying.

Unintended Consequences

Although everything you learn from the Akashic Record can help your soul growth, not all of it is calming. Some people learn past-life information that leaves them feeling anxious or depressed. For example, one woman discovered she had been an executioner in her past life. In this life, she is compelled to do volunteer work with prison inmates. Rather than feeling content to know that she was transmuting karma, she became obsessed with fear that someone she had executed would return to kill her.

In another situation, a woman remembered a past life living in a palace in a foreign country. She lived a privileged life filled with art and elegance. She was loved and very happy. Although the memory helped her understand her desire and attraction to the finer things in life, the contrast to her current life was dramatic. Instead of giving her hope of a better future, remembering her earlier life made her feel depressed.

It's up to you to know how information impacts you and to consider all the ramifications of seeking past-life information. Before you engage in past-life research, you need to examine your motives and consider how different information will affect you. We all want to have been a hero in the past, but what if you find out something you don't want to know?

Another unintended consequence of looking into the past is alienation from your present. Rather than living your present life to its fullest, you may become obsessed with finding more details of your past. Remember that your past is already finished—your growth is in *this* life. Additionally, as you begin to grow in different directions, the significant people in your life (friends, relatives, and spouses) may not be able to grow in the same directions. Rather than helping your life become more focused and helping your relationships get stronger, you may open the door to more stress and fracture.

Another important thing to consider is how this information will affect your religious beliefs and practices. Consider how difficult it was for Edgar Cayce when his Akashic Record readings went beyond health issues and into past lives. He was forced to re-examine all his religious beliefs and disrupt the foundation of his life. While this was ultimately uplifting and helped millions of people, it was a stressful and painful time in his life. If you live in a religious family or environment, exploring past lives may put you at odds with other elements in your life.

You don't need to be afraid that your life will be ruined with unanticipated consequences. Everything you receive has the purpose of enriching your understanding and promoting your growth. You just have to be careful to maintain perspective with what you learn. If you feel compelled to find out information, follow it—just be aware of the major impacts that it may bring.

Keeping Notes

As you look at the clues to past lives through the rest of this chapter, keep a notebook handy. As you explore each session, you'll naturally start thinking of your own experiences. Write them down. Your response to each section will provide valuable information and help create a past life story. Write as much as you can; every detail provides insight. At the end of the chapter, we'll put it all together.

Timeless Tips _____

Journaling is a powerful tool for self-awareness, including uncovering past-life information. If you want more instruction, a great book is *Journalution: Journaling to Awaken Your Inner Voice, Heal Your Life and Manifest Your Dreams* by Sandy Grason (see Appendix B).

Examining Your Preferences

The easiest place to start the journey into your past is to examine your natural preferences. Some of them are easily explained by your childhood or upbringing. Others are at odds to everything you've experienced and seem to have been formed somewhere else.

Especially strong preferences begin early in life. You and your parents may remember that you always wanted to watch a specific type of movie—Westerns, English romance, or science fiction, for example. You may have always loved certain kinds of flowers or been attracted to specific music. You may have enjoyed playing with dolls from certain time periods or airplanes from specific wars.

What we're drawn to in our childhood often continues into adulthood. Many people find that as they reach their older years, the preferences of their childhood become even stronger. Maybe they always liked Spanish architecture but lived in New England, so they bought a colonial reproduction. When they retire, they may decide to move to a hacienda in New Mexico where they feel at home and closer to the natural preference they've had since childhood.

Preferences provide clues to the time and place you may have lived in before. They can also give you a sense of what type of role you played in that society. As you look at the following sections, write down in your notebook your basic responses to these areas. Keep in mind that you have most certainly had more than one past life, and more than one may be influencing your answers. Write everything down, and later you can cluster them into similar times and places. You may be surprised to see many lives revealed in this exercise.

Etheric Advisory

As comforting as it can be to surround yourself with memorabilia from a past life, be careful you're not avoiding the challenges of this life by living in the past.

Time Gates

Most people have curiosity about specific historical time periods. This curiosity can be very strong to the point of wanting to learn everything possible about that time and its events. Some people find they feel more at home in this other time and don't fit in with today's lifestyles. If this is you, you probably lived in the time you're drawn to. You can help yourself feel more comfortable by surrounding yourself with artwork, artifacts, and books from the past period you're drawn to.

Often, the time periods people are fascinated with revolve around wars or pivotal times in history. This is because tumultuous times leave a stronger imprint on the Akashic Record. In addition, turbulent situations often result in untimely deaths, leaving people with unfinished business. You may be drawn to a particular period because you still had things to accomplish in that life before you died. Some of the time periods you're drawn to could have been past lives where you felt very happy and satisfied—a time when you were able to fulfill your dreams. Surrounding yourself with artifacts from this period may help you stay connected to that deep sense of fulfillment.

As you take a few moments to write down the specific time periods, also write down the details that come to your mind. Are you drawn to guns or vehicles from that time? Does the clothing attract you? Are you curious about the technology and science of that day? What are your feelings when you think about this period? Do you feel angry or afraid? Are you overwhelmed with love or sadness? All these are details we'll use to understand your past lives.

Geography: Land of Imagination

When you're drawn to a time period, you're drawn to a certain place as well. Time periods, places, and events are linked. A life during the time period of Christ, for example, was only pivotal if you lived in the Middle East. Native Americans and the Chinese empire wouldn't have been impacted the same way by this period.

You can be attracted to specific areas and cultures without being drawn to a particular time. Do you have a strong desire to see China, Jerusalem, or Peru? Or maybe you're drawn to different climates. Do you only feel comfortable living in the desert? Do you have to live by the ocean to feel alive? Do you have recurring dreams of living in the mountains or flashes of memories of living aboard a spaceship? All these are snippets of past-life information.

Write down in your notebook the climates, places, objects, and flora and fauna you're drawn to. If there's a particular country or city, write that down also.

Historical Figures

There are often clues to when and where you lived before in the historical figures you're interested in. Some people are fascinated with Benjamin Franklin and George Washington, while for other people these are simply the background figures of our history.

You may be attracted to or repelled by a certain historical figure, but either way you may be fascinated and want to know more about them. The historical figures you're drawn to tell you a lot about the qualities you admire and the values you hold. Sometimes these come from your family upbringing and culture, while at other times they seem to come from a deeper place.

> **Timeless Tips**
>
> To have fun finding a famous person you might have been, check out this amusing website: www.selectsmart.com/ pastlives/.

You may be drawn to these historical figures because of their qualities or because you lived in that time period. Maybe you even were one or two of the personalities you're fascinated with.

Write down all the historical figures you're pulled toward and why. What do you like or dislike about them? What do you feel when you examine their life? Does it seem like you know them? If so, how closely? Do you feel as if you understand their motives? These are all important clues to your past.

Art and Architecture

If you didn't feel you had an attraction to any specific geographical place, you may find clues in the architecture and artwork you enjoy or have an aversion to. An antique home can make one person feel comfortable, and another might feel claustrophobic. Both may have lived during that time period; for one person, it was a positive experience while for the other it held hidden trauma.

Think about the houses and architecture you have a strong reaction to. Are you attracted to particular themes, colors, or features? Do your houses have to have balconies, and do you love ornate moldings? Write down whatever you're drawn to and how you feel when you're inside those structures.

Look around your own home and take an inventory of what kind of artwork you have. Often, we hang individual pictures and don't actually notice that they relate to a theme. Is the artwork in your house all related to a certain subject, time period, or culture? Do you only like natural landscapes, or do you prefer pictures of horses or trains? Artwork can be a big clue to your past lives. Be sure to write all this down in your notebook.

Fashion Sense

The clothes you like, your jewelry, and your particular fashion flair are all influenced by your past lives. Do you like gypsy skirts and shawls, long coats and hats, or berets and short jackets? Look at your clothes and see whether they remind you of a particular time or place in history. Look at pictures of different places and see what clothing appeals to you. Do you love jewelry with a particular style? Your clothes and personal effects reveal a lot about your personal past.

Consider the example of Suzanne. Suzanne loves jewelry. She enjoys looking at it, holding it, taking care of it, and admiring the settings and stones. She loves everything about it except wearing it. In fact, she never wears any jewelry at all. She has a strong sense that in a past life she was a trusted maid in a royal household whose job included taking care of the mistress's jewels.

As before, write down in your notebook your fashion likes and dislikes and how you feel when you wear different items.

Activities and Inclinations

Psychologists have often debated whether children are born as empty slates or with an intact and distinct personality. Parents have no doubt. Every parent knows that each child is born with their own distinct personality complete with preferences, abilities, and tendencies. The fact that they are called predispositions should be a clue: they are predisposed from an earlier life. How you played and what you played as a child is part of the Akashic Record puzzle.

Our childhood play influences our activities as an adult. What we decide to do, the education we seek, and the hobbies we enjoy stemmed from the inclinations of our childhood fantasies. Although we can't always see the direction and career we want to pursue, it's part of the fabric of our early predispositions. Taking the time to excavate our early loves and hates can lead us to past lives and into future directions.

Child's Play

Children's inclinations show up early in life. The make-believe activities and artwork of children are very revealing. Some children only want to play cowboys and Indians and have a definite preference for which side they're on. Maybe you played knights in King Arthur's court, ladies in the palace, genies, pirates, or woodsmen. The types of stories you enacted and the roles you played are indications of your past.

> **Etheric Advisory**
>
> It's easy to look at the play-time of kids as merely imagination, especially if they are drawing pictures of aliens and spacecraft or other exotic themes. Give room for more than meets the eye. You don't really know where your child's soul has come from!

The toys you played with and the games you played are also clues. Did you have a stable of horse statues or a hangar of airplane models as a child? Did you draw pictures of certain objects, activities, or animals? Were you always outside investigating nature or playing sports?

In all likelihood, you still have a strong memory of the things you enjoyed as a child. Write them down, including which were your favorites. If you can't remember, ask other family members—preferably one of your parents—and see what gems they may recall. Did your mother save your childhood art? Take a look at it with new eyes for clues to your past.

Career and Hobbies

Most people choose their career based on either what they're good at doing or on what inspires and impassions them. Some unfortunate people never get to pursue the career they were born for but are stuck in jobs with no potential for fulfillment. One thing you can be sure of: your true career was present in your childhood interests and is part of the past-life influences you brought to this life. See whether you can follow the path of your career back into your childhood activities, dreams, or fantasies. What satisfaction do you get from your job? Why did you choose it?

It's also interesting to see what path you took to your career. Some people have a clear direction and simply work until it happens. The intensity of their dedication is a clear indication of a past-life influence. Others want to go in one direction, but obstacles or life circumstances move them along another path. Chances are this wasn't accidental. Still others seem to fall into a career without much forethought, and it turns out to be a perfect fit. Sadly, some people never get to pursue their passion because of family obligations or other life duties.

Personality Types

Your basic personality is also inherited from your past. Are you a born leader? Do you negotiate well with others? Do you prefer to be a worker and let others take the risks?

Children have individual personalities from the day they're born. This is distinct from their family's disposition; you can see the differences between children born in the same family by how they react to the same event. Each child has his or her own distinct reaction. In fact, family structures allow a child's underlying personality to stand out.

Let's look at an example. In the face of an abusive parent, all the children in a family may become angry and resentful and exhibit poor self-esteem. However, they manage their feelings according to their underlying personalities. One child may be timid and grow up to develop a life story around their victimization. Another may be an angry inferno but also exhibit leadership skills in line with their underlying personality. Another child may become a recluse and develop himself or herself within the world of ideas, avoiding interpersonal conflict. How each responds is based on their underlying personality.

Timeless Tips

Personality tests can be quite revealing. Try one at www. humanmetrics.com/cgi-win/ JTypes2.asp.

What happens to us is only one part of the story; how we react is equally important. Make a list of some of the most difficult life issues you've faced. What parts of your personality came to the forefront? What resources did you exhibit, and what did you need to develop? What is your underlying personality type?

The Abilities You Were Born With

No doubt you've worked hard to learn and develop certain skills and abilities. Some were probably harder to develop than others, and were natural. The skills and abilities you had in advance of any training were brought with you from a past life. Mathematical wizards, musical geniuses, and child prodigies all developed their skills in previous lives.

According to Cayce and other Akashic Record readers, people are reincarnating now to create new technologies to help mankind. Inspiration for these is coming directly from your past lives and the Akashic Record, as suggested in Chapter 7. Take an inventory of your abilities and inspired ideas. What do they tell you about who you are?

Emotional and Physical Terrain

Your body is a Geiger counter to gut-level information and an invaluable guide to past-life encounters. As we've discussed throughout this chapter, your immediate emotional response to people, places, artwork, cultures, homes, and so on reveal your inborn preferences from your past incarnations. Too often we shrug these feelings off as curiosities but unimportant. However, uncovering our past-life information can help many areas of this life and heal many long-lasting issues.

To explore the deeper realms of the akasha, we need to use all of our senses—including our emotions. Often called the sixth sense, emotions and physical reactions can read the energy of a situation. Our mind might be engrossed with logical thinking, but our bodies tell us about the underlying reality.

Goose Bumps and Butterflies

Physical sensations are one way your body talks to you. Imagine meeting someone and having an immediate physical reaction, like your skin crawling. Without any wondering, you know this isn't someone you want to spend time with. Sometimes these strong reactions can arouse past-life memories or reveal past-life preferences. Understanding how your body communicates is an instinct, but often our instincts are clouded with too much mental activity.

Reading your body's signals means noticing the sensations you feel. Butterflies in the stomach, tightness in the chest, goose bumps, tingling feelings, hesitations, or feelings of familiarity can be telling you that something is ringing that past-life bell. Take an inventory right now. Are there certain places, subjects, or people that give you the heebie-jeebies, or that make you feel warm and fuzzy inside? Always pay attention and notice what your body is reacting to. Over time, you may find you can read the language of the body quite well and use it as a guide in decision-making and in traversing life's many twists and turns.

> **Library Links**
>
> A good place to look for clues to your past life is in the books, stories, and movies you enjoy watching. Is there a common thread, time period, or story line you're repeatedly drawn to? How do you respond emotionally?

Also note any recurring physical problems you have, especially ones you were born with. Physical issues from birth, as well as birth marks, can be clues. Remember from Chapter 3 that physical problems from past lives can leave imprints in the Akashic Record that create your physical body in this life.

Spiders in the Closets

Fears, phobias, attractions, and aversions all play a role in the emotional landscape of our past-life detection. Phobias that don't develop from childhood events are usually the result of past-life trauma—often incurred at the time of death. Understanding where these come from can help us remove difficult limitations in our life and open the door for opportunity from the Akashic Record. Consequently, many people pursue past-life information to eliminate phobias. At the same time, phobias can lead us to past-life traumas. Let's take a look at a woman who had a strong aversion to American Colonial homes built in the 1600s. She also had an unrelenting phobia about sleeping in a locked house, and insisted that doors always be left unlocked. She had a persistent fear of fire and being burned alive and wouldn't sleep in an upstairs bedroom. You won't be surprised to learn that her aversions, fears, and phobias reveal the time period she lived in and how she died. She lived in the American colonies and died in a fire, trapped upstairs in her home, unable to get outside through the locked-up house.

Instant Likes and Dislikes

In addition to fears and phobias, we have instant likes and dislikes. We're drawn to, or repelled by, people, places, cultures, and events based on past experiences. Have you ever gone somewhere and felt an immediate distaste, even though it was beautiful and appealing? This might represent a past-life influence. Have you ever experienced a very strong fascination, even feeling compelled to visit certain places or meet certain people? You may be trying to finish a past-life drama or revisit a place where you felt deeply loved and satisfied. Strong feelings of being compelled are often markers of past-life events.

> **Akashic Wisdom**
>
> Be kind, for everyone you meet is fighting a hard battle.
>
> —Philo, philosopher in ancient Alexandria

Notice the things that pull you in life. What compels you forward? What are the ideas, areas of study, and places you want to visit?

Passionate Bliss

The things that inspire your passions guide your life. Fulfilling your passions and dreams is what you came here to achieve. Born in the deeds and dreams of your past, your passion indicates your soul's goals in this life. They lead you to your career, your path, and your purpose. We'll talk more about this in Chapter 10.

Write down the things that inspire your passions. How do you feel when you achieve them? What causes, activities, or ideas inspire you? As much as this information tells you about your past, it tells you more about your future.

Recurring Patterns

One of the most important ways to track your past is to pay attention to repeating patterns. Do you always attract the same type of relationship? No matter how hard you try to climb the corporate ladder, are you always blocked at the same level? Do problems repeat in your life?

Not all recurring patterns are negative. You may find that no matter how bad your problems are, you always find a way out at the last minute. Maybe you're repeatedly rescued from your mistakes with a brilliant idea. Patterns point to common threads, beliefs, and assumptions about reality that you bring from the past.

Make a list of the patterns that repeat in your life. Do you see common threads?

Have You Experienced This Before?

Déjà-vu is the strange feeling that the situation you're experiencing has already happened to you. Fractions of a second before things happen, you feel you know they will occur. Everything in the event feels familiar, even though you may not be able to directly place it. You may feel weird, experiencing a strange eeriness about the situation. Sometimes you may think the experience happened before in a dream, although other times the sense is so strong you may feel sure it actually did happen before.

def•i•ni•tion

Déjà-vu is the experience of thinking or feeling that a new situation has occurred before, in the past or in a dream.

Déjà-vu experiences happen to both children and adults and are always significant. They seem to be reminders to us to pay attention to what we're doing. They can indicate we're on the right path or that we're where we're supposed to be. They tend to suggest that there are deeper forces at work in life than what we are fully aware of. As weird as they feel, they are also strangely comforting.

When people visit a new place and feel they've been there before or meet a person they feel they know, it's often accompanied by a déjà-vu experience. When you have this experience, stop and pay attention to where you are, who's with you, and what's going on. Note it for the future; it may fit into a past-life trend.

Instant Recognition

The most common dramatic past-life indication is recognition. This is not a repeating pattern and is more than déjà-vu and more than a sense of familiarity. It's also more than being drawn to a climate or culture. This is the knowing of people, names, places, and features that you could not possibly know. Consider this event that happened to Colin's father, Petty Officer Gordon Andrews, of the United Kingdom:

> I was special operations in the Fleet Air Arm of the Royal Navy during the Second World War. While serving on the *H.M.S. Hood* we were dispatched several times to Malta. The first time I arrived in the Maltese shipyard I had an immediate sense of coming home. I felt excited and alive at being back somewhere that I loved. I knew when I took a left or a right what I would find around the corner. I knew all the streets and even the street names. I knew where to find restaurants and local features. Every place I went was another déjà-vu. I knew this island and loved it. Through all the rest of my life I've wanted to return.

If this has ever happened to you, it was almost certainly a past-life recognition.

Timeless Tips

For past-life stories from different places and time periods, check out www.open-sesame.com/memorybank.html.

In the case of Shanti Devi or James Leininger from Chapter 3, the recognition goes as far as full memory of the life and conditions that were left behind. For some reason, the veil of forgetfulness that separates lives was simply not pulled down at birth. Take a minute to think of the places and people you've had an immediate recognition of.

Dreaming Clues

Another place to find clues to your past life is in your dreams. Especially pay attention to recurring dreams or dreams of other worlds and lands. Our dreams often reveal subconscious information that we're unable to retrieve during daily awareness.

Lucid dreams, where you're aware you're dreaming in the dream, are particularly important. They're often direct visitations from your guides, memories from your past, or represent your soul traveling at night to different places and events. People often report dreams of living in Atlantis or ancient Egypt. Pay attention to these dreams, and keep a dream journal. We'll talk more about lucid dreams in Chapter 18.

def•i•ni•tion

A **lucid dream** is one in which you're aware in the dream that you are dreaming. They usually reveal significant information for your life, answer a question you have, or lead you in a better direction.

Putting the Pieces Together

After completing your notebook entries from this chapter, you're well on your way to discovering your past life. Everything you need is in the life you live, the passions that inspire you, and the feelings that compel you. The places, objects, and people are all signposts to the past.

You probably have information from more than one past life in the notes you've taken. Cluster together the time periods, historical figures, geographical areas, and cultures that seem to go together. You may have two or three distinct times and places. Now look at everything you've written about your predispositions, preferences, aversions, fears and phobias, passions, and dreams. Do some things seem to go with one time period more than another? Think of some of your favorite movies and books. Do they point in a particular direction? Take your time and let the pieces of the puzzle come together.

Let's look at some stories to see how information dovetails into a specific direction.

Timeless Tips _____

If you're interested in learning more about your past lives, check out *The Complete Idiot's Guide to Past Life Regression* by Michael R. Hathaway (Alpha Books, 2003).

A Case in the Civil War

This first case revolves around a young man's fascination. The man worked at a high level in a corporation. He was a strong leader in his company and forceful in his decisions and opinions.

Outside work, he was fascinated by the American Civil War. He was drawn to collecting memorabilia, especially guns and bayonets. The history of the war intrigued him, and he read everything he could. He found that when he read books on war strategies, he often corrected the author in his mind.

Eventually, his fascination became so strong he was compelled to visit key battle sites. He was restless and agitated prior to visiting each one. At the sites, he did not have any memories but felt a strong sense of familiarity. At one location, he noticed his breathing speeding up and his stomach knot in fear. After his trip, he lost his agitation and need to read everything he could on the subject. He felt at peace.

It's easy to see that this man participated in the American Civil War. The location that caused his body reactions was probably the place where he died or where something significant occurred. His personality indicates he was in a leadership role, and his reaction to the books he read implies he was a general or colonel. Whatever he didn't complete in that life was put to rest when he visited the site of his death, even though he had no conscious memories.

Library Links

Fear of death is one of the worst human enemies. It pressures people to try and achieve all their goals and desires in one life. As the soul grows and learns that there are many lives to find fulfillment, compassion and kindness are promoted.

Desert Destruction

Unraveling the next story revolved around the person's physical condition. The woman in this case was born with scoliosis, or curvature of the spine. She developed a love of horses after seeing a picture of one when she was four. Every childhood fantasy and play involved horses. As a teenager, she wore long, flowing skirts with many layers and wrapped her head in scarves. After watching the movie *Lawrence of Arabia*, she developed a deep love and compelling fascination for the Bedouin tribe. She read everything she could find on the subject.

As an adult, the woman's scoliosis acted up and she lived with constant back pain. One day in meditation she asked to understand the origin of her back pain and had the following vision:

> I saw myself as an English man in the 1200s participating in one of the crusades to the Middle East. My job was to care for the horse at the end of each ride. I loved the horses and my horse was my best friend. I was terribly torn during our missions. I believed the heathen had to be destroyed, I just couldn't see these innocent people as heathens.

> As we tore through the Bedouin tent camps, murdering and maiming, I rode in the middle of the pack and avoided killing anyone. I was tortured by the wrongness of what we were doing even though my companions thought it was fright. During one raid I was thrown from my horse and trampled by the horse behind me. He stepped on my back where the curve is today and I was killed. I also saw that my back represented my lack of backbone in doing what I believed was right.

Your Story

You may already have all the pieces of your story and can put together where, when, and how you lived your past life. If you're having trouble, let your subconscious mind have free rein. Let it make up a story. Don't worry about whether it's true or not; you can sort that out later. You can start it with, "If I lived in a past life before, I would …" Let your past reveal itself.

The Least You Need to Know

- ◆ Your past lives exist in the Akashic Record and hold information that is helpful to you in this life.

- ◆ Past-life information is revealed through your preferences, activities, hobbies, fears, aversions, and fascinations.

- ◆ Paying attention to the repeating patterns, emotions, and physical reactions can provide past-life clues.

- ◆ Your past-life puzzle can be understood when you put all the pieces together.

Chapter 9

Healing the Akashic Past

In This Chapter

- ◆ The dynamics of Akashic Record healing
- ◆ Four steps to healing your past
- ◆ Finding your core issues
- ◆ Using intentions and affirmations

Many persistent problems can be healed through the Akashic Record. Understanding the cause and limiting beliefs that were imprinted in the Record provide the pathway to release. Shifting the energy provides personal growth and healing, allowing the entire Akashic Record to grow and evolve.

Healing in the Akasha

According to the Akashic Record, spiritual separation is the cause of disease, and healing is the process of becoming whole. Whenever harm or damage is corrected and there is greater wholeness, healing has occurred. The process of becoming whole requires accepting that the conditions in our life are not external events. We create them through our choices; in other words, through our karma.

Edgar Cayce revealed that the state of your health and the conditions of your life are reflections of your thoughts, attitudes, and beliefs which we can call TABs. Your TABs are formed in your past lives, and present, from the events you've lived through and from your decisions, mistakes, and victories. Some of your TABs enhance growth; some restrict growth and cause physical and/or emotional suffering.

> **Library Links**
>
> Healing and curing are two different things. Curing is the elimination of the signs and symptoms of illness. Healing is becoming whole—removing the underlying cause of illness and identifying with our spiritual self. Healing may or may not occur with a change in symptoms, but it always occurs with an acceptance of self and newfound fulfillment.

Healing requires identifying the limiting TABs that block your growth and then releasing them. Since TABs often develop from core imprints, or past events that color your perceptions, these need to be addressed as well. There are many different methods for identifying and releasing past events, and you may already use one or more. If not, try the steps outlined in this chapter. With whatever method you use, connect with the Akashic Record and allow the information in the Record to assist with your healing process.

The Akashic Record helps you approach healing from a new perspective. It helps you look at your issues not as something wrong within yourself but as a reflection of your desire for growth. Your limiting beliefs, unfulfilled potentials, and incomplete soul growth created both the need and the circumstances for your healing. There are no mistakes.

The Akashic Imprint

As you learned in Chapter 1, everything you've ever thought, said, or done is a vibrational imprint in the Akashic Record. Your level of health, the illness and pain you carry, as well as the immense resources you have are all physical manifestations of the vibrations of your past actions. If you're ill or unhappy, you're physically manifesting your internal beliefs. You can focus on your illness as an external process or consider that your inner wounds created the condition for the illness to take root.

Your akashic imprints direct what lessons you decide to work on in this life, and that creates your circumstances and conditions. Your life may reflect a decision to transmute past karma or to develop a new potential. You may have decided to make a sacrifice for the benefit of those around you. The only requirement from the Record is that eventually, you work on all your limiting TABs and develop all your potentials. The Record compels you to be your authentic self so that your unique perspective and gifts can promote the Record's evolution.

Blocks to Growth

Everyone has blocks to their growth. These are specific beliefs that keep you separated from your spirit. They get in the way of finding the underlying cause of your problem and of living life to the fullest. Removing blocks allows you to realign with your higher spiritual truth and bring more positivity into your life. Akashic healing can highlight your blocks and restrictions, offering you the opportunity to release your limiting beliefs, emotional scars, past programming, and self-defeating patterns.

Library Links

In Shamanic journeying, accepting that our illnesses are part of our undeveloped selves is called "owning your shadow." Wholeness is achieved when the soul journeys outside the body and retrieves the disowned parts of self.

Removing your blocks also allows you to become more aware of the choices you make. Instead of your unconscious TABs deciding your life script, you can choose the life you want. Because developing awareness and love are the prime directives of soul evolution, removing your blocks goes a long way toward helping you live a more authentic and happy life. Becoming conscious of your choices leads to a life full of adventure as you write your script from your passions instead of your fears.

The End of "Bad" Karma

When you cause harm, your karma creates consequences that you must face in order to correct your path. The conditions may seem harsh, but that's what's required for your growth. If you hurt someone by lying about them and turning people against them, you could endure a similar fate unless you develop your conscience, choosing compassion over power. Undeveloped souls have no conscience.

Karma is between you and your higher self, or the Akashic Record, and you can transmute it at any time. All you have to do is demonstrate that you have learned the necessary lesson. The first step is acknowledging your choices and accepting the consequences. The next step is changing your behavior. Like Scrooge in the classic story *A Christmas Carol*, accepting his transgressions was not enough. His enlightenment wasn't complete until he changed his behavior. Accepting the consequences of your past actions is the opportunity to live a life of love, compassion, and service. This is the foundation for healing.

Finding Core Imprints

Core imprints are the underlying causes of our problems that can be expressed through health, career, relationships, or any other part of our life. The Akashic Record can assist your healing by revealing your core imprints so that you can clear them. Most of the time imprints reveal old trauma or transgressions. Other times, however, core imprints push you to challenge your limits and explore new directions—maybe one you've resisted. Edgar Cayce's life is an excellent example of the latter type of healing.

Timeless Tips

An Akashic Record reading can help you identify core issues. To find a reader in your area, go to www.mediumfind.net/.

Edgar Cayce was one of the most prolific Akashic Record readers in history and directly helped thousands of people. Before he could begin his work, however, he had to heal himself.

In 1901, when Cayce was 24, he was working as a salesman for an insurance company when he contracted laryngitis. His inability to speak meant he couldn't work. Doctors told him he would never completely recover his voice. A local stage hypnotist offered to try and heal him on stage, and in desperation, Cayce agreed. While hypnotized, he could speak perfectly well; out of the trance, his voice was once again gone. A second hypnotherapist, Al Layne, put Cayce in a trance and asked him to describe the cause of his illness and heal it. Cayce did.

Although Cayce diagnosed a physical problem and prescribed a physical cure, his real healing involved uncovering his talent. Discovering he was able to diagnose and prescribe successfully in trance showed him his path and purpose. He had contracted in this life to use his voice to help people by providing Akashic readings and healing remedies. His laryngitis pushed him to fulfill his contract.

The Healing Process

The potential for healing within the Akashic Record is unlimited. The key is commitment and intent. It's not always easy and we can be blind to our own issues. Fortunately, the Record Keepers and your guides are available to help, but healing is not an event, it's a process. Your free will dictates the direction, amount of healing, and speed. Nothing is ever forced on you; you are in control of the process.

One way you can use the Akashic Record is through the following four-step process. When you're using this process, ask your guides or the Record Keepers to help.

Often people feel uncomfortable asking guides for help, either because they feel silly or feel they have to solve their own problems. In some cases people are afraid to admit they have a problem—which means it can't be healed at all. Connecting with the Record Keepers and asking for help in seeing, shifting, and healing your imprints and TABs can change your life.

Etheric Advisory

Many of the problems you have can be healed with your own intentions. However, if you have feelings of not wanting to be alive, please seek professional help. Don't wait! You deserve a happy, fulfilling life.

The four steps to releasing an unhealed pattern may be familiar to you. They are:

1. Identify the issue you need to work on.

2. Find the cause or core imprint through the Akashic Record.

3. Expand your perspective and see the bigger picture by connecting to a higher spiritual truth.

4. Shift the energy of the past.

Once this is accomplished, the body's natural processes can go to work.

In the next sections, you'll see examples of how these steps work. It's always a good idea to start any healing process by creating sacred space. You can do this simply by going to a comfortable area free of distractions, putting on soft music, and envisioning the space filled with light. Ask your guides and guardians to be present and available. Envision the highest and best good as your outcome.

Identify the Issue

The first step in the process of healing is to identify the issue. Think of a problem in your life that you've worked to resolve but can't. Maybe this is a repeating pattern for you, a type of relationship you have over and over again, or back pain that keeps returning. Speak the problem out loud or write it down in a journal. Some people feel self-conscious in this process. Don't worry—no one will see or hear your story other than you and your helpers. The truth is that you can't receive help until you acknowledge where you need it, and stating the issue is an important step in the process.

Address all aspects of the issue. When did it start? Who is involved? How do you experience it? Speaking the story out loud or writing it in a journal is an important

Timeless Tips _____

Using this process is another great way to use a journal. If you're still unsure about how to journal, here's a great site: www.amanobooks.com/tips.php.

method for seeing it more objectively. Start at the beginning of the story, and be specific.

Once you've let your deeper feelings out, you may already be clearer. It's amazing how helpful letting something completely out can be. Even though you feel better, continue the rest of the process anyway. There are always deeper levels you can access.

Find the Cause

The next part of the process is to find out where the issue you're working on originated. When was the imprint made? Did it start in this life, or is it residue from a previous life? Is it a karmic debt, an old pact, or some other agreement you've made?

To retrieve past information, you need to quiet your mind. Sit in a comfortable, quiet place where you won't be disturbed. Make a connection to your spiritual helpers or the Record Keepers. You can do this by simply acknowledging them and thanking them for their help. If you want to, you can envision a bubble of light around yourself and invite your helpers inside. This is a safe and comfortable technique. Allow images to float past your mind's eye. Don't try to control them; let them come and go as they wish.

Ask yourself: "If this issue came from a past life, what might the event have been?" Suspend your logical mind and accept whatever comes. Let a story form in your mind. You'll know whether it has legs by how it makes you feel. You may feel goose bumps, tingles, or warm rushes through your body. You may feel you want to cry. These are good indications you've hit the mark. This step takes a little trust on your part. You have to allow the possibility that the images you see in your mind's eye could be real.

Once you have an image of an event, identify the attitudes and beliefs that you formed at this time. You can do this by noticing how you feel and what you think as you witness the story. Ask for help seeing where these beliefs are present in your current situation. If you feel stuck, write the question down in your journal and make yourself give 10 answers, no matter how silly they may seem. Then just write everything you feel about your answers. Eventually you'll strip away the resistance and get to something important.

If you still feel stuck, you might want to have a past-life regression or speak to a reader of the Akashic Record. To understand the difference between the two types of work, feel free to jump ahead to Chapter 19.

Expand Your Perspective

The third step is to understand the larger picture and find forgiveness. It's easy to judge ourselves, other people, or the situations we've been in. In truth, everyone is doing their best to grow—including you! The situation, however hard it is, offers an opportunity to grow.

> **Akashic Wisdom**
>
> I don't feel that we have any choice but to see the Love and the Light that exists within every person.
>
> —Doreen Virtue, Ph.D., clairvoyant psychotherapist

Open yourself to insight into the soul growth underway. Shift to the bigger picture. If you can see the self you were in your past life, dialogue with that person. Ask him or her what is needed and whether there is anything you can do to help. If you want, ask your guides to help clarify. When you feel complete, thank yourself and everyone involved, forgive yourself and all others, and release everyone from the karmic cycle. Thank your guides and the Record Keepers.

Shift Your Energy

The final step in the process is to cleanse your energy field. The human energy field consists of an aura and chakras and is a magnet to energetic forces. Having completed the first three steps, your vibration has shifted. Finalize the shift by cleansing your field of old patterns and making room for new ones. This will help you in changing your old behavior to create the life you want.

You can cleanse your field by imagining flows of energy in the form of light and/ or color washing over and through you. Breathe light in with your inhalations, and breathe the old out with your exhalations. You can also physically clean your energy field by such things as taking an Epsom salt bath. Use a process you're familiar with— and enjoy yourself!

> **Timeless Tips**
>
> If you're not familiar with aura cleansing, an excellent book is *Exploring Auras: Cleansing and Strengthening Your Energy Field* by Susan G. Shumsky and Dannion Brinkley (see Appendix B).

Willingness to Grow

The success of your Akashic Record healing relies on two things: your trust in the process and your willingness to grow. Trusting the process can be difficult, and if this is an issue, you may want to work with a professional energy healer or body-worker to see what magic can happen. After one or two sessions, you should be able to clear problems and issues on your own.

Being willing to grow is evidenced by making concrete changes in your life. Gaining information for the sake of information doesn't promote change. If you don't put in practice what you've learned, everything stays the same. Working with the Akashic Record gives you all the tools. How you use them is your choice. No one but you is judging, and you are the one who benefits.

Truthfully, this work can be very freeing. Inhibitions, restrictions, and fears that have plagued you can be shifted. The separation and isolation you may have felt in your relationships can be healed. You can experience more joy and greater inner peace. Most important is the ability to live in the present moment, making clear and conscious choices rather than being directed by your past.

Walking the Healing Path

The patterns of your life are a direct result of your limitations of imagination. You don't have a more fulfilling life because you can't imagine yourself in one. Or you may be able to imagine a better life, but you can't see yourself living it. If you could, you would. What stops your imagination are the limits you placed on yourself with your underlying TABs.

The four-step healing process you just learned can change your life. You can use it to release physical and emotional problems, create healthy, loving relationships, and let go of things that don't serve you. You can change situations and create better opportunities. As the following stories demonstrate, change happens in ways we don't always anticipate.

Physical Healing

Healing on the physical level is often more challenging than healing on the emotional level, simply because matter is dense and more difficult to change. Fortunately, your body has all the mechanisms necessary to heal. If there are past-life blocks toward healing, removing them frees the natural processes of the body to restore health. If a condition has degenerated beyond a certain point, restoring physical health may not be possible. However, astonishing benefits have been realized using this method.

Remember the woman in Chapter 8 who was trampled by a horse in a previous life? She died in a state of shame and guilt for not standing up for the innocent people being slaughtered. She realized this was the root of her belief that she didn't deserve happiness. Next, she looked for the higher meaning. She accepted that each person there was learning something they had signed up for. She acknowledged that the lesson for her was not to follow the pack but to be her authentic self in all situations. She looked at her life and saw that at work she was not taking a stand she believed in because she thought it would stop her advancement in the company. She also realized there were many times in her life when she had not stood up for what she knew was right.

After clearly seeing her situation, she acknowledged the lesson, thanked and forgave herself and all involved, cleansed her energy, and released everyone from the karmic contracts. Shortly after her inner healing, she found physical healing as well. Learning of a new manual therapy for correcting some types of scoliosis, she signed up for treatment—something she would not have pursued prior to her process work. She responded well and now no longer suffers back pain. Additionally, she changed her life to better express her ideals. She began to voice her views in board meetings and in corporate decisions. Not surprisingly, upon doing this she obtained the promotion she expected to be denied!

> **Etheric Advisory**
>
> Don't make the mistake of assuming you can heal your illnesses with spiritual healing alone. Your illness exists in both realms—spiritual and physical—and needs to be addressed in both realms for the most effective and safest result.

Sometimes the process of healing happens in stages or has gone so far into the physical it can't be easily reversed. For example, Janice suffers terrible pain in her feet. Although doctors can't find any reason for it, Janice's feet are so sensitive she has trouble walking, can't tolerate certain shoes, and can't bear having her feet touched. She feels crippled.

Through the Akashic Record, it was revealed that the pain in her feet originated in a past life as a Revolutionary War soldier at Valley Forge. Her frozen, gangrened feet were crammed into boots that were too small and she was forced to march miles in excruciating pain. Finding the originating event, however, did not cure Janice's foot pain. This may have been because the process was still incomplete. Maybe the underlying TABs had not been found or a higher perspective had not been attained. Perhaps this event was only the first layer in a situation that evolved over many lifetimes. Until more work has been done, the past-life story will not have the power to change Janice's foot pain. Even after completing the process, her feet may still hurt, but she will find inner peace and acceptance and know that healing has occurred.

Situational Healing

As you know, the situations in your life are also representations of your thoughts, attitudes, and beliefs. According to a spiritual teaching called the *Course in Miracles*, all emotions can be reduced to either love or fear. Healing from the Akashic Record can help you let go of fear-based attitudes and realize that people and events aren't the cause of your conflict and distress. It's your attitudes about the people and events that cause your stress.

In fact, you can change the people and events in your life and then recreate the same situations elsewhere, with the next set of people and events. This is because you draw the situations that reflect your inner beliefs that you are here to work on. Until you change your inner beliefs, you cannot change your life.

You can use the four-step process to work on situations, too. Meet Fiona, who is a very talented artist. Her work is exceptional, and everyone can see it—including Fiona. Unfortunately, she finds it difficult to accept money for her work. She repeatedly under-prices it and puts her pieces in shows that draw a clientele who can't pay what its worth. Her continual refrain is, "If only …" It might be, "If only I can sell this art piece, I can get what I need." Or she may say, "If only I had a relationship, I would be happy." Unfortunately, Fiona is blocked in her ability to create her life.

In an Akashic Record healing session, Fiona found that in a past life she gave up her spiritual center for wealth and physical comfort. She was a merchant in the industrial revolution in England. She used child labor and hurt many people, including her spouse, to become rich regardless of the expense. In this past life, she was unable to see the beauty in the world and sold her soul for material gain. In this life, she is producing great beauty and is unable to make any money on it.

During the process, Fiona had a flash of insight. She realized she was as focused in this life on material well-being as she was in that life. She recognized that underlying fears of security and safety ruled her thinking. Once Fiona accepted that her situation was the result of losing her connection to her authentic self, she made a commitment to change her life. She was able to forgive herself and began to look for ways to make the world a better place. She donated her artwork to children's hospitals and taught handicapped children how to access their creativity. In no time, her artwork was selling and her material situation improved—although it no longer had the importance it originally had.

Library Links

Here are a few of the tenets from "The Twelve Principles of Attitudinal Healing," as taught by psychiatrist Dr. Jerry Jampolsky, founder of the International Center for Attitudinal Healing in 1975:

- The essence of being is love.
- Health is inner peace.
- Giving and receiving are the same.
- We can let go of the past and the future.
- Now is the only time there is.
- We learn to love ourselves and others by forgiving rather than judging.
- We can become love finders rather than fault finders.
- We can be peaceful inside regardless of what is happening outside.
- We are students and teachers to each other.

You can find more on his website at www.jerryjampolskyanddianecirincione.com.

Healing Relationships

Relationships offer the greatest opportunity for your growth and can provide the deepest levels of satisfaction on this plane. However, relationships can also be notoriously difficult. Our fears cripple the depth of connection we seek. Relationship fears challenge our need for intimacy versus independence. They challenge our self-worth, empowerment, and compassion. If we meet the challenge, the rewards are plenty—but too often we're trapped in relationships that can't grow. But for some reason, we can't leave.

As we explained in Chapter 4, people repeatedly attract the same unfulfilling relationships until they complete the growth they have contracted in this life. It's important to keep in mind that you choose the circumstances and conditions in your life. However, your only requirement is to show up. After that, you don't owe the situation anything beyond growth. What direction growth takes is up to you. You don't have to stay in bad relationships, but until you clear the underlying imprint, you probably will.

Here's what happened to Cathy. Cathy was raised in a strict family with a psychologically abusive father. Her self-esteem was poor, and as a teenager she avoided dating. Her adult relationships were characterized by her taking care of men who didn't contribute. She tried to earn her self-worth by doing all the work in the relationship herself. She despaired of ever finding a fulfilling partnership.

Everything changed for Cathy after she underwent an Akashic Record healing. In the process, she saw a past life as a man who took huge risks and failed. He died leaving his family holding the bag for the risks he took and the inability to carry them off. Cathy brought tremendous guilt into this life and also an underlying belief that she was incapable of taking care of herself. She had a fear of failure and set up her life conditions to prove she could survive under any circumstance.

Once she saw the pattern, she was free. She acknowledged that she had proven in this life she could take care of herself and everyone else. She thanked everyone involved in the past and present life for her teaching, forgave herself, and called the contracts complete. In her description, "I turned a corner in my mind and the landscape in my life completely changed." In a matter of months, she met her soul mate and the relationship brought all the joy she had every dreamed of.

Changing Patterns

Once you've found the underlying cause of your troubles and reconnected with your spiritual center, your life will start to shift. However, you will still need to take active steps. Old patterns and behaviors are hard to break—especially when they're engrained in your friendships and social life.

Changing patterns may require letting go of people and activities that don't serve your new, healthy self. Maybe that will mean never seeing certain people again, or maybe it just means not being trapped in the roles you play with each other. Either way, as your behaviors change you will be tested and enticed to go back to old ways. At this point, keeping yourself connected to the higher picture is essential.

Akashic Wisdom

As your thoughts are, so is your life.

—Edgar Cayce

Most importantly, changing old patterns requires changing how you think. Your mind is the most powerful tool you have. As we've seen, changing your attitudes and beliefs changes how you think and behave. You can consciously support these changes through the use of creative thinking, intentions, and affirmations.

Creative Thinking

Your thoughts are the creative force you use to craft your life. They are alive and attract life force. Your habitual thoughts, the ones you think several times a day, determine the quality of your life. People who think critical thoughts, who spend their time looking for things to criticize in the people around them, have unhappy relationships. They draw to themselves people with enough things to criticize to keep them busy. On the other hand, people who always look for the silver linings tend to have more of them. They also live longer, as medical studies prove. How you think influences your actions and reactions and creates your life.

When you have a thought, your body has an immediate reaction. If you hear a sound and think someone is in the basement, chemicals cascade through your system whether anyone is really there or not. When you expect unhappiness, unhappy chemicals rule your system. Your unhappiness is reflected all around you in the unfulfilling relationships you create and the unsatisfying job you have.

On the other hand, the power of the mind is unlimited. It's creative and playful. You can keep the momentum of your Akashic Record healing by using the power of your mind to think life-enhancing thoughts. Mind power is second only to the power of spirit. When your thoughts are in alignment with the creative power of the Akashic Record and reflect higher consciousness, there isn't anything that can't be accomplished.

Intentional Thinking

One of the best ways to use your mind power is to form intentions. Intentions aim you toward a goal. Without an intention, you can't manifest your purpose. You know the story—if you don't know where you want to go, you'll end up where you're heading. The problem is that most of us don't have a clear idea of what we want. We have vague thoughts, such as, "I want more money" or "I want more happiness." Obviously, these thoughts live in the delusion that what you want is outside yourself. It's not! You just need to add intention into your thinking.

Here's an easy and quick method for forming intentions. First, get clear about what you want. It's not enough to want money. How will having money make you feel? What will it give you that you don't have now (besides more money!)? If you want money in order to feel free, secure, or capable, then freedom, security, or ability must be part of your intention. If happiness will make you feel alive, then vitality must be part of your intention.

To manifest your intention, let yourself get into a clear, meditative state of mind. Then focus on your intention as if it already exists. See it, feel it, and experience it. Imagine yourself free. What are you doing? Where do you live? Who are your friends? Invest your intention with the power of your emotions. Feel the joy of your intention. If your intention doesn't bring you joy, it's not a productive intention. If you can't generate positive emotion, then you don't have a powerful desire for it.

Powerfully hold your intentions every day. Act as if your intention is manifest. Apply for the job you want, go back to school, or write your book. Make your choices as if you already are free, safe, and capable. Be the person, be the change, and be the attributes you want your intention to create.

Affirmations

While you're living out your intentions and changing your behaviors, you may find that your thoughts, attitudes, and beliefs occasionally slip back into old patterns. Don't get upset when this happens; old habits are hard to break! Just remember they're only habits, and they can be changed. All it takes is mental discipline.

Timeless Tips _____

If you're having trouble making affirmations, here's a great site for instruction: www.affirmations. gems4friends.com/articles/work. html.

Every time your thoughts slip into the old negative beliefs and attitudes, replace them with an affirmation. An affirmation states the presence of the underlying reality. If your intention is to be free, then when you find yourself feeling constrained, replace your limiting thought with an affirmation. In this case, you might choose, "I am a free spiritual being" or "The Akashic Record supports my path and purpose."

Affirmations are directions to your subconscious mind. With an affirmation, you're telling your subconscious what you want to manifest. Your subconscious mind then begins to create your affirmation—what you think you will become. Every time you find yourself thinking a disempowering thought, counter it with an affirmation. Then when you get a chance, spend 60 seconds visualizing your intention in your mind's eye.

Choosing an affirmation that will work for you can be tricky. Here are a few guidelines:

♦ Use present tense. Instead of saying, "I am going to have a loving relationship," say, "Loving relationships are all around me."

♦ Always make positive statements. Rather than, "I am no longer lonely," say, "I am fulfilled and surrounded by love."

♦ Be short and concise. Long affirmations confuse the purpose.

♦ Be focused on yourself and your actions. Rather than, "I deserve for Mark to love me," say, "I deserve and receive love." You can't change someone else, but you can open yourself to being more lovable.

The Least You Need to Know

♦ Healing starts with finding the underlying cause of the problem.

♦ Your thoughts, attitudes, and beliefs (TABs) create your life.

♦ To heal, identify the issue, find the root cause, expand your perspective to see the bigger picture, and shift the energy of the past.

♦ Changing old patterns requires changing how you think. Use intentions to guide your subconscious mind and affirmations to counter old thinking patterns.

Part  3

The Akashic Present

The point of power is in the present moment, and in these chapters you'll gain the insight you need to take control of your life. The conditions and circumstances of your life were decided by you before you were born. You can explore those conditions to find the lessons you've signed up for, uncover your path and purpose, and examine the interconnections of relationships.

In this part, you'll get to search the Record for insights into your love life and the challenges of your life events, and find support in living your authenticity.

"Even this next play is written in the Record, boys.
And it's going to be a touchdown."

Chapter 10

Discovering Your Path and Purpose

In This Chapter

- How knowing your purpose gives your life meaning
- Becoming a purpose detective
- How to follow your path
- Your internal guidance system

Everyone wants to know their path and purpose. People talk about it as if their purpose is outside themselves—a directive that has been given to them. You don't have to search for your purpose; it *is* you. It lives within, directing your path and guiding your choices. You don't have to know your path; every footstep is creating it. You, your purpose, and your path are one. Your life purpose was written in the Akashic Record before you were born. To know yourself is to know your purpose.

Connecting to Your Purpose

Many people are searching for the guiding principle in their life to focus their actions and provide direction. They want to express their core values in meaningful careers and partnerships. Other people have a strong sense that they're alive at this place, in this time, for a reason. They may or may not know what that reason is, but the sense is deep and pervasive. Whether you know your purpose or not, everyone wants to leave the world a better place for having been here.

The Akashic Record holds the purpose and path of every individual and group as well as humanity at large. Before you were born into this life, you consulted with the Record to formulate your purpose and create the conditions necessary to fulfill it. Your purpose is alive and well, kept in your subconscious mind. Your subconscious, however, may not be sending you very many clues!

The good news is that your purpose isn't something you have to find—because it's not lost. It's unfolding in each moment, revealing its direction in every experience you have. Your purpose is part of who you are. Although you can't be separated from it, you can be unconscious of it. Consciously connecting to your purpose is probably the most empowering event in life.

When you connect to your purpose, you find courage and capabilities you didn't know existed. From the moment you make that connection, seemingly disparate events in your life come together. Each separate event now has meaning and context in the whole of your life. Each one provides different tools, and each life experience was essential. Nothing is wasted. Every experience you've ever had seems tailor-made to fulfilling your purpose. Your life expresses a profound authenticity, and there are not enough hours in the day to do all you are inspired to do.

> **Akashic Wisdom**
>
> For the primary purpose of every human being is simply to be fully engaged in this moment, and aligned with the natural flow of reality itself.
>
> —Eckhart Tolle, author

Are you someone who doesn't believe life has a purpose? In some ways, that means you don't believe in yourself. Even if you don't believe in a purpose, it will unfold anyway; you'll simply miss the enjoyment of seeing the connections and meaning in life.

Meaning

The primary benefit to connecting with your purpose is that it gives life meaning. You may have spent years identifying with your job or the roles you play. You may spend time and effort seeking inner meaning through the approval of people around you. Eventually, you come up feeling empty. You're not here to play-act for others. You're here to fulfill a purpose that has nothing to do with your job or activities. It's anchored in the realm of the soul.

Connecting with your purpose doesn't mean you have to change what you do. Purpose has less to do with *what* you do than *how* you do it. A purposeful life is an expression of the values and core truth within your soul. You're not your job, your bank account, your car, or your vacation home. None of these things provide your life with meaning. However, once you're connected to your purpose, all of these develop meaning. Your life purpose makes everything you do, and are, meaningful.

Effectiveness

Purpose gives your life clarity and focus. It becomes easier to see where to apply skills and what wastes your energy. Everyone enjoys the satisfaction of accomplishment, and no one likes wasting their time, skills, and ability. Having purpose provides greater discernment.

Having meaningful goals is motivating and energizing. There's nothing you can't do when you feel connected to your higher truth and are supported in expressing it. Once you're focused on your ultimate purpose, you're able to accomplish your goals faster and with greater fulfillment and satisfaction.

Direction

Purpose provides you with a solid foundation for making decisions. Rather than following what you've been taught or programmed to think and do, you're able to gauge your choices against a higher reality. Everything you do is weighed against whether it adds to or takes away from the expression of your purpose. Ultimately, knowing your purpose provides commitment and allows you to better adjust to the changing world.

If all this talk of change makes you nervous, don't worry: you're not hostage to your purpose. It's not a weight on your shoulders or a task that must be fulfilled. Its function isn't to own your life; it's to guide your life. Understanding it helps you know what's important and what isn't. Once you begin living purposefully, happiness and peace prevail.

Etheric Advisory

Once you find your purpose, you may decide to make big changes in your life. Don't get yourself in trouble by moving too fast. Don't worry: you won't miss anything. Allow yourself to relax and enjoy the unfolding.

Motivation

It's hard to get excited about getting up in the morning to a job with little satisfaction and no prospects for something better. When you can clearly see that an area in your life doesn't work toward your higher path, knowing your purpose motivates and directs change. On the other hand, the same job can suddenly burst forth with meaning when you can see that it fits into your soul's purpose.

> **Timeless Tips**
>
> As you search for meaning and purpose, connecting with inspirational speakers can be uplifting and strengthen your resolve. A good book on the subject is *A New Earth: Awakening to Your Life's Purpose* by Eckhart Tolle (see Appendix B). Or visit his website: www.eckharttolle.com.

When your life has meaning, every day is an adventure. Every day is an opportunity to express your inner truth in exciting and satisfying activities. Your creativity can be set free, and your dreams are inspired.

There are many things that may motivate you: wanting to be a better parent, lover, or friend; wanting to improve your performance at work; or fulfilling a long-held goal. Living your purpose will help bring clarity, fulfillment, and tremendous joy to every goal and activity you engage in.

Support

It may sound as if life will be perfect if only you can connect to your life purpose. If only that were so! Life brings many challenges and sometimes even obstacles to the expression of your purpose. There's no way to completely avoid difficulty or loss. It's a fact of life that everything changes, which means we will lose people we love and jobs we're happy in. Our sense of accomplishment will wax and wane. Having purpose in life doesn't allow you to avoid these things.

It does, however, provide perspective. It lets you tune in to the higher picture and find the meaning in events. It lets you see beyond the horizon. What you go through may be hard, but it becomes bearable when you know there is meaning and purpose in doing so.

Detecting Your Purpose

For many people, and maybe for you, detecting your purpose is the hardest task imaginable. People are full of the directives of their parents, teachers, and society. Listening to the voice within is difficult when there are many external expectations and demands.

If you want to discover your true purpose, rid yourself of all the false purposes that have been engrained in you. It may be that you were born into your family to fulfill the family name or position. If that's true, you will feel excitement and satisfaction in doing so. If you don't, you're living someone else's purpose for you and not your own.

 **Akashic Wisdom**

What is a weed? A plant whose virtues have not yet been discovered.

—Ralph Waldo Emerson, essayist, philosopher, and poet

Your purpose is what compels you at the deepest level of your being. It may not make sense to you, or it may make perfect sense. Often, it is a complete surprise. Gandhi did not start his life thinking his purpose was to liberate India. He probably wouldn't have believed it if he were told. It had to develop and unfold as he lived his life. He was compelled to react according to his deepest principles to the injustice around him. By following his truth, his purpose unfolded.

Understanding your purpose takes time. When you're young, your purpose is to experience life, grow, and develop your skills. When you're older, it shifts to giving back to the world in some way—to using what you learned and create something unique.

Although some people do have a light bulb go off in their heads, in most cases you probably won't find your purpose instantaneously. Your purpose is a journey unfolding one step at a time. At first, it's difficult to see where the steps are taking you. After a while, however, the design begins to emerge. Sometimes you feel you have part of it but not all of it. Patience, commitment, a belief in your purpose, and energy are required at this point.

Key Questions

To start your detective work, you need to have a set of questions that focuses your search. You also want to ask for divine guidance. Your purpose is firmly entrenched in the Akashic Record, and asking for help revealing it can be useful. Consider inviting the Record Keepers and your guides to help in aligning you to the information you seek. Meditate on your arrival at the gates of the Hall of Records and ask your focusing questions to the guides you find:

- ◆ What is most important to me in my life?

- ◆ What are my deepest values and beliefs?

- What gives me joy?

- What would I do if ...?

As you answer these questions, start to apply them to a bigger picture. For example, Susan found that what was most important in her life was making a connection with people. She found her deepest belief was that every person has a divine soul and is invaluable. What gives her joy is watching the light bulb go off in people as they learn something new and feel inspired. When she asked herself what she would do if she had all the money in the world, she knew she wanted to provide teenagers with the opportunity to discover their special gifts. When she formulated this as a purpose, it read, "My purpose is to connect with kids in such a way that they see themselves in their highest light."

> ### Library Links
>
> A scientific study reported in *Business Week Magazine* in 2009, conducted by Dr. Patricia Boyle, a neurophysiologist at the Rush Alzheimer's Disease Center, confirmed what we all know: people who have a purpose—whether lofty or down to earth—live longer, healthier lives than those who don't.

It's true that Susan already had a pretty good sense of her purpose. However, asking these questions allowed her to condense it into a principle that guided her choices. She used her hobbies to fulfill her purpose by inviting kids in her community to join her. Susan is a licensed animal rescuer and rehabilitator and started a community service program through the high school. She invited kids to help by cleaning cages, feeding the babies, and participating in the release when the animals were ready to go. Her purpose wasn't her hobby, although her hobby could be used to fulfill her purpose.

Major Life Events

A good place to look for clues to your purpose is in the conditions, circumstances, and major events of your life. You contracted these based on the purpose formulated in the Akashic Record—the purpose you came here to fulfill.

Fortunately, you've already done a lot of this work in the preceding chapters, so you have an idea of what you've faced and how you've reacted. You've learned what underlying causes and beliefs have impacted you. At first, it might be hard to locate the thread between it all to identify the underlying purpose. The clues to this are in your feelings. When did you feel fulfilled? When did you feel joy? Like Susan, add these experiences to your answers to the previous four focusing questions—and you will be close to finding your path.

Knacks, Talents, and Strengths

You already know that the abilities you developed in a past life are with you today as your special knacks and talents. It makes sense these would be part of the purpose you came here to fulfill. Your personality strengths are also part of the picture.

Your strengths and weaknesses help send you along your path. Some people have a terrible time staying focused in school but can build anything when given a hammer and nails. Obviously, forcing an academic career on a person of hands-on skill could be a waste. Look at your strengths and separate them from what is expected of you. What do you really love doing, and what are you really good at? All of this is part of what you are here to fulfill.

Equally, the most defining moment in a person's life can be stepping outside his or her comfort zone to embrace a project or job he or she never imagined possible. Your strengths take you to the point of growth. It's then possible to step into a new area to develop new abilities or discover strengths you never knew you had.

> **Timeless Tips**
>
> Two great books for finding your strengths are *Now Discover Your Strengths* by Marcus Buckingham and *What Color Is Your Parachute? 2009: A Practical Manual for Job-Hunters and Career-Changers* by Richard N. Boles. See Appendix B for details on both books.

What Intrigues You?

Not everyone feels they have special talents or abilities. Although it's probably not true, you may be having a hard time identifying them. Another avenue to pursue is tracking your curiosity. Some people are driven to understand the mysteries of the universe. Others are curious about different people, places, and cultures. Maybe you are fascinated with concepts of metaphysics and personal development. Whatever captures your imagination and compels you to search for more information is part of your purpose.

Causes you embrace are also clues. Make a list of all the causes you have embraced in your life. Which ones were momentary, and which ones have stayed with you? Do you give money to these causes, or do you get actively involved? The ones you feel compelled to become active in are more aligned to your core.

Purposeful Exercises

At this point, you may be feeling blocked in finding your purpose. There is no universal formula. You can listen to motivational speakers and be inspired. The techniques offered here may help, but there is no one way to find it. You have to explore and dig into your feelings, beliefs, and thoughts about the world. You have to look at your experiences and your reactions to them. Unless you were born knowing, as some people are, then you have to do some work.

> **Akashic Wisdom** _____
>
> Would you like a calling to some great and glorious work? Then imagine a great and glorious work and call yourself to it.
>
> —Joseph John Dewey, New Age writer

Although living your purpose adds meaning, direction, and support to your life, your purpose is rarely about you. It isn't about becoming the best leader in the world, making a scientific breakthrough so your name goes down in history, or getting a Nobel Peace Prize. It's always about giving back to the world. It's about providing something the world needs, whether large like Albert Einstein or smaller like Susan and her teenage animal helpers.

Ultimately, your purpose will unfold as you live—and you'll recognize it because when you're not doing it, your life feels empty. There is only one imperative: live your principles in every situation, and you will be led straight to your purpose.

Simple Access to Your Purpose

You can perform many exercises to help find your purpose. Some are elaborate, and some are simple. Here's a really simple one that taps into the free flow of consciousness. You don't have to make lists of things that compel you or determine your skills and strengths; just let your mind free associate.

Sit down with a blank sheet of paper in a quiet spot where you won't be disturbed. Set a timer for 30 minutes. Write on the top of the paper this question: "What is my purpose?" Don't make a list, per se—just write down or draw whatever comes to mind. Maybe you'll see an image, perhaps a bird or a sailboat. Maybe you'll think of a person, a relative, or an historical figure. Maybe you'll hear a religious passage.

Don't stop with the first phrase or thought that comes, keep asking and answering the question again. Write down or draw as many answers as you can. No matter how hard you're struggling to find new answers, keep going until the timer rings. Don't worry about repeating the same answer more than once, and if you're still getting ideas when the ringer goes off, keep going. Go until one of your answers makes you feel something different. Maybe it will give you energy, maybe it will make you cry, or maybe you will have goose bumps. Whatever brings up strong emotions, develop it.

Purposeful Puzzling

If you like to think and solve puzzles, you may enjoy this process more than the previous one. Again, find a quiet place where you won't be disturbed. Get your notebook from Chapter 8 or several pieces of paper. Take a page in your notebook and make a heading for each of the following, one on each page:

◆ Your knacks and talents

◆ The things that intrigue you and spark your curiosity

◆ The causes you feel strongly about

◆ Your passions and creative outlets

◆ Your strengths and inner resources

Set your timer for 30 minutes and write everything you can think of under each topic until the timer goes off. If you have more to write, keep going past 30 minutes.

Once your lists are finished, look at the causes you feel strongly about, your passions and creative outlets, and the things that intrigue you. Are there any themes among them that emerge? Write down the various themes you find. Look at your talents, strengths, and inner resources. Can they be applied to any of these themes in a meaningful way? See if any of these themes answer the four questions posed earlier in this chapter:

◆ What is most important to me in my life?

◆ What are my deepest values and beliefs?

◆ What gives me joy?

◆ What would I do if …?

Doing this exercise can help clarify how your past actions, enjoyments, and passions reveal your purpose.

Write a Mission Statement

The start of every company or project is accompanied by a mission statement. It keeps the enterprise focused and provides the direction for decision making. After doing either or both of the previous exercises, it's time to write a mission statement for your life. Your mission statement is a one- or two-line statement that reflects your purpose.

Here are a few guidelines for writing your mission statement:

◆ It must be current, alive, and well. Your purpose evolves through your life. Your mission statement should reflect this. If you write a mission statement today and next week it no longer fits, write another.

Timeless Tips

To see examples of personal and professional mission statements, go to www. missionstatements.com.

◆ It should be powerful and able to motivate you and excite your interest.

◆ It should provide clarity and be broad enough to reflect your depth.

◆ It should make you feel empowered and well used in your abilities.

Once you've developed your mission statement, post it someplace where you will see it several times a day (on your bathroom mirror or refrigerator, for example). As soon as it no longer means anything to you, change it.

For example, Colin's mission statement is very basic: To bring hope to our children. He does this through his commitment to creating a better environmental situation and through enriching life by exploring the mysteries of consciousness. Synthia's mission statement is to create a better world by holding a vision of wholeness for the people in her life, including family members, co-workers, and patients.

Staying on the Path

After you've accepted that everyone has a path and purpose—even you—your life will become more focused. But nature is governed by cycles, and so are you. There will be times when you feel fully committed to your path and everything is dovetailing together, making perfect sense. Other times, you'll feel you're swimming against the tide and wondering whether it's worth the effort.

It helps to know that your path was set down in the Akashic Record before you were born. Every footstep falls on that path, no matter how far off course it seems to be. In fact, many prominent people will say that it was the part of their path where they felt most off course where they learned the greatest lessons about who they are and what they're here to do.

The cycles in life also include rest periods, so if you feel like not much is happening, take advantage of the time: do your inner work, pamper yourself, fortify yourself, or just take a break! Sometimes we're too serious, and rest cycles let us know we don't have to work so hard. You're on the path anyway; the only thing you have to do is live by your inner principles. The rest will happen all on its own.

There are signs along the way that support your faith in your direction. Of course, intellectually you know you're on the path because it's where your feet are falling. But sometimes we all need confirmation—especially when obstacles are coming our way.

Synchronicity

Pat and John decided they needed to create an office in their house so they could work on projects together. That night when they arrived home, they found a flyer in the mailbox from a neighbor advertising a new home renovation business. *Synchronicities* such as these happen to everyone. When it happens to you, sit up and take notice. It means you're riding the wave of your purpose and what you need is coming your way.

When synchronicity happens, it's a sign that what you're thinking and planning is moving you in the best direction possible. Pat and John wanted an office in their home, and finding the flyer confirmed that their idea was a good one. Synchronicity does not always arrive to meet a need; it usually

def•i•ni•tion

Synchronicity is the experience of two or more unrelated events occurring together in a meaningful manner.

arrives to let us know we're on the right path. For example, Pat and John may or may not find that the contractor in the flyer is the best one for their job. Its importance was in arriving at a time that confirmed their direction.

Being "in the Flow"

Flow is a close cousin to synchronicity. When you're living your purpose with passion and excitement, events seem to flow together to support you. For example, just when you need more money, a new job opportunity may show up. Or you know you need to clear the air with a co-worker for a project to go forward—and much to your surprise, your co-worker is open and willing to do the work.

> **Akashic Wisdom**
>
> Find purpose, the means will follow.
>
> —Mohandis (Mahatma) Gandhi, political and spiritual leader of India

When you're "in the flow," you're demonstrating the power of your thoughts, attitudes, and beliefs to create your life. You only have to think of a need, and if it's aligned with your purpose, it will be met. Flow is empowering and life enhancing. It allows you to maximize the effectiveness of your energy.

What Resistance May Be Telling You

It's sometimes hard to know when obstacles in your path are tests to be overcome or messages that you're going in the wrong direction. There are many reasons for resistance, and they're not all bad!

Resistance may be telling you that your plans need rethinking. Maybe your timing is off and you're pushing things faster than they can go. Resistance may be a message to slow down and be patient. Resistance holds many messages, and when you bump into it, the best thing to do is take some time away and figure out what the message is.

Sometimes hitting resistance tells you that you're on the wrong track and need to change direction. Usually, though, it's just an indication to recheck, realign, and readjust some aspect of what you're doing. So don't resist the resistance; use it to fine-tune your actions.

Learning the Language

Learning to know when you're on track is like learning a new language. In truth, it's a language you know but may have been trained out of using. Essentially, it all comes down to following your instincts. If you look at the patterns in your life, instinctively you know what the message is and where you got stuck. You know because internally your energy either rises or drops in response.

Fulfilling your purpose increases your energy and leaves you feeling vital and alive. If thinking about your purpose exhausts you, you haven't found the right one. Once again, let's consider Gandhi. He may not have known he would be the one to liberate India, and he may have been tired and discouraged—but the path he was on generated energy, commitment, and vitality. It was impossible for him to ignore it.

Follow your passion; follow what gives you vitality and energy. As you continue on your path, you may find that life isn't easy. Big purposes rarely are easy. But fulfilling them gives you inner peace and the joy of connecting to spiritual reality.

Timeless Tips _____

If you need a little inspiration finding your purpose, this website has what you're looking for: www.abundance-and-happiness.com/inspiration.html.

Manifesting Purpose

The hallmark to finding and living your purpose is the awareness that all parts of your life have come together for this direction. Your ability to live life with integrity brings inner peace. Living your purpose may not be easy, but the satisfaction is extraordinary.

When you live a purposeful life, you find greater levels of self-acceptance and self-love. Once you discover who you are and why you're here, you will draw situations and people toward you. Groups of people come back together to fulfill a common goal. As you come into your purpose, you will begin to meet the people you came here to work with and start the work to complete your common mission.

If you've been wishing for a soul-mate relationship, living your purpose as your authentic self may open the door. True soul-mate relationships involve two people with deep love and trust working together for a higher goal. Finding your purpose and finding your mate may happen simultaneously.

The Least You Need to Know

- Finding your purpose will give you motivation, commitment, direction, and guidance.

- You can detect your purpose by examining your strengths, knacks, talents, and key life events.

- Your purpose will utilize all your past experiences and all your skills and abilities.

- Flow, synchronicity, resistance, and instinct all help you know when you are working to your highest intention.

- As you fulfill your purpose, you may open the door to meet your soul mate.

Chapter 11

Choosing Your Life Circumstances

In This Chapter

- ◆ Creating your life plan before birth
- ◆ Internal and external measures of success
- ◆ Choosing your family connections
- ◆ Through challenge comes joy

Now that you've uncovered clues to your past lives and healed some old wounds, you may be wondering how to apply information from the Akashic Record to your life today. You've already delved into your life purpose in the last chapter and have seen what a dramatic impact living a purpose-filled life can have. The question now is whether the Akashic Record has guidance for your present circumstances. Understanding the process involved in creating your life is the first step toward understanding how to use this information to guide your life.

Akashic Preparation: Your Life Plan

Readers of the Akashic Record describe the process of how the circumstances of life are created. Edgar Cayce tells us that prior to being born, your soul was prepared for the sojourn ahead. You underwent a frequency shift so that you could move out of the dimension of pure soul to inhabit a physical body. As you can imagine, this is not an easy shift and requires significant adjustments.

Even as your soul was being prepared to take a new form, you were preparing the ground for your new life to come. All the Akashic Record information from your past lives was brought into review and used to guide the goals and motivations for your present life. In short, the Record provided the instruction manual for your development. The goal of your present life, however, isn't to relive the past. It's to create something new—to develop new areas of yourself, to make different and better choices, and to contribute something new to the benefit of humanity.

To achieve your life plan, circumstances were chosen to direct and motivate your growth. Particular challenges were designed for you to overcome, and tests were built into your circumstances to see how well you overcame them. Inspiration and excitement were also built in to help guide and lead you. For example, Josh was a young man whose challenge was to live honestly. He grew up in a family where honesty wasn't valued and "cheating the system" was how people got by. He was influenced at a young age by a teacher who inspired him to live a different life. This teacher became a mentor to Josh, who applied himself in school, got a scholarship, built a good life for himself, and overcame the vibration of dishonesty in which he was born.

Later in life, Josh's commitment underwent several severe tests. He was put in situations as an adult where he was asked to lie on behalf of his boss, choosing between honesty and loyalty. With the added consequence of losing his job if he didn't cover the boss's discrepancy, it would have been easy for Josh to lie—thereby contributing to stockholder fraud. Josh's test was built into his life plan to confirm his commitment to his course. No, Josh didn't commit fraud and cover for his boss. He did lose his job as a result, but it opened the door to a much better opportunity and he has not regretted his choice.

As you meet the challenges in your life, all the resources you've developed in the past are available to you—and you incorporate more resources as you grow. Slowly, what begins to emerge is the person you truly are. The process is like an artist sculpting rock to reveal the image that lies inside the stone. With each chip of the stone, your authentic self comes into clearer view.

Guidance and Planning

Your goals, circumstances, and life plan were not handed down by a hierarchical authority. You designed them yourself. Of course, you didn't do this alone; you were given direction by your guides using information from the Akashic Record. The plan you created provides you with opportunities to grow in specific areas. What you do with these opportunities represents your growth edge, the place you are trying to grow beyond to reach new territory.

Your individual needs, however, were not the only consideration in creating your life plan. There are two other very important factors in the process. First, your development is tied to that of your soul group, soul mates, twin soul, and the social needs of the time period. You have agreements with other souls that have to be considered and matched with your own developmental needs. In the time before birth, you and your guides—along with the Akashic Record—determine the best match between your areas of growth with other incarnating souls and historical conditions.

Library Links
Many authorities on the Akashic Record, such as Dr. Bruce Goldberg, indicate that time in the akasha is non-linear. In choosing conditions for your life goals and plans, you are free to move forward or backward in time as your needs prescribe. In fact, many people living today believe that their most recent past life was from a future time period. For example, Mike, a man Colin works with, believes he is bringing new ways of working with computers into the world. The thing is, they don't feel new to him, they are things he already knows. Mike believes it's because he's used them already in the future!

The other factor in choosing your life conditions and goals relates to the larger need of the Akashic Record. Your growth not only benefits you; it also benefits everyone. As the Record strives for evolution, you may be called on to develop specific areas of yourself in order to strengthen or cleanse parts of the Record.

Not What You Do, but How You Do It

According to Cayce, what we do in terms of material accomplishments is not the focus of our life journey. He repeatedly states that "it's not what you do, but what you become" that's valuable. We are meant to become, or live, our spiritual identity. Cayce states that the purpose of each soul's experience is to "know its relationship to its Maker."

This perspective is not unique to Cayce. Most of those who experience the Akashic Record share the same message. They affirm the objective in life is not necessarily material success. The physical world and all the adventures you have are only vehicles to discover your inner self and to extend love to others. You may succeed materially only to fail spiritually, as did Fiona from Chapter 9 who traded her integrity in a past life for money. On the other hand, you may fail materially and gain spiritually as is true when people like Josh do the right thing even though it costs them.

Remember Susan from Chapter 10? Her purpose was to connect with teenagers and support their growth. Her hobby of animal rescue was her vehicle. Sadly, some of the animals they rescued didn't make it, but that wasn't the measure of her success. Success was measured by the growth of love and genuine commitment in herself, the teenagers, and even the animals they worked with to something higher than self. Sometimes how things turn out is not as important as simply showing up for the job and doing your best.

Assessing Your Success

Okay, so you designed some difficult circumstances, found some joyful pursuits, took on some goals for your soul growth, and showed up to do the work. Life unfolds, you run into several tests, and you start to wonder how successfully you're meeting your objectives. If material success in overcoming the conditions and circumstances of your life is not the true measure of success, then how is success gauged?

This is a very important and illusive question. Some New Age spiritual practices and evangelical Christian groups teach that if their supporters follow certain rules, pray, mediate, and live a good life, they will be blessed with material well-being. Therefore, if you don't have material wealth, then you're doing something wrong. You're not following God's will, applying the Laws of Attraction properly, or owning your spiritual power. This can be a trap, leading people to feel spiritually judged because they haven't attained sufficient material wealth.

Experiences within the Akashic Record reveal a larger picture behind our circumstances. This larger picture is more concerned with what you have added to the growth and evolution of the Record than with how much material wealth you have amassed. Wealthy and poor alike can use their circumstances to grow in love, spread kindness and compassion, and be a positive reflection for others—or not. To measure success, we can look for internal and external confirmation.

Internal Measure

Would you be surprised to find that you have a built-in gauge to measure your success? It's part of your emotional matrix. Emotions help guide your path, showing you what's important, what has value, where you're stuck, and where you're tempted to compromise yourself. Every emotion you have provides you with information. Learning to decode it and use it, however, can be challenging.

def•i•ni•tion

Chakras are spiritual energy centers located in the physical body that guide our growth and development. There are seven main chakras in the human body, and each is a center of spiritual energy that relates to a specific developmental challenge and gift.

The part of your emotional matrix that's your "life challenge success" gauge is in your heart *chakra*, the energy center in the middle of your chest. Your heart chakra holds the spiritual energy of unconditional love. As you learn your lessons in this life, your ability to love unconditionally grows.

The seven chakras are:

- ◆ **1st or base chakra:** Located at the base of the spine; governs physical survival, safety, security, and finances

- ◆ **2nd or sacral chakra:** Located below the belly button; governs sexuality, creativity, and the creative aspects of finances

- ◆ **3rd or solar plexus chakra:** Located in the triangle made by your rib cage; governs personal power, willpower, gut feelings, instinct, and manifesting

- ◆ **4th or heart chakra:** Located in the center of the chest; governs unconditional love and living by our principles

- ◆ **5th or throat chakra**: Located in the throat; governs communication and speaking our truth

- ◆ **6th or third eye chakra**: Located between the eyebrows; governs psychic perception, inner truth, and divine inspiration

- ◆ **7th or crown chakra**: Located at the top of the head; governs the connection to spiritual reality and divine will

When you successfully meet a life challenge, you have connected with your higher spiritual identity and it has prevailed. This activates a specific vibration that lights your heart chakra. Often called the heart-light, when it's activated you feel a very deep sense of connection and satisfaction. It's different than self-satisfaction, ego satisfaction, partner love, or even parental love. It's selfless, compassionate, transcendent, and wired inside each of us. You may be very familiar with this feeling, or you may be the type of person who doesn't pay much attention to how you feel. If you're not sure that you've ever felt this, imagine a time in your life when you succeeded against the odds in doing something you truly believed in. Imagine yourself in that moment, and let your body and mind fully engage the moment. Notice how you're feeling and see whether your heart-light is shining. When it is, you can be sure you're meeting your challenges and succeeding.

Another built-in measure of success is your level of inspiration and excitement. Does your life excite you? Are you inspired by what you do and share with the world? If you are, you're sure to be fulfilling the challenges you came to meet.

External Measure

When you start making choices that reflect your higher spiritual identity, your life begins to change. As you transmute your karma through aligning your thoughts and actions with higher purpose, you begin to shift the vibration you live in—manifesting an easier and more secure and abundant life. As your goals come into alignment with higher ideals, opportunity begins to flow toward you and you're able to manifest your dreams.

As you bring good toward yourself, keep in mind that abundance may not look as you expect it to. Do you think security is a certain amount of money in your retirement fund? Or to you, is abundance reflected in having enough money to buy whatever you want? What if instead, abundance meant the security of knowing that you will be able to meet your needs regardless of what's in your bank account?

Although it's important to plan for retirement and use money wisely, many are finding the pension plans and retirement funds they planned on have disappeared in the present economic calamity. True peace and security lie in knowing you have the inner resources to meet life head on. Abundance lies in knowing you are part of the flow of life and that opportunity will open to you. By all means, save money and use it wisely—but also know your ultimate security lies in you and your relationships, not your bank.

Here's a progression many people find when they have successfully overcome a life challenge:

1. The heart center is activated.

2. Life patterns begin to change.

3. Some type of ordeal arrives to test your commitment.

4. Desires, plans, and dreams begin to reflect higher ideals.

5. Life flows, and people, resources, and opportunities arise to assist your goals.

6. You feel more peaceful, with greater calmness and a deeper awareness of the meaning behind life events.

Childhood and Family

It can be hard to accept that you've chosen your family, especially if your childhood was not particularly happy. Although there are many patterns in life that demonstrate the issues you're here to work on, the conditions of your childhood are the greatest reflection of these issues. Family dynamics essentially determine the directions and patterns of your life. The dynamic you were born into is your learning edge.

What's important to remember is that you are not a victim. You may have been badly abused as a child, and there is no justification for hurting an innocent child. This is not about justifying bad actions. It's about finding meaning and growth beyond them. Your parent is not justified in hurting you, but you may find meaning in knowing that you agreed to be born into that situation for a higher purpose. Sometimes it's for your growth, sometimes you sacrificed yourself for another's growth, or sometimes it's to bring a higher ideal into society. Social growth comes first through awareness of such issues, then through social controls to stop them.

Etheric Advisory

It's never okay to rationalize child abuse. If you suspect a child of being abused, report it to authorities. If you or someone else in the home is abusive with your child, send the child to a safe relative and seek help immediately.

It can also be hard as a parent when the situation for your child is not ideal. Although it is our responsibility as parents to provide the best we can, sometimes we take on undue guilt in our parenting skills. Often, even our children don't expect us to be perfect! Here's an experience one woman relates:

> Although my first husband was a good person, we had many conflicts in our marriage especially related to parenting. One day I sat at the kitchen table despairing over the difficulties I felt my children were facing and wishing I had not married their father. My three-year-old daughter climbed into my lap, and cuddling close to me, said, "I remember before I was born when I chose you to be my mother." "How did you choose me?" I asked. She told me that she looked through a "big newspaper" full of names until she found mine. Suddenly my daughter sat up and turned to me, pressing her finger insistently into my chest saying, "And then I found Daddy's name and I chose him, too."

> This interaction helped me to see that my kids were not bystanders in the important factors of their life. I didn't need to feel guilty; everything was as it was supposed to be. I always believed the newspaper my daughter saw was the Akashic Record.

Desert Destruction, Continued

Remember the woman in Chapter 8 whose past life involved participating in the Crusades of the thirteenth century? We saw in Chapter 9 how she obtained healing through the Akashic Record. Let's take a look at the circumstances she created in this life to confront her past-life issues.

This woman went on the Crusades to stand up for her Christian beliefs and principles. The crusaders were on a mission to regain the Holy Lands from the "heathens." During the Crusades, she found a deeper truth that involved the sanctity of all life and the awareness that God lives in every person. It was impossible for her to single-handedly change the course of the Crusades. Her choices were to abandon the crusade or hide her growing agitation. She was deeply conflicted in her loyalties and afraid of social ostracism. In effect, she had "no backbone." She broke her back and was killed when she fell beneath a horse's hooves.

The vibration inherent at the time of her death created the circumstances of her present life. Her objective, determined before birth, was to learn how to stand up for her beliefs. This meant developing inner character and being willing to accept the consequences of her actions, however difficult. To do this, she needed an authority figure to defy and adverse conditions to overcome. She needed the same vibration as what she had just left.

She chose to be born into a chaotic family with an overbearing father. She was born with back troubles that were reflections of how she had died and what she was here to overcome. Her father competed with his children, forcing them into submissive roles. He was adamant in his beliefs, righteous in his actions, and demanded that all those around him agree. Her childhood conditions were perfect for recreating her past-life dilemma.

Although she initially suffered poor self-esteem, through the drama of learning to stand up for herself in her family she began to develop backbone. As she grew in stature and ability to live her truth, she was tested through her job (discussed in Chapter 9). She successfully passed the test and proved her commitment to living according to her higher ideals. Later in her life she left her job, finding deeper meaning and happiness by working for a world peace organization. This allowed her to fully express the truth she had discovered in the Crusades at the cost of her own life.

Leper's Soul

Let's take another look at Janice from Chapter 9, who suffered from sensitive and painful feet. You'll remember that the Akashic Record revealed a past life in the American Revolutionary War, where damage was done to her feet in the winter at Valley Forge. It turned out, however, that this past life wasn't where her foot pain started; it was a continuation of a condition established in another previous life.

Further investigation into the Akashic Record revealed that Janice had been alive in the Middle East near the time of Christ. She lived in a leper colony, and this is where the foot pain started. During her visit to the Akashic Record, Janice relived a traumatic scene where her family abandoned her at the entrance to the leper colony. She was a young girl and stood crying and terrified as her family left, telling her to never come home again. The vibration of abandonment was carried into her life in the American colonies. Her desire to find a place where she belonged and could make a positive contribution resulted in her joining the American Revolutionary Army.

> **Library Links**
>
> When past issues are resolved, forgiveness for others as well as yourself has been attained, and your heart is truly opened and ready to receive, then new roads leading you to love will be revealed.

The unhealed emotions Janice had at the time of her death in both of these past lives were translated into the family conditions she chose in this life. She was born into an aloof, detached family with very little support and encouragement. Her mother was particularly emotionally unavailable. In addition to her foot problems, Janice suffered other physical ailments and was very frail. She maintained distance in her relationships, not wanting to be a burden to others. She suffered from a deep, unconscious fear that she would be abandoned if she needed too much from anyone. Janice's main challenge in this life was to make deep emotional connections with people, to allow herself to receive help, and to trust the commitments people made to being with her. Being able to accept her own value may be the biggest challenge she had to overcome.

Learning from Your Family

It's always easier to see the patterns and lessons in someone else's life than it is in your own. However, the pain of your childhood reveals what you came here to heal. The joy and passion in your childhood is where your inspiration and dreams lie. Take some time to examine your childhood trials and tribulations as well. Where do you feel the most wounded? How does that wounding affect your behavior, relationships, and choices in life?

Pay special attention to the emotional hurdles that repeat in your life. Do you often feel taken advantage of in relationships? Do you find yourself criticizing and judging other people? See whether you can identify the root fear and find a way to live with it without judging yourself or others. Engage the two prime healers: compassion and forgiveness.

The Greatest Gifts

You may have heard that your greatest challenges become the greatest gifts you have to offer the world. In many cases, it's true. What you learn in overcoming a challenge helps everyone else in that situation. Consider two inspirational figures of our times: Tony Robbins and Oprah Winfrey.

Tony Robbins is a high-profile motivational speaker and author of several bestsellers such as *Unlimited Power: The New Science of Personal Achievement*. Although many claim he lived a "normal" childhood, Robbins's parents divorced when he was seven and his mother remarried twice. It may have been normal, but it was certainly not ideal. He went through many difficult periods, culminating in a particularly low period when he was "struggling to pay his bills, overweight, and without direction."

He determined to change his life by finding where his passion and peak performance lay. In helping himself, he developed an approach that has helped millions of people create better lives for themselves, too.

Even more inspiring is the life and contribution of talk show host and media mogul Oprah Winfrey. Named one of the 100 Most Influential People of the Twentieth Century by *Time* Magazine, Oprah best demonstrates this idea. Born in Mississippi in 1954, Oprah was raised by her grandmother until the age of six. She lived with her mother between the ages of six and thirteen until she ran away to escape molestation and abuse. As a last resort, she went to live with her father whose strict rules may have awakened in Oprah the desire to never accept anything from herself that was less than her best. Oprah overcame difficulty and pain and more importantly lives life inspired by her passion for contributing in positive ways to people's lives. Oprah used what she learned to create a forum that has given millions of people the courage and inspiration to change.

Timeless Tips

Here is a great blog entry describing techniques for positive motivation: vladdolezal. com/blog/2009/the-pain-and-pleasure-principle/.

Major Life Events

Major life events—even positive ones such as marriage or the birth of a child—cause stress. Adjusting to any change can be stressful, but major life events come with archetypical problems. Some of the events we go through are inherent in being human, such as being born, reaching puberty, having (or not having) children, and dying. Others are part of our social dynamics, such as changing jobs, buying a house, going to college, or getting married or divorced.

Some life events were lined up before birth to provide the framework for your growth. For example, you may have agreed to marry someone, to bring a new idea or piece of music into the world, or to work at a certain type of job. However, not all life events were preplanned. You came in with a blueprint that you can follow or not. What decisions you make are up to you, and the choices you make create the next round of events.

Gifts and Abilities

It's a mistake to think that everything you have to offer comes only from the challenges you've met and the wounds you've healed. In fact, if this were true, your life would be rather weighed down. It's only because we have so many hurts to overcome that we fall into thinking they're the most important. You are developing new abilities every day, ones that reflect who you are now and what you want to bring to the world.

We can learn as much through inspiration as we can through challenge. You were born not only with a bunch of challenges but also with people and events that bring inspiration, joy, and contentment. As mythologist and writer Joseph Campbell has stated in his teachings, following your bliss is essential.

Most people find pleasure and inspiration in using their gifts and abilities. If you don't have much pleasure in life right now, maybe it's time to stop focusing on overcoming your challenges and start enjoying your gifts. Find ways to include your gifts in your home, look for ways to let your abilities shine in your work, and be sure to include hobbies in your life that stimulate your unused talents. It's important to include joy in your life. If you don't, no one else will make the effort to give it to you!

The Least You Need to Know

- You participated in creating your life plan before you were born.
- Your success in meeting your life challenges is not measured by material success but by internal and external confirmation.
- The conditions of your childhood reflect the issues you came to resolve.
- Overcoming your greatest challenge can become your greatest gift to the world.
- Seek inspiration and joy to power your life.

Chapter 12

Past Loves, Future Partners

In This Chapter

- ◆ The importance of love
- ◆ Balancing love karma
- ◆ The soul-mate relationship
- ◆ Twin souls: the ultimate partner
- ◆ Our animal partners

If this is the first chapter you've turned to in this book, you're not alone. Most people are deeply interested in their love lives. It doesn't matter whether you have a happy relationship, an unhappy relationship, or none at all—chances are you have questions about love. In this chapter, we look more deeply at what the Akashic Record has to say about your romances, past and present.

The Growth of Love

The "prime directive" in the Akashic Record is the evolution of love. While this includes romantic love, it's more than just the emotion of caring for someone or the passion of infatuation. It's the deepest spiritual truth available to humankind. Many mystics describe love as the glue that holds the universe together. According to those who read the Akashic Record, love is the substance of the akashic field, and the ability to feel love is the doorway to higher consciousness. The first step into this doorway is through our relationships.

Seeking love is totally natural; we're biologically wired for it. The deep desire we all have to give and receive love is as basic as eating, sleeping, and dreaming. It's part of the matrix of being alive.

> **Akashic Wisdom** _____
>
> For many people the experience of romantic love is their first experience of spirituality, although they may not know it.
> —Deepak Chopra, physician and author

The experience of akashic love is unconditional. It has no judgment and requires no self-protection. Every relationship, especially primary partnerships, offers an opportunity to develop unconditional love. Relationships aren't easy, but every obstacle successfully met brings you closer to your true self. Every intimacy you welcome allows you to express yourself more completely. The journey of love is that of becoming fully yourself.

According to Edgar Cayce, Madame Blavatsky, Dion Fortune, and others who read the Akashic Record, there are two key purposes for the soul's development of love: to become whole and to develop spiritual mastery. Relationships offer the perfect opportunity to discover both.

Finding Wholeness

You're already whole and complete just as you are. Everything you need as a fully self-actualized, spiritual being already resides within you. The problem is the misconceptions we encounter through our many lifetimes. The process of living seems to bombard us with messages of not being good enough, successful enough, beautiful enough, smart enough, and so on.

When we believe these messages, we give away our sense of wholeness. We become less than we truly are and lose parts of ourselves to the judgments and manipulations of those around us. Becoming whole is simply bringing all the parts of who we are back under our own control. Being whole is living an authentic life—one that is designed for our inner growth and not to impress the world.

Do you seek wholeness through relationships? No other person, even your soul mate or twin flame, can complete you. You are already complete, and only you can access the entirety of who you are. Relationships allow us the opportunity to express the deepest and truest parts of ourselves. They help us see ourselves more honestly and provide an opportunity to feel the joy of connection. However, they are strongest and most fulfilling when they are made of two complete, whole people enjoying an adventure together, rather than two people dependent on each other for completion.

If you've been focusing on relationships to become whole, consider that it might be a diversion allowing you to avoid your inner work. To enter a soul-mate relationship, you must be on the path to owning your wholeness—starting with loving yourself. In learning self-love, you can begin to accept others without the need to change them or control their actions. It's only when you love yourself that you can face the world with an open heart, ready to love unconditionally and without judgment.

Spiritual Mastery

The biggest misconception is that life is merely physical. Our focus on the physical has led many people to believe that gathering wealth, status, and accomplishments is the most important pursuit in life. Of course, material well-being is important to our health and happiness—but in and of itself, it doesn't create fulfillment. The wholeness we seek is the knowledge of our spiritual identity. When you know you are a spiritual being having a human experience, you begin to explore higher realms and develop spiritual mastery.

Ironically, once you accept your spiritual identity, it's much easier to attain material goals. You become able to use the spiritual laws governing the material world to attract what you need.

The hard part of mastery is responsibility. Once you realize you are a powerful spiritual being with unlimited ability, you also realize you are responsible for everything your thoughts and deeds have created. This is the evolution of the Akashic Record.

Responsibility requires that you use love as the basis for all that you create—not the codependent love of the karmic relationship, but the spiritual love that unselfishly seeks the highest good for all. To live in love is to expand beyond the limits of self-awareness into the awareness of universal consciousness, which is pure love. This is the goal of the Akashic Record and the direction relationships take us.

Progression of Relationships

Relationships offer a reflection of your personal growth. Because no single person can mirror another completely, each of us has many different relationships to reflect the myriad parts of ourselves. Some connections are deeply fulfilling, showing us the best of who we are. They increase our understanding and ability to see the best in others. Some are trials that test us. All are opportunities to increase our ability to love unconditionally by seeing the inner divine in everybody.

There are many types of love relationships falling into three general categories. Each of us experiences all of them through the course of our development. These are karmic relationships, soul mates, and twin flames. You may experience all of these in the course of one lifetime or over the course of many.

Karmic Relationships

You may yearn for the joy of a soul-mate relationship yet pull back from the intimacy and vulnerability such connection brings. Many people have wounds from relationships that need to be healed before a soul-mate connection is possible. *Karmic partnerships* are those that we contract to complete very specific and often difficult past lessons. These relationships are not always fun, but be assured they have a role to play in your development.

def•i•ni•tion

A karmic partnership is a primary relationship that is based on the mutual need of two souls to balance their karma. They help each other by providing the conditions necessary for their karmic lessons.

All relationships have past karma, but karmic partnerships are more focused on balancing the past. In these relationships, both people are drawn together from mutual need. The attraction is often quite strong because it reflects a deep desire for completion. If you're involved in a karmic partnership, it may not be as fulfilling as a soul-mate connection—but the forces that attract you are equally powerful. They're directed by your higher self and by your need to grow, and they are essential to you.

Karmic partnerships provide the circumstances you need to complete your past. In some cases, one person may agree to support the other's growth at the expense of his or her own. Two people may come together to heal injuries they inflicted on each other in a past life. Or they may agree to be an impartial mirror reflecting the best and worst of each other. These relationships may be abusive, codependent, addictive, or simply unfulfilling.

The growth required may involve learning about consequences, developing self-respect, or understanding responsibility. The possibilities of what your relationships are teaching you are endless. What's important is to learn to see each person in a loving light, no matter what actions you need to take in the relationship—including leaving them.

Characteristics of the Karmic Partnership

Are you wondering whether your relationship is a karmic partnership? Keep in mind that most people have at least one karmic partnership in their lives, and most have many. Learn what you need to learn, accomplish your mission, and love anyway—and the relationship will either evolve or reach completion.

Karmic partnerships are characterized by:

- A strong attraction with limited compatibility
- An addictive need to be with the other person
- A repeat of family patterns learned in childhood
- Focusing more on your relationship than on your own personal development
- Control, manipulation, and communication issues
- Sacrificing your personal dreams to be together
- Neglect, abuse, or violence

Of course, a karmic partnership won't have all of these components, and your relationship may be different. Use these as guidelines when evaluating your romantic situation.

Karmic Example

Sharon and John are an excellent example of a karmic relationship brought to completion. They met at a party given by mutual friends and immediately felt a strong attraction to each other. Here's their story in Sharon's words:

> "When I met John I felt a magnetic attraction. He wasn't my type but I thought about him all the time. We got together and no surprise, we didn't have much in common. The attraction got stronger anyway. Our dates were spent talking about our disappointments and difficult childhoods. John could never measure up to his father's expectations and thought of himself as a failure. My parents divorced when I was young and I never saw my father again. I craved male attention.

> "My strong attraction to John turned into a compulsive desire to rescue him from his childhood pain. I believed through my love he would feel successful, get a good job, and love me. Of course I was really trying to heal my own pain

by making myself important in a man's life. John wanted to rescue me too. He wanted to be my hero.

"Our marriage was a disaster. John didn't feel successful, couldn't hold a job, and wasn't much of a husband, never mind hero. I began to think of him in terms of all the ways he let me down, all the ways he was a failure. Instead of rescuing each other we re-enacted the disappointments of our childhood. As time went on John's sense of failure increased as did my feelings of male abandonment.

"Eventually we decided enough, and agreed to a divorce. As I was cleaning through the debris of our marriage I suddenly saw my lesson in our being together. My epiphany was seeing that John, and everyone else, is made up of both his failures and successes, but I had defined him only in terms of his failures. I realized that how I look at people is a choice. I can choose to see people as their successes or I can choose to see them as their failures. How I see them doesn't change who they are, it changes who I am. This single realization shifted my life completely. I began to look for the positive in everyone. You can call me Pollyanna if you want, but so what? Maybe she's not such a bad role model.

"My ex and I have become good friends. I'm sure we agreed to help each other learn what we needed before we came into this life. Now we're both married to our soul mates and very, very happy."

Evolving Relationships

People in karmic partnerships often stay together out of guilt and remorse. After all, it's their karma. This fatalistic attitude has nothing to offer either person. Karmic partnerships are about growth. If there's no hope of progress, you have some decisions to make. Not every karmic partnership ends as Sharon and John's did, however. In fact, many become abusive—and instead of solving karma, they create more. How long someone should stay is different for everyone. It depends on whether you've learned what you came to learn, whether it's possible to learn what you came to, or whether the relationship has become unable to grow. Of course, responsibility to children is a factor, too.

Karmic relationships can become soul-mate relationships if your partner is from your soul group, which we talked about in Chapter 5. Once the karma has been balanced and the karmic patterns are healed, you may find an underlying soul connection. If this is true, the joy that you will uncover is almost unimaginable. It's just as possible, however, that once you've completed your karmic balancing you'll find karma was the only connection between you. Like Sharon and John, you're now free to find your true soul mate.

If your mate is abusive, it may not be possible to complete your karmic balancing. Maybe you already have completed what you came to do and just don't realize it. Sometimes the only way forward is to leave. There's no guilt in this! You showed up and did your best. Staying won't help things get better if one person isn't able to grow.

Soul-Mate Reunions

The soul-mate relationship is the one everyone wants. It's the true love that you've read about in storybooks and dreamed could come true for you. You may have been told true love and soul mates only happen in fairy tales. It's only a fairy tale if you think a soul-mate relationship doesn't require work; the depth of connection is every bit as true as the stories you've read. Everyone has a soul mate, so go ahead and keep seeking yours. It's totally worth the journey!

Edgar Cayce gave many life readings that dealt with soul mates. He revealed that they have a deep and abiding commitment to each other, lasting centuries over many lifetimes. Dr. Brian Weiss, a psychiatrist, has performed past-life regressions on patients with relationship troubles. His book *Only Love Is Real* (see Appendix B) beautifully demonstrates that every person has a soul mate—someone we have loved and grown with through many past incarnations.

Soul mates have a profound and true connection with each other. Through countless incarnations, they help each other grow and develop in the most positive aspects possible. Soul mates journey through many lives, tracking each other through trials and suffering to help each other find happiness. Dr. Weiss states that love is the only reality, and soul mates are dedicated to finding that truth with each other.

Timeless Tips _____

You can get a list of Dr. Brian Weiss's books as well as other good information about love and past lives at his website, www.brianweiss.com.

Soul-Mate Timing

People spend their lives seeking their soul mates. Depression often occurs when people believe they don't have or deserve one. Everyone has soul mates, but the timing of your meeting and the ordeals you go through before finding each other can be huge. Remember, this was preplanned before birth. You can work to attract your soul mate, but ultimately timing has to relate to the larger picture. Your job until then is to keep growing.

The worst feeling in the world is meeting the person you know is your soul mate only to find he or she is not available. The emptiness is unbearable, but don't despair. If you've met your soul mate, then you know he or she does exist. You're not in control of the future and don't know what changes are in store for you or your soul mate that may bring you together. At the same time, act with integrity. If your soul mate isn't free, don't pursue him or her. Trust your path; what is yours will come.

As explained in Chapter 4, it's possible that it's not in the plan for you and your soul mate to be together in this life. Meeting him or her may be a reminder of your journey and what lies ahead in a future life. Use the meeting to look at your life and see all that you have to be grateful for. Use the knowledge of your soul mate's existence to inspire your life with love. Any love spent in the universe is never wasted, whether it's spent on your soul mate or someone else.

Don't forget that you have more than one soul mate. Meeting one person who you can't have a relationship with doesn't mean that there isn't another soul-mate relationship ahead for you. According to Edgar Cayce, each person can have as many as 25 different soul mates. Some say we have a different one for each of the major growth horizons we face. You may have a spiritual soul mate, a companion soul mate, an adventure mate, and so on. If you're taking a break from the intensity of this type of relationship, maybe you're integrating the lessons of many lifetimes.

The Perfect Fit?

One of the biggest myths about soul mates is that once you find yours, you'll live happily ever after and there will be no major issues or conflicts to work through. Now *that* is a fairy tale! You can be sure you'll live a life of passion and joy, but you will have conflict, too. Some soul mates believe that myth so strongly that they fracture at the first conflict, deciding the person must not be their perfect mate after all. In reality, they weren't ready for the honesty required. Soul-mate relationships provide the safety to go to deep places of healing, and hidden aspects within each person are allowed to surface. Deep wounds from many lives can emerge for healing. The depth of connection offers a special opportunity to work on our most profound aspects of growth. However, this isn't easy and requires exceptional commitment. When conflict arises, instead of running away or compromising, the soul-mate challenge is to reach to the heart of the issue and heal it. This type of love allows complete honesty. There's no need to protect yourself. You're supported in the hardest work you have to do, and your mate can expect the same from you. Equality is the true hallmark of this type of love. Soul-mate relationships work because each person honors the contribution of the other.

The Ultimate Betrayal

Believe it or not, even soul mates can have affairs! When this happens, the betrayal is the worst pain possible. The trust and sharing between soul mates creates an energetic link that when severed literally breaks the heart. As hard as it is to understand, this, too, is a contract. But let's be clear— the contract is for the challenge; the outcome is ours alone.

If your mate had an affair, it wasn't because you contracted to be betrayed. If you had an affair, your contract didn't include hurting your partner. Your contract was to accept a challenge from an outside person influencing your relationship. How you handle it, whether you have an affair or whether you strengthen your love with each other, represents your personal growth.

Attracting Your Soul Mate

There are many ways to attract your true love. You can use visualization techniques and positive thinking, but actually you're attracting your soul mate with every thought, action, and deed. Everything you do and are is a beacon into the akasha that connects you with your soul mate. As the connection gets clearer and brighter, you're both getting ready to fulfill the contract ahead. The best way to strengthen your beacon is to keep your spiritual light clear and focused, stay connected to your dreams, and follow your heart.

Changing outmoded beliefs about love and relationships can help brighten your beacon of light into the akasha. Techniques can be helpful to clarify your intentions and keep you focused on your highest ideals. This prepares the ground for a conscious, connected, loving, and joy-filled relationship.

Here are some tips for attracting soul-mate relationships:

◆ Visualize the type of relationship you want, and send love to this vision every day.

◆ As you clearly see what you want, pay attention to your thoughts, feelings, and sensations. Which ones help you, and which ones hinder you?

◆ When you've identified a block, find a higher perspective and release the TABs that created it.

◆ Align yourself with the highest and best good, and express gratitude for the life you have.

◆ Relax and trust the design of your life.

◆ Enjoy your life; this is the best way to light your beacon.

Recognizing Your Soul Mate

Now that you're spending energy attracting your soul mate, how will you know when you meet him or her? When soul mates meet, they have an immediate and intense connection. It's more than the strong attraction of a karmic bond. Soul mates feel like they've known each other forever. They're highly compatible, share similar life experiences, and know almost immediately that they will be together.

When you meet your soul mate, other strange things may begin to happen. In fact, everything in your life may change in unexpected and positive ways. When you meet your soul mate or twin soul, you may experience any or all of the following:

◆ Increased sense of déjà-vu

◆ Increased synchronicity

◆ Deep feelings of knowing the other person

◆ Your life takes a new, more positive direction

◆ You have a heightened sense of purpose and direction

◆ Your life undergoes a spiritual acceleration

Twin Flame Soul Mates

Your twin soul is not only the one soul mate who you share the most with—it's the one who you share your mission with. The idea that your mission is shared with another soul may be quite emotional for you. We're conditioned to believe that we're alone in the world. The truth is that you're not alone and were never meant to be. When your soul was created, it was created with a twin—and you're both there to help each other.

As mentioned in Chapter 4, a twin-soul relationship is the most fulfilling relationship it's possible to have. You can expect a deep connection and feeling of being truly known and seen in the very deepest part of yourself.

Recognizing Your Twin Soul

Signs that you've met your twin soul include all the signs of meeting any other type of soul mate. In addition, it's common for twin souls to share a psychic connection. They may have shared dreams, call each other on the phone at the same moment, and know what each other is thinking and feeling no matter how many miles separate them. Everything they do is magnified. Every spiritual impulse is amplified, and every gift is suddenly heightened.

Potholes Along the Road

Twin-flame relationships can have the same pitfalls of other soul-mate relationships—plus one or two more as well. You can consider a twin-soul relationship as the final test to be sure your path of wholeness and self-mastery is complete. Consequently, there are a few issues to watch out for.

If you've found your twin soul, it's easy to forget that you're not simply two halves of a whole. You're each whole and complete on your own. The twin-soul connection is a gift of simpatico, not a need to find your other half. It's easy to lose your self-mastery when you start giving away your personal power to someone outside yourself.

Another common issue is thinking you know everything there is to know about your twin soul. Because you're so connected, it's easy to assume you know what the other person would think, say, or do and inadvertently overlook his or her input. It's easy to take him or her for granted. This is very dangerous and a sure way to send you back to a karmic partnership to sort yourself out!

Finally, just as a twin-soul connection amplifies your spiritual impulses, it also amplifies your negative patterns. This is a great opportunity to clear your darkest self, but it's also scary and intense. You have all the support you need to grow. When you focus on love and amplify its frequency, you can illuminate and transform any area of darkness.

Animal Partnerships

Animal partnerships can be every bit as important as human partnerships. People who have made connections with animals know the powerful spirits that live within. In her book *Many Lives, Many Loves* (see Appendix B), Gina Cerminara writes that the Cayce readings reveal "Animals have an equal place in the oneness of life."

> **Akashic Wisdom** _____
>
> As a man deals with animals so shall he be dealt with by the forces of life in general.
>
> —Edgar Cayce, from an Akashic Record reading

The strength, depth, and loyalty of human and animal relationships are legendary. Animals have surpassed humans in every regard when it comes to selfless love. They offer solace to the lonely and teach us the finer aspects of unconditional acceptance. Is it so strange to think they have a place in the Akashic Record? And if they do, do they reincarnate as well?

Animal Reincarnation

In his book *A Bridge Across Forever* (see Appendix B), Richard Bach tells the story of seeing his dead cat's soul reincarnate into the body of his new kitten. Although the story is very moving, there's little direct evidence of animal reincarnation.

Theosophists such as Charles Leadbeater believe that animal souls are not individualized and when an animal dies, its soul goes back into a common "soul soup" with all the other souls of that species. Some forms of Hinduism believe souls progress from animal form into human, called *transmigration*, but do not go backward unless there's some egregious sin committed in human form.

def•i•ni•tion _____

Transmigration is the evolution of a soul from animal to human form.

Modern-day channels are divided on the issue. Some think animals are advanced souls that don't have to take form but do so for our benefit. Others think animals are on their own soul path and animal souls can only reincarnate within their own species. Still others think souls can take any form they want—human, animal, extra-terrestrial, and so on. They don't limit a soul to a particular form or judge the superiority of one form over another.

While the Hindu ideas of animal reincarnation and those of the Theosophists don't put a high value on animal souls, animal communicators such as Anita Curtis have a much different perspective. Animal communicators intuitively communicate with animals, and the information they reveal about mundane issues of the animals' lives that can be verified has been shockingly accurate. In regard to reincarnation, communicators say that animals talk about having past lives and of frequently staying with a specific family through many reincarnation cycles. The biggest difference between animals and humans, they say, is that animals have direct recall and continuity of memory from life to life.

Animal Soul Mates

Many people believe they have soul-mate relationships with the animals in their lives. The bond they describe has many of the same characteristics as human soul mates. They have an immediate connection when they meet, trust each other completely, feel a strong psychic link, and often seem to read each other's minds.

Animal soul mates seem to validate the idea of some type of animal reincarnation. Here's a personal story from Synthia:

> "I found my cat Lamar in an alley behind a grocery store in East Lansing, Michigan. I was walking one evening with my friend Glen to his car. The cat seemed to take an instant liking to me and followed us. When I opened the car door she got inside so I kept her. For the next sixteen years she was my best friend. We went through many difficult moves and life changes. I didn't always have the best situation for her, but we always stayed together.

> "She was sixteen years old when she died. The night before she died there was no indication she was ill. However, she did something strange before I went to sleep. I was reading and as usual, she came and lay on my chest. Then she placed her paw on my right cheek and looked directly into my eyes for many minutes. I laughed and gave her an extra pet before turning the light off and going to sleep. The next morning she went out on the deck, lay down in a pile of leaves, and went to sleep. She never woke up. When I saw her body I knew her paw on my cheek was a message. I felt she was saying good bye and giving me a clue as to how to recognize her 'next time round.'

"Many years later I found another abandoned cat. It took weeks before she trusted us enough to become part of our family. One day, after she had been with us for a while, she lay down on my chest and put her paw on my right cheek as she looked directly into my eyes. I was deeply touched as I welcomed Lamar back home."

The Least You Need to Know

- The expression of love leads to wholeness and spiritual mastery.

- Relationships that are based on balancing karma can be very strong but not very fulfilling.

- True-love stories are describing soul-mate relationships.

- You can have more than one soul mate.

- Twin souls are the most intimate, intense, and fulfilling relationship you can have.

- In all likelihood, animals reincarnate and provide long-term soul-mate relationships with their people.

Chapter 13

Akashic Challenges

In This Chapter

- How challenge serves you
- Designing your health issues
- The purpose of personal crises
- Remembering your essence

One of the hardest issues in life is trying to understand the purpose of suffering, pain, and loss. How is it possible to make sense of a horrible tragedy? How can we believe that souls would agree to be victims of natural disasters, torture and mutilation, war crimes, concentration camps, AIDS, cancer, and worse? The answers found in the Akashic Record may surprise you.

Understanding Challenges

Accepting that everyone preplans the major conditions in their lives before birth is difficult in the face of profound suffering. An enormous number of Akashic Record readings have focused on this, and the answer every time is the same. People do, in fact, agree to horrific conditions and events in their lives. In order to comprehend this, we have to examine why. As we do, our definition of "victim" may be challenged.

There's no easy answer as to why a soul willingly agrees to suffer. The reasons are complex, and the benefits are myriad. The old concept of karma as retribution—you hurt someone and you'll suffer the same fate in your next life—has evolved. Karma is no longer payback, but rebalancing. Lying, cheating, killing, or any of the other ways of harming people represents an internal imbalance that must be rectified. This calls for teaching, not vengeance. Readings from the Akashic Record reinforce this concept over and over.

Sometimes challenges are your soul's way of pushing you in a particular direction. Health professionals, for example, often go into their profession to find ways of healing themselves or other family members. People forced into a profession they don't want may get ill or go bankrupt to be free to follow their dreams. Challenges can be a way to get your attention and move you toward your life purpose. Equally, they can be the mechanism to resolve your past karma.

> **Akashic Wisdom**
>
> Each of us has designed our life with as many obstacles and challenges as we could create along with a variety of options and possibilities to overcome those same challenges. Remember this, you can never become a great sea captain if you only sail calm waters.
>
> —Dannion Brinkley, author and transformational speaker

Reasons behind life challenges can be called paths of karma. It's a mistake to think that someone who is suffering, including you, somehow deserves it. You don't know what path of karma anyone else is on or what motivation is in place, so you can't judge what's deserved and what isn't. In fact, every path is ultimately motivated by one thing: the desire to increase love.

The Path of Rebalancing

When one person hurts another, the action needs to be balanced through growth. Figuring out the best way for this to happen occurs before you're born, when you meet with your guides and plan your life. In this session, you design the lessons that balance your karmic debt. Because karmic debt is about growth, not payback, similar actions don't necessarily require the same conditions to regain balance.

For example, let's imagine two different men each torture or murder someone. One man feels no shame or remorse, believing the victim deserved his or her fate. This person has no conscience. His lesson will look like vengeance because he needs to learn what it feels like to be the victim of his own actions. His next life he may be killed in the same cold-hearted manner. Rather than "an eye for an eye, a tooth for a tooth," this plan promotes the man's awareness and growth. Specifically, it provides the opportunity to develop a conscience.

Imagine the second man, however, was acting from deep inner turmoil and pain or was on drugs when the crime was committed. Afterward, he's crippled with remorse and empathy for his victim. Rather than needing to develop conscience, he needs to heal. His healing may take the form of living his next life serving and protecting people as a police detective, medical provider, social worker, or any number of other jobs that give back to society. By giving back, he can redeem his own self-image and rectify his past mistakes. His life design will enhance and support others who he may have wronged in the past. This will allow him to regain balance.

As different as they look, both of these life designs rebalance the karma for the same type of crime.

The Path of Duty

People agree to difficult conditions to fulfill past promises. They may feel a sense of duty to a particular ideal, activity, group, person, or lifestyle. Duty that crosses over from one life to another is often the result of vows or pacts that were made under intense emotions. In your life-planning session, you may insist on keeping past obligations alive in your present life. Although the pact may no longer be relevant, the emotions that created them are still strong and very real.

Some souls feel a strong commitment to a family line or ideal and reincarnate into the same genetic family through many generations and lifetimes. This has been claimed of royal and political dynasties. The sense of loyalty to the family name, business, belief system, and heritage is very important to these souls. It's interesting to think that the decisions made to benefit the family in one lifetime become the conditions they inherit in their next life.

The path of duty can create positive soul growth when the call is to a high ideal. A vow to vengeance or another low-level impulse will result in incurring more karma, requiring more rebalancing. Often, this path is simply misplaced loyalty resulting in one person refusing to grow until others in the pact are ready. They waste their life going nowhere, serving an ideal that has passed.

Healing around misplaced duty requires supporting loyalty while teaching forgiveness, compassion, and the ability to let go of the past and move on.

The Path of Awareness and Healing

We're all on a path of growth to develop our awareness. We're also healing our belief in separation. Sometimes the most difficult situations give birth to profound growth and healing. Instead of viewing challenges as punishment for something you've done wrong, consider difficulty as opportunity. In the face of specific challenges, consider what part of yourself you're being asked to develop and or heal.

Timeless Tips

Remember the Apollo 13 space mission? Two days after takeoff, an electrical failure caused an explosion in the oxygen tank. With limited time and only the materials on board, the crew and ground support were pushed to find a solution. No one wasted time wondering what they were being punished for—and neither should you. Sometimes we're forced by circumstance into our best and greatest growth. Face every obstacle as a choice you made to grow and heal.

The Path of Sacrifice

As souls raise their awareness, they begin to put service to others ahead of their own personal gain. They may design life conditions to assist others. This may require major sacrifices on their part. The conditions they accept are often tragic and seemingly senseless. The fact that a two-year-old child has leukemia, for example, makes no sense until you consider the opportunity they give their parents for exceptional growth.

Sacrifice can be the motivation in all the following circumstances:

♦ Being willing to be the "bad guy" so others can rebalance their karma

♦ Being born in poverty-stricken areas to bring the light of awareness to disenfranchised souls

♦ Suffering terminal illness for the growth of those around you

♦ Agreeing to die young to stimulate your parent's growth

♦ Agreeing to be a victim of horrendous crime to stimulate positive world action, as in the concentration camps of World War II

♦ Those who work behind the scenes with no recognition to increase love and compassion

The purpose of sacrifice is to provide an avenue of growth for others. People on this path often have exceptional calmness and acceptance of their situation. They inspire those around them with their positivity and courage.

The Path of Service

We're all in service to the divine; some people are simply more aware of it than the rest of us. People on this karmic path design their lives to bring enlightenment to the planet. They release personal attachment and are geared to the masses. Winston Churchill, Mohandas Gandhi, Nelson Mandela, Winnie Mandela, the Dalai Lamas, Martin Luther King Jr., Mother Teresa, and others who give selflessly to the cause of the advancement of humanity are clearly on this path.

Less grand but every bit as impressive are the people who provide service to others in innumerable ways every day, in all walks of life. Motivated by love, they lead the way to helping the Akashic Record evolve.

Health Tests

Your health is a reflection of the life you live now and the lives you lived in the past. Your physical condition may be an imprint of your death in a previous life. It becomes the basis of the lessons you're learning in this life. Your physical body and the conditions you suffer are messengers for your soul's mission.

Are you wondering what good a healthy lifestyle is if you've contracted an illness? For example, if you've contracted to learn from a heart attack, what difference will it make to lower your cholesterol and increase your exercise? Aside from maximizing the quality of your life, the reason is because the future is mutable. If you learn the lesson of your health challenge, you can change the direction of your life.

The Akashic Record suggests that during the life-planning session, multiple futures are designed. Like a kaleidoscope, changing directions will precipitate different designs. There are crossroads in every life where one outcome is chosen over another. Conditions are set up in advance, and how you respond determines what design is enacted.

Akashic Wisdom

I have noticed even people who claim everything is predestined, and that we can do nothing to change it, look before they cross the road.

—Dr. Stephen Hawking, theoretical physicist

Transmuting Health Karma

Here's an example. Joan had trouble all her life communicating her deeper feelings. Raised by an abusive parent, she was afraid her love would be rejected, her feelings laughed at, and that she would be punished for her anger. She learned early to keep her emotions to herself. She also learned early that cigarettes could help. She started smoking at the age of 13. When she was angry, she smoked a cigarette to hold it in and calm herself down. When she was sad, instead of talking about it she smoked for a pick-me-up. In most situations, instead of speaking her mind she used cigarettes to suppress her expression—holding back her thoughts and feelings while blowing smoke out into the world. Not surprisingly, she developed lung cancer in her early 40s.

Smoking may have been the mechanism that caused Joan's cancer, but the real source of it was her inability to be authentic with the people she loved. Once she was diagnosed with cancer, everything changed. She chose to look into the deeper issues of her life through counseling. Before she died, Joan was able to express to her children and husband what she felt and who she was inside. The family underwent tremendous growth. Joan's illness and eventual death provided an opportunity for everyone, including Joan, to resolve dysfunctional family patterns.

If Joan had learned earlier in her life how to own her emotions and express what she felt, she may not have needed cigarettes to cope. She also would not have needed the healing that lung cancer provided her soul. In Joan's planning session, she designed her childhood and family contracts to provide the conditions she needed to fulfill her life mission: claiming her authentic self. She also contributed to the healing of the rest of her family.

In the planning session, Joan created multiple outcomes to cover the different choices she could make in her life. Her illness was motivated along multiple karmic paths of service, growth, and healing. At any point along the way, Joan's desire to be her authentic self could have prevailed. She could have sought counseling as a teenager, stopped smoking early, and lived different choices. The design of her life would have shifted. This is true of everyone. Nothing is predestined except the lesson you came to learn. It's up to you when you learn from your conditions.

Illness and Disease

We're conditioned to think that illness and disease is life destroying, but is it possible it can be life enhancing? It's often said that without health, we have nothing. It's true that fulfilling your highest dream is difficult without good health—difficult but not impossible.

Consider Dr. Stephen Hawking, the famous theoretical physicist paralyzed with a type of Amyotrophic Lateral Sclerosis (ALS). Despite progressive paralysis, Hawking has made exceptional contributions to the fields of cosmology and gravitational physics. His discoveries are on par with Albert Einstein's. Hawking's true genius, however, may be his ability to transmit difficult concepts to laypeople. Believing science should be accessible, he's written best-selling layman's books and a children's book to help open the mysteries of the universe to everyone.

Many people wonder what Hawking might have accomplished and how far he might have risen if he didn't have ALS. Studies in the Akashic Record say that illness and disease are part of the soul's larger plan. Dr. Hawking offers this assessment of the impact of his illness: "I'm sure my disability has a bearing on why I'm well known. People are fascinated by the contrast between my very limited physical powers, and the vast nature of the universe I deal with." Dr. Hawking may have made more discoveries without his illness—or not—but would they have made the same impact to the everyday person? Did he have a deeper design along his karmic path?

> **Etheric Advisory**
>
> Although we design our illnesses to heal deeper levels of our selves, don't make the mistake of blaming the victim for being sick. Ultimately, every choice is to increase love.

While Dr. Stephen Hawking demonstrates the Path of Service, many illnesses, such as Joan's, are designed to help an individual heal the part of himself or herself that lost connection to that person's spiritual identity. In addition, some people's soul path is to bring attention to a specific condition by getting the illness in order to focus resources on finding cures.

Childhood Illness

Nothing is harder to bear than the suffering of children. Every parent wants their kids to be healthy, well adjusted, and happy. When childhood illness strikes, it can be incapacitating to the parents and other siblings. It also forces incredible feats of growth. The impact of childhood illnesses, accidents, or death on families has been captured in story lines of many books and movies. They are emotional, devastating, and inspiring.

The Akashic Record suggests that families come together to enact these tragedies for the benefit of all concerned. Every person involved grows from the situation. The child may be on the path of sacrifice, offering to suffer for the growth provided to everyone. In doing so, he or she is transmuting lower-level impulses into higher impulses and undergoing immense soul growth. As tragic and painful as it is, the life that ends early has not been wasted.

Many parents today are challenged by children with forms of autism, Attention Deficit Hyperactive Disorder (ADHD), or Attention Deficit Disorder (ADD). According to a national survey and a study conducted by the Centers for Disease Control (CDC), reported by *About.com* in 2009, 7 percent of parents of 6- to 11-year-olds have been given a diagnosis of ADHD or ADD for one or more of their children. The disorders are characterized by slower emotional development, learning disabilities, hyperactivity, and defiance of authority.

Akashic Readers such as Shaun Martinz, author of *Remember Who You Are: Insights from the Akashic Record* (see Appendix B), say these disorders are common in the highly developed souls being born today called the Indigo and Crystal children. These souls have high levels of creativity, new ways of thinking and perceiving, and a highly developed ethical code. They're bored by the restrictive modes of teaching currently in use and see through authority. Although highly challenging to parents, Indigos are bringing new ideas and concepts into the world. Knowing this helps parents guide these kids and manage their own feelings. Indigos are born into families who are answering their own call to growth.

Terminal Illness

Terminal illness brings tremendous change to people's lives, as Joan's story demonstrates. Each person's motive for agreeing to a terminal illness is their own; however, some trends appear in Akashic Record readings. For example, people with cancer are often those who put other people's well-being before their own. They often suppress their own needs for others.

Robert Schwartz reports a conversation with the angelic realms in his book *Your Soul's Plan* (see Appendix B). It provides an Akashic Record explanation for the AIDS epidemic. He quotes the angel as saying, "(AIDS) ... points to a pattern of self-hatred among humankind, a culmination of centuries and generations of movement away from Spirit, movement away from light, and a belief in the self as the body and separate from All that Is." The story Schwartz relates demonstrates how the growth of individuals is linked to the growth of society through agreed-upon events. The person with AIDS was learning self-acceptance while the people around him were facing their own judgment, fear, and loathing—brought to the surface through confronting this disease.

Matt was a young man diagnosed at 19 with an aggressive form of Multiple Sclerosis (MS). He was given a prognosis of three to five years to live. Prior to becoming ill, Matt had a perfect life. He was the center of his family and a leader among his crowd at school. Everything seemed to go his way. Matt says, "When I started to get really sick I suddenly understood that everything I had done for my friends and family was nothing compared to what was ahead. It was my job to show them that we are more than bodies and that our awareness doesn't end with death. It was my job to show them how to die; to show that there is nothing to fear. I soon realized this lesson was for everyone, that our society is afraid to die."

"As the disease advanced I was paralyzed and in a wheelchair. People didn't want to look at me. They didn't see me; they saw a disfigured body and seemed afraid that even to look at me would reveal that they, too, were trapped. Whenever I could catch someone's eye I winked and smiled and told them through my inner peace the truth: That we are more than this. We are not trapped inside bodies; we are free and death is not forever."

Personal Crises

Every personal crisis is designed to fulfill someone's karmic path. There are no exceptions. Even accidents and mistakes are part of your path. It's said that it took Thomas Edison 10,000 attempts to make a light bulb. Do we remember his 10,000 failures or his one success? Each "mistake" he made was part of discovering the final answer. Our personal crises are the same.

There is no formula that matches a type of crisis with a particular lesson. Everything is individual. Making sense of the patterns and challenges in your life is your life's work. No one else can tell you what it means, but they can guide your understanding. Every challenge is designed with a way out. If you're having trouble finding it, don't hesitate to seek professional help from a psychotherapist or alternative health provider, Akashic Record reader, or a good life coach. You are never alone; there's help in places you may never have thought to look.

Financial Ruin

Lenny came into this life to learn the lesson we're all here to learn: that we are spiritual beings. He was born into a highly successful family where his mother worshipped his father and everyone in the family tried to live up to his father's stellar example. Lenny's father was rich and successful. He was an upstanding member of the community, serving on the local hospital charity board and teaching in the high school's Junior Achievement. Lenny felt he could never measure up. He did poorly at school and started several businesses but lost them all. He saw himself as a failure and suffered from depression.

Lenny finally made it big with an Internet business in the 1990s. Within a few years, he was earning a million dollars a year. His new success didn't make him happy. He was still depressed and covered it with ostentatious behavior. In fact, Lenny had been so focused on material success that when it came and didn't make him happy, he felt lost. Was his value to society based on his material success, or was he worth something more than money? This crisis of success was the beginning of his transformation.

The Akashic Record indicates money issues represent confusion around power and spirituality. Is it hard to see yourself as a powerful person? Are you afraid of what having power means? Maybe you identify money with exploitation or are afraid that having money will separate you from your friends. Did you make a past-life vow of poverty?

A lack of money may indicate questions of self-worth. Do you feel you don't deserve money or that it will separate you from spiritual truth? Having or not having money is irrelevant. What is important is knowing that you're a spiritual being with unlimited power and inner resources to take of yourself.

Addiction

Drug or alcohol addiction is a terrible waste of potential. It sidelines people from fulfilling their dreams and achieving soul growth. Often, addiction is the result of an old pact and the person is unable to move forward until the pact has been fulfilled. Sometimes it's the result of deep self-hatred that's presenting itself for healing. Sometimes the addiction is a challenge the soul sets up simply for the growth obtained in overcoming it.

Timeless Tips _____

Indigenous people have believed addiction is a type of spiritual possession. Spiritual treatment is gaining ground in different treatment programs. If this thinking resonates with you, you'll find more information on this website: moonviewsanctuary.com/addiction-treatment/spiritual-addiction-treatment.html.

Addiction is often a replacement for love. Not believing in their own lovability, substance abusers numb themselves to escape. According to Robert Schwartz in his book *Your Soul's Plan*, a soul may design the challenge of substance abuse simply to learn that nothing can replace relationships or the importance of loving and being loved. Addiction may simply be the means of forcing a soul into this awareness so they will focus on healing their relationship issues.

The power of addiction is such that it can take many lifetimes to break free. Or it can happen in a single moment of awakening.

Natural Disaster, War, and Mass Murder

Service, sacrifice, rebalancing, and learning—all paths of karma can be found in disasters involving masses of people. Each person brings their own karmic plan to the disaster. Mass events involve more than the people directly impacted. The entire world is part of the karma of such events. Everyone who witnesses it, responds to it, or ignores it is part of the lesson.

It's not good enough to use karma as a reason to accept suffering or injustice. We can't ignore starving masses, epidemics, disabilities, disease, or the victims of disasters based on the belief that it's the karma of those involved. It's our karma to be witnesses. Are we inspired to contempt or apathy by another's pain, or are we inspired to compassion?

Akashic Planning

At this point, it's clear that the challenges in your life are not chance events but part of an elaborate plan for growth. Terrible things don't happen because you deserve them or want them but because you agreed to them out of a higher motivation. You're not here by accident, and what happens to you isn't an accident, either.

Readings from the Akashic Record are clear that in one way or another, suffering is the result of separation from our essence. Whether you suffer to enhance your own growth or in service to another's growth, the experience is an opportunity for spiritual alignment. Transform your fear, anger, and everything that keeps you separate from unconditional love by focusing your life on finding the edge of growth. Awareness will bring more fulfillment, meaning, and purpose to living. The purpose of life reveals itself when we shift from thinking of it as a game of chance—or worse, as punishment and reward—and look at it instead as the journey home to our essence.

In the face of the wisdom within the Akashic Record, it becomes impossible to think of ourselves as victims of fate. Fate is something we help arrange, and the word "victim" implies there is no power or purpose in the plan. Avoiding difficulty would be like avoiding death. It would stop any forward progress at all. This is not to say that growth doesn't happen from inspiration and positive energy. Of course it does. In fact, when we remember the truth of who we are, separation will cease to exist and pain and suffering will no longer be present.

The Least You Need to Know

- You agreed to the challenges in your life in order to promote your soul growth.

- Life challenges are motivated by different karmic paths and are not about punishment and reward.

- A health challenge can be life enhancing by moving you to grow in new directions.

- Life crises are geared to help us remember who we are as spiritual beings.

Part 4

Akashic Imprints

How much of the future is predetermined, and what outcomes can we change? The Akashic Record is described as mutable, a constantly changing and interactive field of energy. How the future is created, how prediction works, and what science is discovering about time are examined in these chapters.

The consciousness contained in the Akashic Record reaches beyond that of humans. This part looks at some of the other realms contained within the akasha and explores the significance to us.

"C'mon, Bessie. You're in touch with the Record.
What's Farmer got in store for us?"

Chapter 14

Afterlife in the Akashic Field

In This Chapter

- ◆ Accessing the afterlife
- ◆ Death and resuscitation
- ◆ In-between lives
- ◆ Planning the next cycle

Our fear of dying creates more pain and suffering than any other force on the planet. Religious teachings all promote an afterlife, yet people still wonder, "What will happen to me when I die?" The Akashic Record asserts that our awareness continues after death. It affirms that life is continuous and meaningful. This chapter looks at what happens when we die as seen through the Akashic Record accessed through hypnotic regression, Electronic Voice Phenomena (EVP), and near-death experiences.

Into the Spirit World

One of the difficulties of truly believing in life after death, or in being able to imagine what the afterlife may be like, is that once someone is dead it's hard to communicate. The veil that separates the dimension of life from the dimension of death is difficult to penetrate. Although many claim to receive messages from the other side, unless you have personal verification it takes a leap of faith to believe the messages are real. Various religions provide descriptions of the afterlife that are remarkably alike. Descriptions from the Akashic Record are similar as well, with some important differences.

The biggest difference is the concept of judgment. In research of life after death, there's no external judge examining your worthiness. Instead, after death you undergo a life review with the support of a team of guides and assess your own development. The assessment determines what will be involved in your between-life sojourn as well as the conditions for your next incarnation.

There are reports of people visiting hell. It's described as a horrible place where souls are trapped inside their own beliefs and negative perceptions. This scenario is captured well in the 1998 movie *What Dreams May Come* with Robin Williams. The point is that the Akashic Record version of hell is self-created, not a punishment from a heavenly being. Anyone can leave as soon as they can see beyond the fear and limitation that has become their reality.

Research into life after death is growing. A variety of techniques and avenues of study are being explored. Some are scientifically based and others are based on psychic phenomena. In the following sections, we take a look at some of the more prominent areas of research.

Readings from the Record

Past-life readings from the Akashic Record have offered much information on what happens after death. The readings explain the life review process, the Halls of Learning within the Akashic Record, the evolution of the soul, and the purpose of life. This is reinforced with information gathered through methods of new science as well.

Readers such as Edgar Cayce, Madame Blavatsky, and Theosophist Rudolf Steiner have spent considerable time investigating conditions of the afterlife in the Akashic Record. Everyone who reads the Record can gain afterlife information, and there are numerous books on the subject, some of which can be found in Appendix B.

Hypnotic Regression

Hypnosis is a technique to relax the conscious mind and allow access to the subconscious. The subconscious holds our memories and connection to the akashic field. Hypnotic regression uses a trance state to regress a person. The technique is often used to help subjects recall childhood events and repressed memories of trauma, and to uncover motivations for self-destructive behavior. The discovery that people can be regressed back to previous lives happened almost accidentally.

Hypnotic regression has become a useful tool to understand the process of reincarnation, past lives, the afterlife, and even events from pre-historical times. It has the advantage of being uncensored by the conscious mind's natural skepticism. It has the disadvantage of unproved scientific validity due to the impressionable nature of people while under hypnosis. Pioneers in the field of life-after-death hypnotic recall are psychiatrist Dr. Michael Newton, Dr. Helen Wambach, Dr. Raymond Moody, and Dr. Bruce Goldberg.

Electronic Phenomenon

Electronically capturing voices or images of people is called *Instrumental TransCommunication* (ITC). Researchers believe the recordings are imprints on an electronic medium from people who have died. ITC developed from the spiritualist movement of the early 1900s with the advent of the camera. It became very popular in paranormal research in the 1970s, and interest in this area is expanding once again.

One type of ITC is Electronic Voice Phenomena (EVP). EVPs are the recordings of spirit voices, usually on tape recorders, with no currently understood physical explanation. An EVP can range in quality from being almost unintelligible to being clear, understandable statements. Another form of ITC captures visual images of people who

def•i•ni•tion

> Instrumental TransCommunication (ITC) is the process of electronically capturing voices or images of people who are dead.

have passed away on monitors and television screens. ITC images are clearly recognizable. ITC researcher Mark Macy, author of *Spirit Faces: Truth About the Afterlife* (see Appendix B), has provided the most detailed ITC photographs.

Techniques and equipment have been developed to encourage all types of ITC events, and there's a growing body of supportive research. The information received includes descriptions of the afterlife as well as technical and scientific information.

Timeless Tips

If you want to make your own EVP recordings, here's a site that will tell you how: www.trueghosttales.com/how-to-record-evp.php. To see ITC images of those who have passed away, check out this website: www.worlditc.org/.

Additional pioneers in ITC include parapsychologist Konstantin Raudive, author Raymond Bayless, and Friedrich Jürgenson, the Swedish man who discovered EVP. In 1982, engineer George Meek and psychic William O'Neill built a device called a Spiricom that allowed two-way conversations with the dead.

Near-Death Experiences and Resuscitation

A near-death experience (NDE) is the experience of dying and being brought back to life. Some people are "dead" for only seconds. Some, like Dannion Brinkley, author of the best-selling book *Saved by the Light* (see Appendix B), are clinically dead for more than 20 minutes. Unusually, in the course of his life, Brinkley has had three near-death experiences.

A rich source of afterlife information comes from people who have died and been resuscitated. The information revealed in the event is profound. According to a Gallup Poll taken in the early 1990s, 23 million Americans have been brought back from the verge of death. Of those, eight million have had a mystical experience during the time they were being resuscitated.

NDEs are an opportunity to hear firsthand what exists on the other side. People experiencing an NDE share common elements and reveal that life is meaningful and death is not the end of existence. Dr. Raymond Moody and Dr. Kenneth Ring are pioneer researchers in this field.

The typical NDE begins with the death of the physical body. During the process of dying, many people report feeling intense pain and fear as their body fights for survival. At some point, the soul levitates from the body and dispassionately watches from above the efforts to save it. Once out of the body, people often notice inconsequential things such as how attractive they look or how much they weigh. At some point, usually as they are leaving their body, people report having "their life flash before their eyes."

Next, the person finds himself or herself traveling very quickly toward a bright, white light, often traveling through a tunnel. They're aware that if they pass through the tunnel, they will physically die. In the light, people often see loved ones who have already passed welcoming them "home."

> **Library Links**
>
> Skeptics say that people who undergo an NDE were never actually dead, even when their brain, heart, and metabolic functions ceased and they were pronounced clinically dead. The reasoning is that by definition, people don't "survive" death; therefore, the person didn't die and the NDE doesn't prove the existence of life after death.

Souls are met at the end of the tunnel by a guide. The guide is described as a "being of light," and the person discovers that they, too, are an emanation of light. They are in a light-filled world, and the beings they meet are beautiful, wise, and loving. The ND experiencer feels very calm, peaceful, and filled with incomprehensible love.

For many people, their NDE ends after traveling into the tunnel of light. At this point, they're resuscitated and their awareness returns to their body. Emotions on returning are mixed. Some people are elated to know that life continues after death in a wise and wonderful world. Their life takes on new meaning, and they completely lose their fear of death. Others are angry at having to return to a body filled with pain in a world they don't want to be in. Either way, dying and returning isn't an accident. There's a purpose to fulfill in being here, and life for the experiencer is never again the same.

Akashic Record Life Review

All of the sources of afterlife information relate a life-review process. Although time has no meaning on the other side, people who are dead only briefly seem to end the experience at the tunnel of light. Others who are dead longer experience the Akashic Record life review.

Dannion Brinkley had his first near-death experience when he was struck by lightning. While dead, he was taken through an Akashic Record life review. He describes watching his life from a second-person point of view and experiencing every event—not only from his own perspective but also from that of every person with whom he interacted. He was able to know firsthand the pain or happiness he brought to each person.

In one of his lectures, Brinkley reports watching the wave of his actions ripple outward. Each person he was kind to spread kindness; each person he was cruel to spread cruelty. In his review, he came face-to-face with the selfishness in which most people, including him, live. This process offered him the opportunity to change.

During the life review, no one else is passing judgment. Says Brinkley, "When the panoramic life review ended, despite the many obvious mistakes I had made in my life, I experienced no retribution—no judgment and no punishment. I was the only judge presiding over my day in court!"

The life-review process is key to creating the conditions of the soul's next life as well as his or her between-life sojourn in the afterworld. The awareness a person gains when face-to-face with all of his or her actions, both good and bad, makes clear the areas requiring growth. Most souls are eager to make amends. They're limited only by their own development, wisdom, and insight.

Visions of the Future

During their sojourn to the other side, ND experiencers are often shown information important for humanity. They return with visions of the future, technological advancements, and/or scientific breakthroughs. Along with this information, they're given tasks or directives to carry out. These usually involve acting on the information they've been given to benefit humanity or more simply to spread kindness in the world.

Here's an excerpt from Dannion Brinkley's ND visions: "One by one, the Beings of Light approached me. When they did, a small black box emerged from their chest and sailed toward my face. Before impact, the boxes would open to reveal pictures, or what I now call visions, of the future."

Brinkley had difficulty understanding the visions and what they meant. "However," he continues, "it is amazing to me still, how much of what I saw, the day I died in 1975, has come to pass over the years. After viewing over one hundred visions, the Beings of Light gave me one last assignment. I was told to create Centers for stress relief on Earth. And then I was told it was time to go back."

Researcher, inventor, and lecturer Mellen-Thomas Benedict had an ND experience lasting more than an hour and a half in which he was able to ask questions of the "light of God" and was shown answers. He returned with information that became the basis of several scientific breakthroughs.

> **Library Links**
>
> For more information on Dannion Brinkley, go to www.dannion.com. For more information on Mellen-Thomas Benedict, go to www.near-death.com/experiences/reincarnation04.html.

Life Before Rebirth

NDEs provide descriptions of the afterlife, but they don't tell us the entire story. In an NDE, the soul returns to the same body rather than being reborn—cutting short the afterlife experience. Using techniques of hypnotic regression and information from Akashic Record readings, the larger picture emerges.

Many spiritual systems believe that when a person dies, he or she suddenly becomes enlightened. However, this isn't the picture that surfaces. At death, you'll remain at the same level of awareness in which you lived. Regression information indicates there are different etheric levels to receive souls of differing development. For example, some souls are not ready to die. They think death is nothingness, and because after they've died they still have awareness, they simply don't believe they're dead. These souls either stay connected to the earth or enter a lower-level etheric plane. According to author Mark Macy, these souls group together and recreate in the etheric realms the communities they were used to on Earth. Eventually, the Earth plane loses its hold on them and they awaken, moving on to the life-review process.

According to the medium named Staci in Robert Schwartz's book *Your Soul's Plan* (see Appendix B), there's a distinct building, or hall, in which life reviews and pre-birth planning sessions take place. After a soul emerges from the life review, it spends time healing from its Earth experience and integrating its lessons. There are great Halls of Learning where souls are allowed to finish studies they began on Earth or perfect musical or artistic talents. Scientists often continue working on problems they were solving before they died. Souls also receive counseling around the issues they had in life, and new perspectives are attained.

Nothing is forced. Through their life-review process, souls came in contact with their growth edge. If they want, they now have the opportunity to learn and grow. Or they can rest and rejuvenate as long as necessary. Your personal desire to gain understanding and your motivation to expand determines where and what you will do in the period between lifetimes.

Guides

Many people have questions about their guides and the role they play. Most regression sessions and NDEs report the presence of guides that help each soul in their post-life journey. Some people report meeting their guide after they've passed through the tunnel of light. Others say they were aware of a presence during their entire passage into the light. Either way, your guides help orient you to the transition ahead.

According to Dr. Michael Newton, author of *Journey of Souls: Case Studies of Life Between Lives* (see Appendix B), guides stay with an individual soul through many lifetimes. He has found that everyone has one master guide who has been with them from the time of soul creation. You also have one or two secondary guides who are in training to become master guides. A master guide can oversee many members of a soul group, so you may share your master guide with others in your circle. Many psychics claim we can have multiple guides—some who stay with us for our entire soul development and some who are only for specific passages along our journey.

Guides are responsible for supporting the direction of your growth. They act as teachers, guiding your path during life and helping with the transitions between lives. They assist in the life review and also in the planning sessions for the soul's next incarnation. You may be interested to know that one of the functions of your master guide is to begin your training as a beginner guide for others. For many people, it's comforting to know that we're never alone on our journey.

Library Links

In *Journey of Souls: Case Studies of Life Between Lives,* Michael Newton describes guides as having different teaching styles. Some, he says, "give constant help to their students on Earth while others demand their charges work out lessons with little overt encouragement."

Many people wonder why souls are not met directly by God when they die. In fact, some are. Mellen-Thomas Benedict believes he was met by "the light of God," who answered his questions and showed him the beauty and sacredness of life, the universe, and humanity. Light seems to be as direct an experience as we can have with God, or the God force. More direct interaction would, it seems, "blow our circuits." Dr. Newton's assessment is that guides have the job of direct interaction with us, presumably until we are ready to stand in the presence of God.

Homecoming

Another consistent feature of NDEs is the feeling people have of coming home. They're welcomed by the souls of family members who have passed away—and while this is a wonderful reunion, it isn't the source of the feeling of "home." It seems that people remember where they are. They realize they're returning to the home they had before they were born.

Although in reality we are beings of light, to make the transition easier souls present themselves in their human form. They usually reproduce themselves in a perfected image of their body at an age they enjoyed. Their bodies in death are different from their physical bodies only in the light emanations that stream outward.

Most souls welcome their time in the etheric planes. The demands of a physical body are completely lifted. They're in beautiful surroundings filled with music and light. They welcome the relaxation and rest they receive. In short, they're in no hurry to return to Earth. When the time is right, however, everyone does return. The Earth journey is our opportunity to put in practice the ideals developed in the etheric planes.

Regression information reveals that advanced souls enter training to become guides. As your soul develops, you'll spend more and more time in the etheric planes. You'll receive training and eventually act as someone's secondary guide between your own incarnations. At some point, you will have "zero point" karma and you won't need to reincarnate unless you want to return as an ascended master to help steer the direction of humanity.

Input for Life Planning

The final part of your sojourn through the etheric planes is determining your life plan, mission, and conditions of your next incarnation. Your life review has provided the information you need. Your time spent in the Halls of Learning has helped integrate your experience and fine-tuned your skills. Now you simply need to determine what issues you want to explore, what you want to express in the world, and how to set up the game plan.

You may want to develop your awareness, heal old wounds, or deepen a love connection. You may want to express the highest ideals of spirit in the most challenged environment or help humanity rise to a higher frequency. You may want a life to simply enjoy each breath. Your guides will lovingly support and direct your choices, and together you will design a life to give you the most opportunity for the expression you seek.

The ultimate goal of life is to move beyond the concept of separation and know that we are all one. In each life, you are encouraged to be the powerful and creative spiritual being that you are. You have power to bring joy to life and creativity in the expression of your divine nature. In your essence, you are love—and the gift of compassion and forgiveness is yours to give freely in the world. The work you've done integrating your past experience will provide the foundation for sailing the stormy seas we all encounter.

Prior to being born, you will be prepared for the transition to come. As you emerge from the birth canal, the veil between the dimensions will slowly be lowered and your time in the etheric planes will become a dim memory. But it will still be there, and at odd moments when you hear a certain musical tone or see a particularly beautiful image, you'll feel as if you almost remember. You'll feel you're seeking something and don't quite know what it is until you look into the eyes of someone who you know you have known before—and the lights shine brighter and you sense that feeling of "home."

The Least You Need to Know

◆ There is no judgment in the afterlife.

◆ Methods exist to understand what happens when we die, including near-death experiences (NDEs), hypnotic regression, and Instrumental TransCommunication (ITC).

◆ When you die, you will be met by loved ones and guides, taken through a life review, and allowed time to integrate your Earth experience.

◆ The afterlife experience is peaceful and allows you time to explore the Halls of Learning and fine-tune skills and abilities you have been developing.

◆ The creation of your next life is based on the life-review process and your integration during your between-life sojourn.

The Physics of the Future

In This Chapter

- ◆ How solid is the future?
- ◆ Quantum reality
- ◆ Do predictions come true?
- ◆ Reading your record for clues to your future

The Akashic Record has been defined as a recording of all that is, all that ever was, and all that ever will be. It contains every event, thought, action, deed, and intention—past, present, and future. Psychics who tune in to the akasha offer readings on future events. However, this raises many questions about the nature of reality. Can the future really be read, and if the future already exists in the Record, can it be changed?

Shifting Futures

The future is not predetermined. If it were, we wouldn't have free will— and the Akashic Record, or universal consciousness, could not evolve. However, if the future is flexible, how can it already exist in the Akashic Record—and how can we read events ahead of time? This is a clear dilemma. In order to read the future, events must at least be partially formed.

def•i•ni•tion

Precognition is the direct knowledge or perception of the future, obtained through extrasensory means. A premonition is a type of precognition that involves a sense, or feeling, of a future event.

A lot of people don't believe it's possible to read the future, yet most people report having unexpected precognitive experiences. *Precognition* is the direct experience of knowing the future—not by a logical extension of the present but through extra-sensory perception, or ESP. You don't have to be a psychic to be precognitive. It happens to people more often than you'd think and has probably happened to you.

Have you ever had a dream of the future that came true? That's considered precognition. Other precognitive events are daytime visions, unexpected thoughts or feelings that guide your actions, or just simply "knowing" that something is going to happen. According to Rosemary Ellen Guiley, author of *Harper's Encyclopedia of Mystical and Paranormal Experience* (see Appendix B), precognition is the most common type of ESP and happens most often in the form of dreams.

Intuition is a type of precognitive ability. Having a gut feeling, or hunch, is one way of recognizing future directions. Businesspeople, detectives, and scientists rely on intuitive hunches every day—and most of the rest of us do, too. We're simply not aware of how much our intuitive reactions impact the decisions we make. In fact, precognition is hardwired into our physiology—a fact established in recent research conducted by scientists Dean Radin at the Institute of Noetic Sciences and research psychologist Dick Bierman at the University of Amsterdam.

Personal Precognition

You have multiple precognitive events happening every day just below your level of conscious awareness. This was demonstrated in independent experiments conducted by Radin and Bierman. Subjects were presented with stimulating events while their physiological responses, including heart rate, blood pressure, and changes in brain waves, were measured. It was discovered that people react to events seconds before they happen.

Seconds may not seem like very much time, but it can be the difference between avoiding an accident or having one. Have you ever reacted to avoid something before you consciously registered the danger? People in this situation often report that "something else took over." That something else may be instinct reacting to precognitive stimuli. Research now is focused on the question of how far into the future someone can consciously extend their hardwired ability.

Most precognitions of the future predict unpleasant events such as death, illness, or accidents. Some people preview natural disasters, plane crashes, or the outcome of war battles. Guiley reports that spontaneous future cognition is usually of events that happen to a close relative or friend or involve very large numbers of people. You may have experienced this with a vision of a relative dying or suddenly seeing that a friend was going to have an accident. The benefit of these spontaneous events is that people can, and do, change their behaviors. People refuse to get on a plane after dreaming of it crashing, then react in horror when they learn it did.

If precognition is a survival benefit, as Radin's research seems to suggest, then developing the ability to read the Akashic Record future may be a skill we are meant to develop. Edgar Cayce predicted that as consciousness evolves, people will become not only more precognitive but also more psychic in general.

Interestingly, psychic experiences of all kinds are currently on the rise. Every day, people in all walks of life are noticing more synchronicity and intuitive knowing. When the phone rings, do you know who it is before you look at the caller ID screen or pick up the receiver? Do you reach for the phone to call someone, only to have the phone ring as that person calls you? Are your dreams giving you advice about your business dealings? As these happenings increase the drive to understand, our mind and consciousness expand.

Divination

In some ancient cultures, such as the Greeks and the Mayans, decisions were made based on consultations with oracles, shamans, or priests. Predicted outcomes seen in signs and visions guided the actions of leaders. Today, psychics, mediums, channelers, and remote viewers (see Chapters 2 and 16) all make predictions about the future. How successful they are isn't easy to measure; if they've warned of disaster and it's successfully averted, their accuracy is difficult to determine. More importantly, what does their ability to predict tell us about the nature of the future and the Akashic Record?

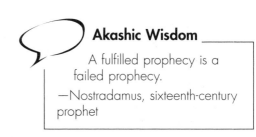

Akashic Wisdom

A fulfilled prophecy is a failed prophecy.

—Nostradamus, sixteenth-century prophet

Many people are afraid of predictions, believing they create a self-fulfilling prophecy. For example, if you're told you'll have an accident on a certain day, then you become extra nervous and create the accident you're trying to avoid. The question arises: If large numbers of people believe that something will occur, can the belief create its occurrence? Examining how people and consciousness affect the future requires a shift in how we look at reality—a shift best described by quantum physics.

Changing the Future

The future is an extension of the present, and changing our actions changes the future. Researchers describe the future as a sea of possibilities. Predictions are based on which possibility holds the most energy or is most probable based on current conditions. The most probable outcome is the most easily "read" outcome. However, from the moment a prediction is made to the moment it comes to pass, many things can change—and a different outcome can occur from that which was seen.

The future in the Akashic Record is described as looking like a sea of shimmering, shifting possibilities; some gaining energy and becoming stronger and brighter, then fading as conditions change and other possibilities becomes stronger and brighter. As time goes on, the most probable outcome gains in energy until all others fade away—and the future becomes fixed in the present moment and then becomes a solid fact of the past. You can see that predictions made within a day or two of an event have more likelihood of being accurate. In fact, future vision seems to depend, at least in part, on what day you looked and what the probabilities were on that day.

However, the future is more complicated than this picture suggests. For example, by viewing the future, is energy added to that outcome—making it more probable? Or does seeing the future create actions that make it less probable? Are all possible futures contained in the Akashic Record? These questions can best be answered in the study of quantum physics, and understanding how the Akashic Record holds the future may require understanding the dynamics of quantum reality.

Akashic Mechanics

The existence of the Akashic Record becomes harder to believe when talking about the Akashic field holding not just the future, but all possible futures, or worse, providing a medium for the future to affect the past. It begins to sound like science fiction. However this description of the Akashic Record is consistent with the foundational tenets of the field of physics known as quantum mechanics (QM).

QM has changed the way we see the world. It's changed our understanding of how matter and energy behave, and how time, matter, and energy interact. In the world of quantum physics, not only the future but the present exists in a sea of possibility that isn't solidified until it's observed. In QM the future and the past are connected such that the future can change the past, called past causality, something that can be explained in mathematical equations and demonstrated in laboratory experiments. Suddenly the mystical Akashic Record is more concrete than the "real world" described by QM.

The advent of the study of QM was met by scientific skepticism. Albert Einstein, whose equation $E=MC^2$ opened the door to QM, was never able to accept the world it described. Yet putting quantum theories into practice has enabled physicists and chemists to create new and advanced technology. It stretched our imagination beyond credulity but has also opened a new world of possibility. Inadvertently, it explains the anomalies of the Akashic field and the Record held within.

The Mystery of Particles and Waves

At one time scientists believed that matter was composed of the basic building blocks of atomic particles. Energy, they believed, was a force that existed as a wave. Einstein's equation, $E=MC^2$, changed everything by asserting that energy and matter are the same substance existing in different states of vibration. So does that mean energy is really made of particles or that matter is really the condensation of a force field?

Experiments to determine the underlying reality of energy and matter revealed something nobody expected. At the level of subatomic particles, energy and matter can be either a particle or a wave. Sometimes they can be both simultaneously, called a "wavicle." The wave-like and particle-like properties of matter are central to the study of quantum mechanics.

Here's the dilemma: particles exist in a finite place and time while the energy of waves is not limited to a specific time-space location. Theoretically a wave can propagate in an area until it exists in all locations at all times. So how can subatomic matter be both everywhere at the same time and still be located in one specific finite place? And how does that affect the Akashic field of consciousness and predicting the future?

Probability and Intention

According to Heisenberg's Uncertainty Principle, we can't predict the future at all. At least not when based solely on the information from the present. The Uncertainty Principle explains that it's impossible to determine both the position and the velocity, or speed, of a particle at the same time. You can either locate it in space, or determine how fast it's moving. Once you've located it in space it's no longer moving, and if it's moving, it's not in one finite location. This makes predicting its future place or velocity uncertain.

def•i•ni•tion

Quantum superposition is the combination of all possibilities for an event existing simultaneously.

It becomes even more uncertain because the particle is also a wave. The wave-particle duality resulted in the development of a theory called *quantum superposition*. This is the combination of all the possibilities for an event existing simultaneously, as it does in the Akashic Record. For example, when looking at an atom all the possible positions of its electrons exist in a field of probable locations, known as the quantum superposition of the atom. Superposition occurs when matter is in its wave form. The future exists in superposition within the Akashic Record, occupying all possibilities at once. It waits to be fixed in time and space by the arrival of the present.

When is matter a particle and when is it a wave? According to QM, matter exists in superposition as a wave-form until the moment it's observed. At that point the wave collapses into a particle with a definite location. With the atom, the subatomic particles exist as a superposition, or field of possible locations, until the moment the atom is measured. The act of measuring the atom changes the subatomic positions from potential to exact location. What that location will be is unknown and may depend on who is looking!

The future within the Akashic Record holds all possibility in superposition. The present represents the moment of observation when the multiple potentials collapse into one that unfolds into the present reality. Which of the many possible futures condenses into an actual event is not predetermined but it isn't random either. In QM it's based on how the observer interacts with events.

Schrödinger's Cat

Scientific revolt occurred in response to the theory of superposition. If you've followed the discussion this far you're probably in agreement! It simply doesn't make sense in the world outside of subatomic particles. What makes it worse is that in QM not just the future but the present exists as a sea of possibility until it's observed and becomes fixed.

This dilemma became famous with the thought experiment known as Schrödinger's Cat. In the experiment a cat is locked in a box with radioactive material. If the material decays it will activate hydrocyanic acid that will kill the cat. The experimenter doesn't know until he opens the box if the cat will be alive or dead. QM theory says the cat is both alive and dead until the moment when the box is opened and the cat is observed.

It's impossible for us to believe that the cat exists in both realities. Scientists theorize multiple universes existing simultaneously where in one universe the cat is alive and in the other it's dead. For us, both universes exist within the Akashic Record. Reality is starting to look much less solid than we've ever thought!

What decides whether the observer views the dead cat or the living cat? The observer, of course! The cat and the observer are interacting with each other. The cat is alive or dead based on who opens the box. And the quality of the person is based on the choices they've made in their life, one choice leading to the next leading to the next. The question becomes, which outcome do you believe? Which universe do you live in, and do you have a choice?

> **Library Links**
>
> In his later years as he worked on dilemmas created by the multiple universe theory, Schrödinger is reported to have stated to a colleague, "I wish I'd never met that damn cat!"

Are you expecting to see the dead cat or the living cat? Your intentions determine the precise location within the sea of possibilities that will become your reality. The Akashic Record holds it all. What area shines the brightest depends on what area you are energizing.

Holographic Access

The reason QM makes no sense in the world we know is because we believe that time is linear. Reality is a hologram and in a hologram all time happens simultaneously. (If you don't remember what a hologram is, recheck Chapter 1.) When everything is happening concurrently, time is a device the universe uses to separate events so that we can distinguish cause and effect.

QM describes the behavior of holographic reality. We can access the past, the future, and separate locations in the present through the holographic mind. In a hologram, the whole exists within each of its parts. Since we're part of the hologram, developing our precognitive skills is really developing our ability to look within. Chapter 18 explores different ways to do this.

When we tune in, we're connecting with vibrations. The waves of future potentials are vibrations of different amplitudes. The future with the highest amplitude is the one we see most easily. Emotions enliven future events and increase their amplitude. Events that will have a huge emotional impact have much larger amplitude than other possible futures. Consequently, many people felt 9/11 before it happened. This was demonstrated clearly with a spike in the random generator monitored by the Princeton Global Consciousness Project (see Chapter 5) one hour before the events of 9/11 unfolded.

Akashic Predictions

So can the future in the Akashic Record be read or not? The Akashic Record is available for us to access. When you do, you can look at the many different possibilities of future events. You can highlight which possibilities are most likely to happen given current events. However, you can't say with certainty that what you've seen will occur. Different readers will have a different take on the future based on their own quality of being. What they see is a reflection of their own interaction with what the record holds. A reading always reflects the level of consciousness of the reader.

Kevin Todeschi, author of *Edgar Cayce on the Akashic Records* (see Appendix B), states that the future is based on calculations of evolving probabilities. According to Todeschi, the Record is not involved in simply predicting the future, it's interested in tracking the best opportunities for growth. In his readings Cayce was speaking from his higher self who selected information from the Record that would best help the development of the seeker. In doing that, he shaped the direction of their future.

Trusting the Future

How accurate can the Akashic readings be in predicting the future? The reason to make a prediction is to provide a path forward. They allow people to change the future, thus avoiding the prediction, or to prepare for it. Understanding that predictions are not written in stone, can you rely on their information?

Cayce has certainly been the preeminent reader of the Akashic Record. Over the course of his life he gave over 14,800 readings. Some of his readings included predictions of social and environmental upheaval. It's claimed his overall readings have been 85 to 92 percent accurate. Let's look at some of his successful readings as well as some of the ones that seem to have fallen short.

Cayce's Predictions

Cayce began giving readings around 1901. Over the next 50 years he correctly predicted the following events:

- The beginning and end of World Wars I and II

- The fall of the stock market in 1929 and the lifting of the Depression in 1933

- In 1935, Cayce predicted the coming holocaust in Europe

- In 1939 he predicted the deaths of two presidents in office (Roosevelt and Kennedy)

- 15 years beforehand he saw the creation of the State of Israel

The success of these predictions was astonishing at the time, especially since at the time of the readings there were no indications that history was moving in the directions he saw. The most probable outcomes were already well established due to the strength of choices society had made over a period of decades.

On the other hand, some of his predictions of earth changes have been equivocal at best, and many have simply not happened at all. He predicted dramatic changes in the earth's surface between 1958 and 1998 due to a tilting of the earth's axis, which clearly did not occur. Although the following predictions have not happened, there are those who think they still could. Cayce predicted:

 Etheric Advisory

The danger of predicting a catastrophe is that people can make significant change in their life based not on their gut instinct but on what other people tell them.

- The eruption of Mt. Etna along with sinking or rising in the Mediterranean. Although Mt. Etna has erupted many times since this prediction, the combined rising of the Mediterranean has not happened.

- By the end of the century New York, Los Angeles, and San Francisco would be destroyed.

- Much of Japan would go underwater.

- The shifting poles would cause some coastland to become submerged as other lands would emerge, including the lost lands of Atlantis.

- Southern portions of Carolina and Georgia would disappear.

- ◆ The Earth's axis would be shifted by 2001, bringing on reversals in climate.

- ◆ The waters of the great lakes will empty into the Gulf of Mexico.

- ◆ The possibility of a third world war which would begin in the Middle East.

Could these changes still occur? Many people believe that Cayce's focus on earth changes has changed people's consciousness enough to have diverted or delayed these events. In light of other prophecies, some people expect these changes will still occur, perhaps within the next five years.

Reading Your Future

Reading your personal Record for clues to your future has the same pitfalls as those of reading global events. The future hasn't been finalized. You can look at the general nature of your future and you can look for trends, but specific events are more elusive. More importantly, why do you want to know?

You may want advice on important decisions, or information on your career, love life, or spiritual path. As Todeschi reports, the Record is interested in your growth. In that regard, Akashic readings by their nature will focus on what will help you most. It won't help you win the lottery, or best an opponent, or pull your lover away from their spouse. It will help you see yourself and your growth more clearly so that you make the choices that will bring you the happiest future. See Chapter 18 for tips on how to read the Record yourself, or Chapter 19 for tips on how to pick a reader.

Precognitive ability can be amplified by stimulating brainwave frequencies. Brainwave research shows that combinations of audio frequencies stimulate changes in consciousness that increase precognitive and clairvoyant abilities. If you want to increase your ESP ability, listening to specialized audio programs can help.

Timeless Tips _____

You can obtain computer downloads of brainwave-activating audio programs at www.daael.com/precognition.htm. Another great resource is the Monroe Institute, which you can access at www.monroeinstitute.org.

The Least You Need to Know

- Everyone has precognitive events. They are natural, and our system is hardwired to be able to receive information from the future.

- The theory of quantum mechanics describes the Akashic Record and helps explain how the future can be read.

- Reality is holographic in nature, so we can access the future because the whole exists in each of its parts.

- Readings from the Akashic Record reflect the bias of the reader due to the influence of the observer on events as explained in QM.

Chapter 16

Future Passages

In This Chapter

- The difficulties the world faces
- Predictions for the future
- Future outcomes
- Creating positive change

We have seen that the future exists as probabilities. Predicting the future is based on seeing which probability has the greatest amount of energy enlivening it. The more people focus on an outcome, the more likely it becomes. We're approaching a time in history when the world is focused on change. The change is predicted to be cataclysmic, cleansing, and transformative. This chapter looks at the predictions for our times and how we can positively impact unfolding events.

These Are the Times

Before we look at where we're going, let's look at where we are. This is a time unlike any before in our history. We're seeing tremendous leaps forward in science and technology. We're capable of astounding medical advances and creating technology that's changing the world. Many people are opening to new paradigms, and a change in consciousness is evident.

At the same time, the abuses of the past are coming full circle. We're seeing the results of misusing the natural resources of the planet. We're facing the cumulative impact of over-fishing the oceans; over-developing farmlands; destroying the rain forests; and dumping untold amounts of pollution into the air, water, and ground. Our politics have degenerated into deception and spin. The present is the product of our past actions, both good and bad.

The difficulties the planet faces are immense. As the world population grows, the competition for resources is increasing while the world economy is in depression. The destruction of the environment weakens the earth's ability to sustain life. Climate change is causing an increase in epidemics, new viral strains, and violent "super storms." You don't have to take our word on this; the evidence is in the daily news.

External pressure is causing people to feel increased internal stress. Racial and class tensions are growing. Food shortages in small countries such as Haiti have resulted in riots as people fight for food to survive. At this time of high global tension, the ability exists to destroy the planet with nuclear weapons.

The picture is grim, but it's part of a larger wheel that's turning. According to the Akashic Record, we've been in this situation before. The hypothetical continents of Atlantis and Lemuria both reached this precipice. The situation is an opportunity to balance the karma of the past and correct the path we're on. We simply have to take the right steps into the future. The Akashic Record readings suggest there are many positive elements to the opportunity at hand.

Library Links

Consider the following facts about plastic bags, which were first introduced in the 1970s. For more, see *The Environment Equation* by Alex Shimo-Barry (see Appendix B):

- Every year, between 500 billion and 1 trillion plastic bags are used worldwide, and fewer than 3 percent are recycled.
- In the United States alone, 88.5 billion bags are used and fewer than 1 percent are recycled.
- The average household uses between 1,400 and 1,500 plastic bags per year.
- It takes 12 million barrels of oil a year to make the 88.5 billion plastic bags used in the United States.
- Plastic bags take up to 1,000 years to biodegrade, emitting toxins into the soil as they break down.
- Plastic bags pose an environmental hazard that kills countless animals every day.

Battle of the Souls

Edgar Cayce claims the souls who lived in the end times of Atlantis and Lemuria have been returning in large numbers over the last several decades. They're reincarnating now to correct mistakes of the past and to help shift humanity in a positive direction.

The conditions of today are said to be a repeat of those that occurred in Atlantis. On one side are those who believe that the material world is more real than the spiritual; they desire material advantage, power, and success at any cost. On the other side are those who believe the spiritual world is more real; they desire growth, higher awareness, greater connection to our spiritual source, and universal well-being.

The discord, however, is not among people or even nations. It's a tension within each of us. It's our own base desires competing with our spiritual yearnings. External conditions are simply the expression of our internal conflict.

According to Akashic Record readers, this battle has been confronted and lost at least twice before. This time, we can do it differently. We can change the framework. Instead of each side fighting against the other, it's time to transform the battle. There's no need to give up material well-being for spiritual growth. Both can exist simultaneously. Applying spiritual principles to material problems can advance both. What we need is a complete change in paradigm.

New Frequency

Akashic Record readers say the new paradigm is coming. The planet, it is said, is receiving transmissions of higher frequency from a spiritual source. In Chapter 1, we described how matter and energy exist along an electromagnetic frequency spectrum. Humans exist along a very narrow frequency band, and our specific level of vibration determines where we are on the continuum. We're limited to what we can perceive by our level of vibration, meaning that our window of perception opens to those areas that vibrate close to our own rate.

Check back to the diagram shown in Chapter 1. You can see the limited range of human perception. The Akashic Record readings suggest that as new frequencies arrive on the planet, humans are vibrating at higher rates. The effect is that our window of perception is widening, and our awareness is beginning to increase. Mayan astronomers foretold this event in their prophecy more than 2,000 years ago.

An increase in spiritual awareness is evident. It's permeating scientific thinking, as we will see in Chapter 17. People are reaching for new ways to understand the world and to stretch beyond duality and limitation. The new science is leading the way. Akashic Record readers suggest the qualities being developed are compassion, unconditional love, and greater awareness of spirit in matter. The global challenges we face are asking us to look toward the highest and best good of humanity and life on earth, leaving the conflicts of nations aside. It's also suggested that time is accelerating. Acceleration is part of the quickening of vibration. As everything vibrates faster, time speeds up and the law of cause and effect becomes more obvious. As each thought expresses itself in the material world, the way in which your thoughts create your reality become evident.

What the Future May Hold

Predictions are based on probable outcomes and can therefore be changed. Prophecies have identified this time period as pivotal and many predictions foretell difficulty and social collapse. Reading the details can leave you feeling depressed or overwhelmed, especially in light of today's headlines. However, there's a solution for every problem, and the purpose of predictions is to focus on finding solutions and creating change. Let's look at the following information with a heart to creating positive change in our lives and in the world.

The Mayan prophecy, Nostradmus, and Edgar Cayce have all been cited as predicting earth changes for the times we're in. Many other channels and psychics, such as Gordon Michael Scallion, have also predicted earth changes. The Mayan calendar is said to be ending with a bang, with a new Golden Age emerging from the ashes. This story is also part of the Hindu Kali Yuga calendar, which is also ending at this time, heralding a difficult transition into a golden era. The take-home message is this: it's okay to let go of the old; it hasn't been working, anyway. What's important is to be prepared for difficulty and use positive solutions to create the world we want to live in.

Etheric Advisory

Don't let destruction scenarios make you feel powerless or depressed. Each of us can make a positive contribution to change by living as the person we want others to be and each day learning from our past mistakes. Working with others and finding common ground is the key. Anyone who has experienced working within a highly motivated team of positive individuals, like firefighters, knows that good spirit, friendship, camaraderie, and a commitment to creating the best outcome makes the difference between success and failure.

Mayan Prophecy

The Mayan prophecy relating to 2012 is receiving a lot of attention these days. If you're interested in learning more, read *The Complete Idiot's Guide to 2012* (see Appendix B). The prophecy is based on a series of calendars that are the most accurate ever devised. The Mayans were exceptional. They were advanced in mathematics, architecture, and astronomy, understanding concepts such as the progression of the Equinox, the exact length of a year (365.25 days), and the eccentricity cycle of the earth's orbit. The Milky Way was central to their cosmology, and they understood Earth's movement with our solar system around the Milky Way. The Mayans had a unique concept of time—one that fits well with the modern views of quantum physics. However, the main reason the Mayan prophecies are being looked at is because they're proving to be correct.

The prophecy is based on the end of two Mayan cycles: the Mayan Long Count calendar of 5,125 years and a Mayan Age of 26,000 years. The end of the calendars coincides with Earth and the solar system crossing the plane of the galaxy. These three events come together over a 36-year time span. During this period—one we are now in—major changes have been predicted.

The calendars are said to end on December 21, 2012, although there is controversy about this date. The term "age" is often replaced with the term "world," and the Mayans chronicle three of four previous worlds, or ages, in their creation documents. Past ages may relate to the times of Atlantis and Lemuria.

The ending of an age is a time of reconciliation. It's claimed that the self-destructive patterns of society come to a head and are destroyed. Everything that was out of balance gets realigned, and the disharmony of the human spirit gets adjusted. It represents the end of the old and the beginning of the new. It's a positive change amid trials and tribulations.

The end of our current age will be difficult. It's predicted that people will distrust governments and religious leaders. There will be economic collapse, famine, and shortages of resources, leading to riots and fighting. Natural disasters will increase as will pestilence and epidemics, causing many people to die. The *Chilam Balam*, a key Mayan document, states that this age will end with destruction by fire: "Stones fall from the sky and heaven and earth shall be universally consumed by fire."

That's the bad news. The good news is that the Mayans also foresaw "marvelous gifts" and "great opportunities." It's believed that when the earth crosses the plane of the Milky Way, energy from the heart of the galaxy—the Hunab K'u, or spiritual center—will flood the earth. The new frequency will return spiritual awareness to people and raise the level of consciousness.

The *Chilam Balam* says the New Era reunites people with the wisdom of the past. Masters return to spread wisdom and help people through the transition. People unite as one and create a new and better world, which the Mayans called the Golden Age of the prophecy. It's a time when people live in balance and harmony with the cycles of nature.

The Predictions of Nostradamus

Nostradamus is one of the most famous prophets of all time. Born in France in 1503, his predictions were written in four-lined poems that are ambiguous, vague, and difficult to interpret. Nonetheless, he has a large following of people who believe he is extremely accurate in forecasts that span 500 years. He used a technique called *skrying*, in which he concentrated on a bowl of water until he saw visions in the reflections.

def•i•ni•tion

Skrying is the ability to produce visions by staring into shiny, reflective objects such as water, crystal balls, and mirrors. It's a technique that was used by the Mayans, the Aztecs, gypsies, and fortune tellers.

Nostradamus saw events he couldn't comprehend or describe. There was no framework to understand or vocabulary to describe the sight of tanks, airplanes, and nuclear bombs. Consequently, his predictions are clumsy and difficult to interpret. They're usually not clear until after the event they describe has happened, giving them minimal value for creating change. He has been credited with predicting the rise of Napoleon, Hitler, World Wars I and II, and the attacks on September 11, 2001.

Still to come are predictions of a major comet whose path across the sky, and possible collision with Earth, coincides with earthquakes and volcanoes. The earth changes will bring famines, droughts, and social upheaval. This will pave the way for an anti-Christ precipitating World War III. After the destruction of the anti-Christ, the earth enters a period of peace.

Nostradamus suggests that to avoid or survive the coming changes, people should prepare themselves spiritually and intellectually. He urges people to be aware of their survival abilities.

Remote Viewers

As we mentioned in Chapter 2, remote viewing (RV) is a technique in which the viewer projects his or her consciousness to another time and place. This protocol was developed by U.S. intelligence after World War II. It was initially introduced to the public in 1974 by Russell Targ and Harold Puthoff. Remote viewing is used to view objects, people, places, and events.

In experimental programs, targets are given to viewers in sealed envelopes as a set of coordinates. Neither the project manager nor the remote viewer knows what the target is. Without opening the envelope, the remote viewer goes into an altered state of consciousness and provides details of the target site. What he or she sees are a series of impressions. When all the impressions are put together, a picture of the target emerges. Neither distance nor time is an obstacle to the viewer's perceptions.

Remote viewing has been used to find missing people, provide government intelligence, and predict the future. Major Ed Dames, once part of the Military Remote Viewing project, now owns a private Remote Viewing Institute. When asked to remotely view the time period after 2012, his group is uncharacteristically blank—not because the world has ended, but because the change is so extraordinary that the world is unrecognizable.

On Art Bell's *Coast to Coast* radio show on December 3, 2000, Ed Dames claimed that time itself changes after 2012. "Something happens on earth, in the past, that affects the entire earth in the future, all at once, and when you look around everything is different. You appear to be somewhere else, and in fact you have leapt onto a different trajectory, a different time, a parallel time if you will."

Alternate Futures

The predictions for the era we're in provide three possible scenarios. They range from total destruction to intercession from a higher intelligence to complete planetary transformation. Maybe only one will come to pass, maybe two of the three, or maybe all three will happen in succession. In quantum reality, whatever future we focus on is the one in which we'll live.

Often, people think that all they have to do is think positive thoughts and the future they want will come to them. Actually, while positive thoughts are essential, we have to match them with positive action. We have to hold a vision and work toward creating it. Too often, positive intention is mistakenly used to turn a blind eye on the troubles of today. Sticking our heads in the sand won't make our problems go away. Clearly seeing what exists, visioning the best possible outcome, and working toward it will. We can't fix what we refuse to look at, but we do have to look beyond the circumstances and focus on solutions.

Of course, it's possible that something completely unanticipated will happen. If frequency is increasing, our paradigm may shift so rapidly that we can't possibly foresee the outcome.

Predictions of Destruction

Most of the current prophecies see the immediate future as one of hardship and difficulty. The world economy collapses. Social anarchy ensues as governments lose control with no money to enforce laws and enact policy. Hospitals are undersupplied, and grocery stores are empty. Mobs leave the cities looking for food, traveling as gangs into the countryside. It's our worst nightmare. The more we focus on this as an outcome, the more likely it is to occur.

Nostradamus talks of a third world war along with economic and ecological disaster. He describes what could be a nuclear bomb. The Mayans' destruction by fire can be interpreted as volcanic eruptions or nuclear detonation.

Timeless Tips

If you're interested in other predictions for this time, this website has all the prophecies and predictions for 2012: www.2012supplies.com/what_is_2012.

Although these predictions are framed as a cleansing, it's hard to see annihilation as something good. It's true that institutions, corporations, and governments need to be cleansed of corruption. So, too, do the recesses within each of us. However, the path being described has the potential to destroy the good with the bad. If we let our fears direct our thinking, we may well find ourselves in this scenario. Reaching to higher ideals is essential at this time.

Intercession

Many forecasts predict that as the planet is thrown into catastrophe, there will be an intercession that changes planetary events. The Mayan prophecy of energy arriving from the Hunab K'u at the center of the Milky Way can be viewed as an intercession. Some believe there will be a spiritual intervention and angelic realms will interact directly with human realms. Still others believe that the damage we can do with nuclear annihilation will draw the intervention of alien species.

Apparently even the Tibetan monks have an opinion. It's claimed they have used techniques of future visioning, and have seen turmoil and conflict in world affairs around the time of 2012. It's reported that they see an extraterrestrial intervention that saves humanity. The continuation of life becomes a completely new adventure. Science and technology find the physics of spirituality to be more fascinating and rewarding than material physics and chemistry. In this intercession scenario, life goes on as usual with greater awareness. Complete destruction or transformation are both avoided.

Transformation

The complete transformation of society is another commonly seen outcome of today's events. Sources such as remote viewer Major Ed Dames, the Mayan prophecy, and present-day channels describe something we can't exactly conceive: the Golden Age. As Dames's group suggests, it's as if time itself has changed or we've moved into a different dimension.

The question is, "Do we have to go through catastrophe and cleansing to get to transformation?" If we manage to go straight to transformation, will we need an intervention—or is transformation within our own power to achieve?

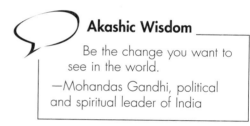

Akashic Wisdom

Be the change you want to see in the world.

—Mohandas Gandhi, political and spiritual leader of India

Empowerment

Some say this time period is a test meant to push us beyond our known limits and force us to use our higher abilities. Transformation is ours because we surrender to our higher good.

Destruction and intercession are both unacceptable outcomes. It's time to take the mantle of authority and change the world ourselves. We are responsible for the mess, and we are responsible for correcting it. We are spiritual beings with unlimited spiritual ability. This time period is pushing us to learn the laws of spirit and cooperate with the laws of nature to correct the problems we face.

According to Dr. James Hurtak, author of *The Book of Knowledge: The Keys of Enoch* (see Appendix B), regular cataclysmic changes are agents of evolution meant to quicken humans and push them to the next phase. He suggests humans are on the verge of either mastering the "physical continuum and progressing beyond this world" or starting over. Mastering the physical continuum would certainly be something beyond our imagination!

Creating the Future

The takeaway message of quantum physics is that we create reality. Like mystics and positive thinkers have been promoting, how we think, feel, act, and intend creates the world in which we live. Some of this is individual. We create individual reality in the form of relationships, jobs, where we live, and the joyfulness of our life. Some of it is within the consensual reality of the rest of humanity. The country we live in has an agreed-upon framework of public policies, national direction, environmental perspectives, and humanitarian beliefs. To some degree, we participate in holding together the consensus of society.

Changing how we view reality and creating positive change in our own life has a ripple effect into the world. We can't change the world by fighting it. We can only change by being different ourselves. More and more people are anchoring new frequencies and expressing them through their lives. Communities are forming of people who view reality in terms of unlimited potentials. They're joining together to create something new and different.

The Power of Intention

There is a considerable amount of current scientific research being applied to the power of the mind. Highly respected scientists such as astronaut Dr. Edgar Mitchell, Dr. Dean Radin, and renowned systems scientist Dr. Ervin Laszlo are engaged in discovering how the mind and matter interact and in finding out what the mechanisms of paranormal (psi) phenomenon are. A careful review of the literature suggests there is ample evidence that the mind does interact with and affect matter, as we discussed in Chapter 5 when we talked about random generators.

Researcher Lynne McTaggart, author of *The Field* (see Appendix B), discussed the findings of her current research on Art Bell's Coast to Coast radio program on September 2, 2009. She reports that in experiments developed by Dr. Gary Schwartz, the bio-photon emissions of a leaf can be enhanced over that of a control leaf by having a group of people imagining the leaf "glowing." This has been successfully replicated six times. The results have shown a significant difference between the target leaf and control leaf.

Believing that quantum physics describes a world in which we are all connected, McTaggart seeks to demonstrate that the power of intention can be used to create change in a troubled world. Her intention experiments focus on creating peace and cleaning pollution. Her first Peace Intention Experiment focused on reducing the violence in Sri Lanka. Thousands of people spent 10 minutes a day for 8 days sending their intentions of peace. The results were evaluated by a team of scientists and statistical experts.

What happened during the time of the experiment may not be as revealing as what happened afterward. She reports that during the eight days of holding intention, violence in Sri Lanka quadrupled. However, in the weeks afterward, violence decreased by 75 percent. She believes the course of the Sri Lankan civil war was changed for the better. Spikes in the random generator readings were seen during the 10-minute period people were meditating each day. McTaggart is continuing her experiments with intentional programs by focusing on lowering global temperatures and cleaning pollution.

Timeless Tips

To find out more about the Peace Intention Experiment and other intentions experiments underway, go to www. theintentionexperiment.com/ the-peace-intention-experiment.

Intentional Visioning

The experiments of McTaggart and others demonstrate the power we have as individuals to change the course of events. Random generators spike when large groups of people focus their collective attention on one area. Interestingly, the highest spikes of the random generators at Princeton University were during Princess Diana's funeral and the events of September 11, 2001. Events that capture the attention of the entire world are potent times—and when focused in positive directions can make powerful change in the world. We need more leaders who can engage that moment and guide the world in new directions.

We can all use the power of collective intention. As individuals, we can form intentions and hold them for just 10 minutes each day. We can form meditation groups and hold intention collectively. In this time of polarization, when some politicians sometimes can't speak civilly to one another, we don't have to agree on everything to make coherent change. We don't have to agree on the cause of global warming or whether private or government forces should correct it. All we have to agree on is that we love our children, respect nature, and want the freedom and liberty to pursue happiness. We can change our paradigm in the blink of an eye and behave like the powerful, creative, and spiritual beings we are.

Positive Action

Backing up our positive intentions with positive actions firms the cement of the future we're creating. We live in a capitalist society where consumerism drives the economy and the direction of policy. Be a proactive consumer. Every dollar you spend is a vote. Decide which products represent the ideals you want to grow in the world. Maybe you want to buy American, organic, green, local, or whatever makes sense to your ideology. If prices seem too high to buy according to your ideals, form co-ops. Prices will come down as more and more people drive the market.

Be responsible for the waste you produce. Do you know the size of the floating garbage dump in the Pacific Ocean? It's massive. Just the eastern patch is twice the size of Texas and contains millions of tons of toxic plastic garbage. Take active steps to properly recycle, compost, and dispose of all your refuse. Plastic six-ring can holders, fishing string, and cans with holes in them all increase the suffering of the animals that get caught in them. As suffering increases for one, it increases for all. This is the universal law: we are all interconnected—more so than you think—as the next chapter will explain with the quantum theory of entanglement.

Timeless Tips

A Place Called Hope is a wild bird rehabilitation center run by Christyne Cummings-Secki and Todd Secki. In addition to caring for injured birds of prey, they provide information on living in harmony with the wildlife around us. Visit them at www.aplacecalledhoperaptors.com.

Aligning to Your Highest Ideal

We may not all agree on what we believe in, but some ideals surpass belief systems, religions, and political persuasions. Simple kindness is one. Respect and care for our elders is another. Loving our children is something we can all agree on. If we agreed on just those three things and aligned to them when making decisions, choosing our paths, and in our behavior toward each other, the world would change.

The Least You Need to Know

- The difficult times we're in reflect the cumulative consequences of choices we have collectively made in the past.

- Predictions from the ancient Mayans, Nostradamus, remote viewers, and Akashic Record readers predict cataclysmic events as part of a cleansing.

- Destruction, intercession, and transformation are three possible outcomes futurists have seen for the world.

- Science is demonstrating that the mind can powerfully interact with matter.

- Holding intentions of our highest ideals and acting on those ideals can lead to a new and better world.

Chapter 17

The Akashic Realms

In This Chapter

- ◆ Levels of the akasha
- ◆ Our perceptions of reality
- ◆ Intelligent life in the universe
- ◆ Our place in the cosmos

The Akashic Record is said to contain all knowledge. Not limited to human experience, it is the knowledge base of all eras of time, all regions of space, and all dimensions of reality. The Record also contains descriptions of other forms of consciousness, including alien intelligence. This chapter looks at some of the information of the inner dimensions of the Record.

Within the Akashic Record

The Akashic Record is described as an energy field resonating with diverse energetic imprints. Although it was often viewed as nothing but a reference source, or library, current understanding accepts that it's more—that it's also the substance of universal consciousness. It has awareness. It changes, grows, and evolves with consciousness throughout the universe.

The akashic field of consciousness is the matrix that creates interconnection between all things. We've learned that it influences reality as much as it records it. What we can see of the Akashic Record is limited to what we can perceive. Consequently, our idea of the Akashic Record and what it contains has changed over time and is still evolving.

Ancient texts reveal the Record contains different planes, or dimensions, of reality. Traditionally, the dimensions have been represented as levels on a transcending ladder of awareness and mastery. With quantum physics, we understand the levels are interconnected and equally important aspects of reality. One level is not better than the next; they all have purpose and function within the whole.

Each plane in the akashic energy field vibrates at a specific rate that maintains that dimension. Hindu philosophy tells us that we're not distinct and separate from these planes; they actually relate to our own energy field, called the *aura*. Each of us has an aura, which—like the akashic dimensions—has seven layers. Through our aura, we connect with the different levels of reality. Each layer of the aura has a corresponding chakra, or energy center (see Chapter 11). Chakras link the aura to the body. As we grow in awareness, we receive information from more levels of the aura—interacting with additional dimensions of reality. As you can see, we are woven into the structure of the universe.

def•i•ni•tion

Our **aura** is our own personal energy field that maintains our physical form and dimensional awareness. It exists in seven layers, or levels of awareness.

Traditional Planes of Reality

According to ancient Hindu texts, there are seven dimensions existing in the same space but at different vibrations. The rates of vibration relate to the seven musical tones, the colors of the rainbow, levels of awareness, and so on. It's important to remember that we co-create reality. As we grow and evolve, so does our ability to perceive and understand; consequently, descriptions of the dimensions have changed through time. Today, psychics see additional levels that exist in higher frequencies. We've grown, and reality has grown with us. Here's an overview of the traditional Hindu designation:

- ◆ **1st—physical plane:** the realm of minerals and the consciousness of crystals

- ◆ **2nd—etheric plane:** the realm of plants and the consciousness of nature spirits, elementals, and devas.

- ◆ **3rd—mental plane:** the animal realm and the consciousness of humans, aliens, and animal totems

- ◆ **4th—akashic plane (or astral plane):** the realm of angels and ascended masters; universal consciousness. It's the central realm of all seven levels— the hub that allows the interaction between them all. Although the Akashic Record is the oneness behind all dimensions, access to the Record resides in this realm.

> **Akashic Wisdom**
>
> This universe, composed of seven zones ... is everywhere swarming with living creatures, large or small ... so that there is not the eighth part of an inch in which they do not abound.
>
> —*Vishnu Purana,* ancient Hindu text

- ◆ **5th—template plane:** the higher angelic realm and that of spiritual consciousness

- ◆ **6th—celestial plane:** the realm of the archangels and that of enlightened consciousness

- ◆ **7th—causal plane:** the realm of pure awareness, pure energy, or the god force; divine consciousness

The planes of existence represent different formulas, or mixtures, of energy and matter. The lower planes express more of the material aspect while the higher planes express more of the energetic/spiritual aspects. This doesn't mean the consciousness existing within the physical realms is less spiritual than the consciousness of other realms, however. Consciousness connects to its source. Each realm has a connection to universal consciousness through the Akashic Record. The trick isn't to climb the staircase of awareness; it's to maintain awareness on all levels simultaneously.

The Multiverse

Quantum physics has opened the door to new realities. As we discussed in Chapter 15, Heisenberg's Uncertainty Principle, not to mention Schrödinger's cat, have elicited new thinking on the nature of reality. The cat in Schrödinger's box simply can't be both dead and alive at the same time.

In 1957, scientist Hugh Everett proposed the solution: the *multiverse,* or multiple possible parallel universes. Each possible observation, he thought, created another universe. The multiverse theory is also called the Many Worlds Theory (MWT),

def•i•ni•tion

The **multiverse** is multiple possible universes (including ours) that together comprise all reality as described by quantum physics. The different universes within the multiverse are sometimes called parallel universes or alternate universes. The term "multiverse" was coined in 1895 by psychologist William James.

which more accurately states that our single universe contains many worlds. New worlds split off the one we're in as alternate choices are made. Instead of one world line, we have a many-branched tree with every possible quantum outcome. While this theory boggles the mind, it also provides fuel for the development of string theory, which supports the multiverse model of reality.

The multiverse solution to quantum mechanics energized new mathematics that provided models of reality with 11 dimensions. Scientists such as Lisa Randall at Harvard University and Raman Sundrum at John's Hopkins University suggest that our visible world of four dimensions is embedded in a higher-dimensional universe. Professor Stephen Hawking, one of the most brilliant scientific minds since Albert Einstein, has stated that "these other dimensions of the multiverse do in fact exist and are as real as the one in which we are experiencing right now."

In fact, hidden dimensions seem to make up more of the world than the physical parts we see and measure. Although science doesn't know what these other dimensions might be like, it seems the ancient texts weren't so far off in their description of multiple dimensions of reality.

Perceptions of Reality

The multiverse theory has consequences that are difficult to grasp. Essentially, each of us lives in our own reality. We decide which universe we inhabit and with whom. This creates unlimited confusion! For example, the people in your life may make different decisions than you—and your decisions place you in one world, while theirs are in another. Yet they're still here, in your world. Or does a version of them continue in your world line while another version exists in another world line? Do we have multiplicity of selves? It's enough to make you crazy! The difficulties become insurmountable and beg direct understanding.

When we stop thinking of the Akashic Record and different levels of awareness as being independent of us, we no longer have to speculate. We can experience them directly. According to Ken Wilbur, author of *The Theory of Everything* (see Appendix B), we can access information in three ways:

- ◆ Through our senses (standard science)

- ◆ Through our minds (mathematics and logic)

- ◆ Through spirit (direct experience)

We're finding that our minds and senses, although extraordinary tools, contain their own biases and set of limitations. Only direct experience can take us to the heart of the universe to know the Akashic Record. The layers of our aura connect us to the information we seek.

Timeless Tips

To learn more about string theory, check out *The Complete Idiot's Guide to String Theory* by George Musser (Alpha Books, 2008).

Karl Pribram, neurophysiologist at Stanford University, has a new understanding of how the brain stores memory. It's not stored in specific locations but in patterns of neural energy, the same way patterns are encoded on holographic film. In other worlds, our brains are holographic. Through the holographic nature of reality, we have access to all other parts—including direct experience of the akashic realms. We simply have to tune in to the layers of our own aura for direct experience.

Experiencing the Record

Edgar Cayce channeled his own higher self, who read the Record directly. Dion Fortune astral projected into the Akashic Record and interacted with different akashic dimensions. Rudolph Steiner had direct awareness of akashic realms. A considerable amount of information about the Record has come from channeling, including information from ancient Hindu texts that were channeled by various gods. All of these are forms of direct experience.

Direct access requires inducing an altered state of consciousness because our daily awareness keeps us focused in the physical and blocks out contact with other realms. Altered states, on the other hand, are trances with various levels of mental alertness that allow connection to other realities.

Altered States of Consciousness

Changes in consciousness correspond to changes in brain wave activity. Electrical transmission in the brain emits frequencies, or brain waves, that can be measured by an electroencephalograph (EEG). As we mentioned in Chapter 2, there are four basic brain states—beta, alpha, theta, and delta—that we all experience every day. When you're in an alpha brain state, your body is deeply relaxed yet your brain maintains a sharp and focused awareness. Alpha is the doorway to the slower theta brain state, which produces an even deeper state of awareness.

Normally, each side of the brain produces a different brain wave. In meditation and altered mind states, the left and right sides of the brain synchronize—and the greater the synchronization, the deeper the trance. In a trance, you may experience mental relaxation; clarity; insight; inner vision; the ability to access the akasha, uncovering hidden potentials; and the ability to contact guides, angels, and other realms.

> **Akashic Wisdom**
>
> There is no one reality. Each of us lives in a separate universe. That's not speaking metaphorically. This is the hypothesis of the stark nature of reality suggested by recent developments in quantum physics. Reality in a dynamic universe is non-objective. Consciousness is the only reality.
>
> —M.R. Franks, author and life member of the Royal Astronomical Society of Canada

Although we aim to induce altered states with different practices, they can also be induced by fever, illness, and drugs. You may have experienced altered states when you were very sick, perhaps hallucinating or actually entering other realms. Hallucinogenic drugs have been used by shamans and ancient cave dwellers to access different planes of existence.

Multidimensional Awareness

Humankind is opening to the ability to perceive other dimensions as part of everyday reality. As the Record evolves, an entire range of dormant human abilities is coming to the forefront. It's part of our collective soul plan to express our true spiritual nature, inspiring higher states of consciousness and pushing us beyond old paradigms.

Multidimensional awareness is the ability to be aware on more than one plane or in more than one place simultaneously. In this state, people have interacted with other beings—both from this and other dimensions. The range of information retrieved has been dramatic. Encounters with other realities and intelligences have resulted in an expanded view of the universe and human capabilities. They have impacted religion, psychology, and philosophy. They have produced tangible results, inspiring new technologies and scientific breakthroughs (see Chapter 7). In fact, many stories from religious texts, such as the adventures of Krishna in the Bhagavad Gita or Ezekiel in the Old Testament, describe receiving information through multidimensional awareness.

Alien Intelligence

Are there other sentient beings in the universe? Can we interact with them? According to the Akashic Record, there are many sentient beings interacting with humans—including aliens. The existence of off-planet intelligence is not disputed (at least, not scientifically). What is disputed is whether they are advanced, whether they visit Earth, and whether there is alien-human interaction.

> **Akashic Wisdom**
>
> Our sun is one of a hundred billion stars in our galaxy. Our galaxy is one of billions of galaxies populating the universe. It would be the height of presumption to think that we are the only living thing in that enormous immensity.
>
> —Wernher von Braun, rocket physicist and astronautics engineer

The subject of unidentified flying objects (UFOs) has been part of the underground media since the late 1940s. Some say this corresponds with the beginning of a change in paradigm. Prior to breakthroughs in nuclear physics, the idea of space flight was impossible. The advent of hydrogen-powered rockets opened the door for space exploration, and once it was possible for us, why not for space beings?

As we began to conceive of other worlds, the collective imagination of the planet provided UFOs as the next boogie man. There was an explosion of science fiction stories, movies, and comic strips focusing on aliens and spacecraft. At the same time, ordinary people began reporting lights in the sky, strange encounters, and eventually alien abductions. Was this, as some say, the impact of a changing paradigm on collective imagination? Or is there evidence of interaction?

Ancient Astronauts

There is a prevalent belief that humans did not evolve naturally on this planet but were genetically seeded. It's believed off-planet intelligence has visited the planet extensively through the years, leaving behind relics and influencing genetics, cultures, and technology. Proof is seen in images that have been recorded in cave drawings, biblical records, and ancient monuments. Here are some examples:

- A series of caves in what is now the desert region of Iran display prehistoric paintings depicting circles of fire in the sky that look like modern-day UFOs.

- Sumerian petroglyphs show rockets traveling through the sky, which Sumerian expert and author Zachariah Sitchin deciphers as "gods" coming from other planets in flying machines.

- In the Old Testament, Jacob witnesses an aerial object which he called a sky ladder, and Ezekiel saw four flying objects looking like "a wheel within a wheel." Ezekiel was taken to heaven in a chariot of fire.

- Egyptians described gods that arrived in flying boats and disks of many colors.

- Aztec and Mayan murals depict rockets flying across the sky and men in garments that look like today's space suits.

- Native cultures throughout North and South America refer to "Star" nations from where they originated.

Ancient cultures add to the mystery by exhibiting advanced mathematics and astronomy and by unexplained technological accomplishment in building the pyramids of Egypt, Japan, and Guatemala. Readers of the Akashic Record have said that many of these skills came from Atlantis and Lemuria, but the Record also confirms that alien intelligence exists and interacts with Earth.

Close Encounters

We've all heard the claims of alien encounters and UFO abductions. Maybe you've even seen lights in the sky that clearly didn't belong to planes. Since the 1950s, sightings and claims of close encounters have been increasing. They began to draw serious public attention in the 1980s with the publication of Bud Hopkins's book *Missing Time* (see Appendix B). Hopkins is an artist who saw a UFO in the 1960s. His sighting created an avid interest that led him to research the claims of UFO abductions. Using hypnosis, he recovered details of abduction experiences that have fascinated many. Hopkins was the most prominent researcher in the field until joined by the late Dr. John Mack in the 1990s.

Dr. Mack of the Harvard School of Medicine began studying abductees in the late 1980s. Initially believing abductees were mentally ill, he simply gathered data and observed. Eventually, he became convinced that there was a genuine phenomenon happening to mentally healthy individuals. He wrote the book *Abduction: Human Encounters with Aliens* (see Appendix B) on his findings, risking professional censure and ridicule.

People have three typical experiences. In the first, the abductee is suddenly woken from a sound sleep and is aware but unable to move. They're caught in some type of force field and float out of the room and into a UFO. They describe seeing the classic extra-terrestrial—a small stature with a large, egg-shaped head and huge, almond-shaped, emotionless eyes. Abductees typically say they saw babies that represent a hybrid of alien and human genetic material.

Another common encounter starts with people traveling in a car and seeing a UFO. They experience electrical failure and suddenly find themselves several miles away with two or more hours of missing time. They have no memory of what happened during the missing time or how they came to be at a new location.

The third type of encounter happens in an altered state, where the experiencer is taught different types of information. They are often taught healing techniques, given scientific breakthroughs, or provided with technological instruction. People enjoy these encounters and seek them out. The beings they interact with are described as taller and more interested in the human condition than their smaller counterparts.

Whether these encounters are real or not, the experiences are vivid, extraordinarily similar, and seem to be describing objective reality.

Library Links

The term "crop circles" was coined by Colin in the 1980s to describe swirled plants in crop fields that form intricate patterns. His research of 30 years shows that many crop circles are made by people; however, a higher mind seems to be guiding the process. People who make crop circles report feeling compelled to, they experience interactions with strange lights in the sky while making them, and are inspired to create particular designs. Is it possible they are being directed by and interact with intelligence that is extra-terrestrial in nature? If so, what is the message? Could it be an intervention to awaken us to a reality outside our current way of thinking? Colin believes we need to remain open to all possibilities.

A Different Explanation

Consciousness researcher Graham Hancock, author of *Supernatural: Meetings with the Ancient Teachers of Mankind* (see Appendix B), sheds a different light. According to Hancock, today's UFO enthusiasts are looking for a nuts-and-bolts explanation for alien-human interactions when they should be looking at consciousness.

Hancock explains that the images found in cave drawings, such as the renditions of spaceship-like objects and images of faces that look remarkably like the extra-terrestrial descriptions of modern abductees, are a reflection of altered consciousness. Ancient man and shamans used hallucinogenic drugs to induce altered states and explore the "boundaries of reality." The images they drew, says Hancock, are the visions they saw of different dimensions while in altered states, dimensions UFO experiencers are entering as well. What makes Hancock's theory different is that he believes the visions represent objective experience of alternate realities. In these trances, often referred to as dreaming or visioning, a guide is present who takes the seeker through a series of experiences. What is remarkable is the similarity of what people in trances see and experience. They typically meet the same guide and see the same places in their visions, indicating an underlying coherent and reproducible reality to the realms they visited.

Government Disclosure

Not surprisingly, governments have conducted their own investigations into the claims of UFOs and alien encounters—the most famous being the crash at Roswell, New Mexico, in 1947. Initially announced as a UFO crash, the U.S. military immediately retracted its statement and announced the crash was a weather balloon. Colin is a friend of the son of the Army officer, Jesse Marcel, who was part of the first response team at the Roswell crash site. Jesse Marcel Jr. adamantly disagrees that what his father saw was a weather balloon.

Unfortunately, the reports on this and other UFO investigations have not been available to the public. Withheld as a threat to national security, governments worldwide downplayed both the existence of an alien presence and their interest in it. The Akashic Record might suggest that the time was not right for a full discussion of the topic. Timing in the akashic field is based on a larger picture.

No government or person has the right to control the growth of consciousness, and the picture has begun to change. Governments worldwide are releasing their UFO investigations under a disclosure agreement. The following countries have opened their secret files:

- France: March 2007: news.bbc.co.uk/2/hi/europe/6486287.stm

- Brazil: May 2005: www.rense.com/general65/braz.htm

- The United Kingdom: March 2008: www.foxnews.com/story/0,2933,510180,00.html

- Canada: March 2009: www.sott.net/articles/show/180422-Government-of-Canada-Provides-Open-Access-to-UFO-X-Files

- Denmark: February 2009: www.icenews.is/index.php/2009/02/06/danish-ufo-files-now-open-to-public/

- Uruguay: June 2009: www.abovetopsecret.com/forum/thread471181/pg1

Our world is changing before our eyes—and with it our perceptions of reality. Government files are showing that we're not alone. If we accept the concept of right timing, then we have to accept that growth in the akashic field of consciousness has resulted in the timing of this release of records. Curiously, the United States is resisting disclosure despite mounting public pressure.

Soon, we will undoubtedly have collective experiences—and a new reality will be born which will encompass an extra-terrestrial presence.

Our Place in the Universe

Paradigm change happens in slow increments over time until a tipping point is reached, after which nothing is the same. Many think we've been involved in a paradigm shift since the time of Einstein's equation $E=MC^2$. The advent of quantum mechanics and space travel has brought us to within seconds of the point of no return.

Dr. James Hurtak of the Academy for Future Science (AFFS) experienced a mystical encounter with "Higher Superluminal Intelligence" in 1974. His encounter resulted in writing *The Book of Knowledge: The Keys of Enoch* (see Appendix B). The Keys provide a blueprint for the evolution of humankind into higher states of consciousness.

We're on the verge of knowing that we are not alone in the universe and that we are, and always have been, part of a larger galactic collective. Hurtak declares that humankind is on the threshold of becoming a conscious and responsible part of this collective. The evolution of the Record requires that we expand our consciousness and move into other realms of existence. Hurtak sees a difficult passage ahead, but the outcome is assured. We will change paradigms no matter how difficult the birthing is.

The Least You Need to Know

- ◆ The Akashic Record describes many levels or dimensions of reality.

- ◆ Ancient texts and quantum physics agree that there are more dimensions than the four we can measure.

- ◆ We can learn to change our brain states and alter our consciousness to access other realms.

- ◆ Off-planet intelligent beings have interacted with the planet since the beginning of life on Earth.

- ◆ The paradigm shift underway will take us into conscious interaction with other life in the universe and with other dimensions of reality.

Part 5

Keys to the Library

Do you want a personal Akashic Record reading or the ability to enter the Records yourself? In these chapters, we discuss different types of Akashic Record readings along with the pluses and minuses of each.

In addition, the tools introduced in Part 1 will take you further into your own intuitive exploration of the Record. We'll use lucid dreams, astral projection, remote viewing, and other techniques to sharpen your perceptions. By the end of this part, you'll have everything you need to use the Record to guide your life and create the future you envision.

"I dreamed that the tortoise wins in the end."

Chapter 18

Tapping Your Psychic Abilities

In This Chapter

- Paranormal abilities and the Record
- Aligning with the Record
- Remote viewing training
- Tuning in to channeling
- Understanding lucid dreams

The tools we need to access the Akashic Record exist within each one of us, and if the readings are correct, humans are moving into a time when we will use these tools as part of everyday reality. We already have the necessary abilities; they're simply waiting to be developed. As we fully enter the quantum reality, it's claimed that the blocks to our growth will disappear. In this chapter, we look at some skills and methods you may want to develop as an Akashic Record reader.

Science of the Mind

New abilities thrive when coupled with intellectual understanding. The universe as an interconnected whole is not a new concept; it's fundamental to Eastern philosophy, where our knowledge of the Akashic Record is based.

As Western science grows, it seems to support ideas of the ancient texts, including the realization that we have abilities of the mind that we haven't yet developed.

Etheric Advisory

People are often afraid of the paranormal because it seems too strange and out of the ordinary. Actually, paranormal abilities such as precognition, telepathy, and clairvoyance are natural, and psi phenomena is more common than you'd think. People from all walks of life experience paranormal abilities throughout their lives.

Paranormal abilities, also called psi phenomena, are explainable through the Akashic Record. If quantum physics and holography describe properties of the akashic field, as it appears, a mechanism for psi abilities and phenomena is available. As you understand that these abilities are normal, natural, and explainable, you may become more interested in developing them.

Psi abilities divide into three main categories:

- Extra-sensory perception (ESP)
- Mind-matter interaction
- Life beyond death

You've probably unthinkingly performed each of these in everyday life. You may successfully engage in ESP when you know who's on the phone when it rings. Praying for a sick friend is an example of working with your mind to influence matter, and dreaming of your grandmother after she passed away may be communication from the other side. This part of us is really far more prevalent than we give credence to!

Examples of ESP include telepathy (passing information from mind to mind), clairvoyance (seeing at a distance), clairaudience (hearing spirit voices), intuition (knowing information that is not logically obtained), precognition, and reading the past or future in the Akashic Record.

Paranormal researcher Dean Radin (see the following sidebar) defines telepathy as "feeling at a distance," and telepathy may be the foundation of ESP abilities. You may experience this type of psi phenomenon daily. Many people get a sudden urge to call a friend, only to find the friend desperately needed them at that moment. Or maybe you're an empath, sensing other people's feelings and being able to help them.

Mind-matter interaction involves influencing a physical object without physical contact. It often includes healing, prayer, and effecting outcomes as in random generator studies (see Chapter 5). Many people have experiences of feeling the impact of healing prayer and long-distance energy treatments.

Life beyond death deals with concepts of life existing outside the physical realm. It looks at reincarnation, what happens when we die, how life is designed, and what other realms of reality might be like. Akashic readers are used in this area quite regularly. You may have contacted a medium yourself to talk with a deceased loved one.

The fact of psi phenomena is unarguable. It happens, and it's recorded and studied in laboratory settings. Forensic psychics are used in police investigations. Precognitive dreams and experiences occur.

Library Links

Although there are many paranormal researchers, Dean Radin and Russell Targ are two of the most respected. Russell Targ, senior research physicist at the Stanford Research Institute, has received government grants for 30 years to study remote viewing, a form of clairvoyance. Prior to studying the paranormal, Targ worked in the development of laser and plasma physics. Dean Radin is the head of the Noetic Science Institute, which studies consciousness. For 16 years, Radin has conducted studies of psi phenomenon in academic and industrial settings, including Princeton University, the University of Edinburgh, the University of Nevada, and SRI International.

Psi and Quantum Physics

One of the difficulties with psi phenomena is that mind effects, such as telepathy, happen over a distance. Thoughts are transmitted irrespective of space. Past explanations of psi phenomena have focused on an exchange of some form of subtle energy. Yet energy is unable to move faster than the speed of light—and the speed of thought is instantaneous. Experiments show ESP events are simultaneous. Quantum physics has the same problem.

The mechanism behind psi phenomena may lie within our understanding of the quantum akashic field. Telepathy research suggests that humankind is connected at a deep level. Research of mind over matter indicates there are links between mind and the external environment. Subatomic particles in quantum mechanics (QM) operate the same way. In QM, it's explained with a theory of non-locality, meaning objects separated in space can influence each other. Einstein called non-locality "ghostly action at a distance."

Non-Locality Within the Akashic Field

In 1982 at Paris University, physicist Alain Aspect and his team proved the theory of non-locality. They performed an experiment demonstrating that subatomic particles instantaneously communicate with each other regardless of how far apart they are. Somehow, each particle always knows what the other is doing and responds accordingly.

The experiment demonstrates that quantum particles can affect each other at different locations without any apparent force or energy exchanged. Instead of energy, it seems information is exchanged. Locally, effects happen as a transfer of some type of energy or force. You push me and I move. In non-local exchange, there's no direct transfer. It sounds far-fetched, but in reality we experience this all the time (in love, for example). We can feel the impact of love from across the room or across the ocean. In general, all of our emotions are non-local events.

However, instantaneous transmission breaks the speed of light, which can't happen. It's a big no-no in physics—one of the few laws that still hold in the quantum world. So how is instantaneous transmission of information possible? The universe is a hologram and everything inside is connected. Non-locality reinforces the realization that the universe is an interconnected whole. It's the arena where the action of subatomic particles are seen to have consequences in the world—the point where the observations of quantum physics coincide with the observations of psi phenomena.

Entanglement and ESP

Non-locality has interesting implications that help us understand psi phenomena. Physicist Nicolas Gisin demonstrated in experiments in 1997 that in order for two particles to exchange non-local information, they have to know each other to be somehow connected. Once a particle has "met" another particle, they become *entangled* and are able to transfer information non-locally. Gisin took unrelated photons and introduced them, creating entanglement. There's no limit on the number of particles that can be part of one entanglement. Information can be spread to an entire group of related photons instantaneously. Once connected, they're always connected. It begins to sound like biologist Rupert Sheldrake's morphic field is a species entanglement.

def•i•ni•tion

Entanglement describes how particles of energy or matter become entwined with each other and continue to interact and influence each other regardless of how far apart they are.

Dean Radin believes entanglement explains psychic abilities. In fact, some believe entanglement is part of the process of cellular differentiation in the growth of an embryo. Information exchange is needed to organize a developing embryo— something that has never been explained by conventional science. If so, psychic abilities are as innate as life itself. It's part of our cellular and human nature.

Learning to Access the Akasha

There are many ways to access the Record, and all involve psi phenomena. Everyone has psi ability, although some people are naturally better at it than others. Perhaps the people who are naturally good at it developed these skills in a past life, or perhaps they've had less cultural training telling them to ignore intuitive information. All that's needed is to embrace the concept and be open to possibilities.

If you're ready to explore your psi abilities, you'll want to start with easy and safe techniques. Psychic abilities are natural, but learning them isn't always safe. Just as swimming is a natural ability, you wouldn't throw someone into the water who couldn't swim. Starting in the shallow end of the pool ensures you won't drown, and drowning is an apt description of what you'll feel like if you develop your skills too quickly. Getting inundated with information can be overwhelming. It becomes difficult to make boundaries between your everyday responsibilities and the internal download. Maintaining your priorities can be challenging.

It's always best to find a good teacher (the resources in Appendix B are a good place to start); however, many people do teach themselves. Knowing yourself and why you're seeking to expand your abilities is key. Do you want to know and express your creative self? Are you curious about the mysteries of life? Do you feel compelled to develop your skills for no known reason, or are you looking to impress people with other-worldly ability? Wanting to impress people or to use these skills for material gain is the type of motivation that can backfire and keep you from developing your skills.

Timeless Tips

Finding a reputable training center or teacher for developing your intuitive skills is important. One way to find a credible source is to go to trainings at well-established conference facilities such as the Omega Institute in New York State, Kripalu Yoga Institute in Massachusetts, the Association for Research and Enlightenment in Virginia, and the Eslan Institute in California. Organizations like these tend to attract credible teachers and verify their legitimacy.

Remote viewing, channeling, and lucid dreaming are three safe methods of developing your ability to read the Record. We discuss all three in more detail later in the chapter.

The Qualities of a Good Reader

To be successful at reading the Record, you need to approach it in the right manner. You need to be unbiased, neutral, and in alignment with higher ideals. Neutralizing your biases is difficult, however, because most of the time you don't even know what they are. If you enter the Record believing in advance what you'll see, you're limiting what you'll find.

It's important to stay neutral. You may obtain facts or ideas that are completely unbelievable to you. Don't put up blocks to receiving by ridiculing your insights. Accept what you receive, and if it makes no sense, is too outlandish, goes against your beliefs, or doesn't match your ideas, just hold it to one side and don't judge it. Give yourself permission to not be an expert. Pretend you know nothing. Let everything you receive be held as a possibility awaiting further insight.

Stay in alignment with the ideals represented in the Record. Entanglement shows how important it is to be in a relationship with the aspects of the universe you want to exchange with. To be in alignment with the Record, you need to approach it with non-judgment, acceptance, unconditional love, and compassion. These are the qualities that open the door to the mystery of the Record and the secrets it holds. Anything less will leave you on the threshold.

Starting Your Approach

Psi ability begins with clearing your mind of chatter. The non-stop dialogue going on in your brain must be quieted so you can shift from everyday awareness into deeper brain states. One way to shift your brain state is through meditation.

Timeless Tips

Find out more about how you can learn to access your own Akashic Record by visiting www.SacredInsights.com.

If you already meditate, use your personal technique before trying the remote viewing and channeling exercises that follow. If you don't have your own meditation technique, here's a simple format:

1. Find a quiet, comfortable place to sit. Keep your eyes partially open, and don't focus on anything in a hard way. Just keep a soft gaze. Closing your eyes is fine, too, as long as you don't fall asleep.

2. Take three deep cleansing breaths to clear your lungs and mind. Then relax. Keep your attention on your breath. Follow it in and follow it out. Allow thoughts to come into your mind, and let them go out. Don't hold on to any thought. If you find you're thinking of something and not letting it go, return your attention to your breath. Continue letting things come and go.

3. If you're visually oriented, light a candle in a safe place and gently watch the flame. Let your mind be still.

4. With every breath in, bring in light and peace. With every breath out, let go of tension and chatter. Systematically release the tension in your muscles from the top of your head to your feet.

5. When you're still and quiet, proceed with the technique you want to use to access the Record.

Remotely Sensing the Akasha

Remote viewing, which we discussed in depth in Chapters 2 and 16, is often considered a form of clairvoyance—but there are some big differences. With clairvoyance, practitioners look for vivid and clear pictures. They allow the sensations they receive to provide additional information. For example, if they see a tall man with black hair wearing 1800s-style clothing and a gun belt, they'll augment that information with how they feel about the man or what he's doing. They'll make comments such as, "He makes me feel nervous, like he's after someone," or "He's sad, like he's lost someone he loves." In clairvoyance, what is seen is married to what is felt emotionally—and all becomes part of an interpretation.

Remote viewing is different. Vivid pictures with a lot of clarity are considered to be manufactured by the imagination. They're disregarded in favor of impressions, shapes, textures, smells, and other non-distinct pieces of information that together reveal a target. The point isn't to interpret information but to gather it.

Clairvoyance is usually performed by a psychic or medium at the request of individuals seeking information. The details may not be proven true or false for a long time, if at all. Remote viewing, on the other hand, is geared toward immediate verification. This makes it an excellent training tool!

How to Remote View

There are three steps to practicing remote viewing. First, you need to establish targets. Targets are pictures of scenes that are unknown to you. They are given an associated designation number, and that's what you focus on while you try to see the target picture.

Next, you induce a relaxed altered state while you remotely view the target. Draw or write your impressions as you receive them. Drawing is recommended, because often shapes that seem meaningless turn out to be central features of the target you're viewing.

Finally, you look at the target and see how many of your impressions can be verified. Don't look for exact renditions; instead, look for your impressions to match pieces of the picture.

Establishing Targets

To establish your targets, you'll need the help of two other people. Ask the first person to gather 5 to 10 pictures. They should be impersonal, and it's probably best to cut them out of magazines. The picture can be of anything—a rocket launch, a landscape, a dairy truck, anything. Have your friend place each picture in an envelope that can't be seen through and seal them.

Timeless Tips _____

If you don't have friends to help, this website has targets where you can test your abilities: www.greaterreality.com/rv/instruct.htm.

Give the envelopes to a second person and ask him or her to mix them up and put a designation number on each one. The number can be a mix of letters and numbers, such as MC2L. Neither you nor the person who made the designations on the envelopes knows what's inside. The person who chose the pictures doesn't know what designation number stands for which picture. This makes it a double-blind experiment.

Finding the Target

Pick any envelope and focus on the designation letters. Follow these steps:

1. Use a meditation technique and induce a change in brain states. You can use the meditation we described in an earlier section or any practice that you're used to. How you get there isn't important; what matters is being able to let your mind become still. Some people visualize an empty screen or blackboard.

2. Disregard the vivid images of your imagination. Say the target designation number to yourself. Allow shapes, impressions, and colors to form in your mind. Notice your emotions. Note textures and movement. Avoid trying to identify what you're seeing or feeling; just draw and/or write down your impressions.

3. After you've written down impressions, return to a meditative state and repeat the designation number to yourself. Remain open to receive another impression. Repeat this process each time you receive an image. Give yourself a set amount of time in which you are committed to receiving images—say, 5 or 10 minutes.

4. After you've written or drawn all your impressions, open the target envelope. At first you may be dismayed as you see that you didn't identify the picture from your impressions. However, notice how many impressions you've received that are in the picture. These are hits. As you get better, you'll have more and more hits. Eventually, you'll be able to accurately describe the pictures.

Viewing the Record

Once you've gotten good at remote viewing, you can use it to view the Record. Start by having the names of people you don't know put in an envelope with a designation code the same as you did in the previous sections. Say the designation code out loud to yourself, and intend to see a detail of the person's past life. Stay clear and empty, and write down impressions as they arrive. You may find some remarkably significant impressions when you share them with the target people.

With practice, you'll be able to remotely sense and view the Record without using the envelope technique. Simply holding the name of a person in your mind as you stop your thoughts will allow a flow of impressions. As you begin to trust yourself, you'll get better and better.

Tuning Your Channel

Channeling involves acting as a conduit for spirits to speak. Being a good channel requires accessing a high spiritual guide, removing your own influence, and increasing your commitment to live by spiritual laws.

As with all methods of psychic development, care needs to be taken when establishing your channeling abilities. There are two basic forms of channeling: a trance channel and an aware channel. If you act as a trance channel, you'll enter a deep trance and be unaware of the information coming through you. Some people find this disconcerting and don't like the feeling of being out of control. Other people are reassured by knowing they're not influencing the information. If you decide to be an aware channel, you'll enter a trance but maintain part of your awareness on the proceedings. Your objective awareness acts as an observer as your spirit guides communicate through you. This allows you to maintain a level of control, which may feel safer. On the other hand, you'll have to train your observer self not to influence the information you receive.

Etheric Advisory

The ability to channel is not about being more spiritual than anyone else. It's about being open to other realms. The act of channeling may help you become more spiritual, but you will have to do your own inner work. It's not a shortcut—it's a support structure.

Channeling is a key method used to access the Record. Edgar Cayce channeled his higher self, who worked directly with the guardians of the Record. Many psychics today access the Record by channeling alien intelligence or guides from the angelic realms of consciousness.

The guides you channel can be from the realm of angels and ascended masters or from the realm of archangels. You may find you can enter the Record and channel the Record Keepers directly, who can take you to the individual records you wish to view. Not all the information you seek will be available to you. Some of it may be withheld because the time isn't right. Some may be withheld because it breaches rules of privacy. You can be sure that if you are working directly with the Record Keepers, you will receive the information that will meet the highest and best good of all.

Pros and Cons of Channeling

Like most things, channeling has both positive and negative aspects. You may decide to channel to better discern your path and purpose. While channeling will give you this direct access, it won't protect you from your own growth. If you need to learn lessons, your spirit guides won't warn you away from the learning. They'll help you through your trials, but they won't help you avoid them.

Many people say the best part of channeling is the profound sense of peace and spiritual connection that pervades their lives. If you listen to your guides as you move through your challenges, you can look forward to growing more mature, creative, and inspired.

On the other hand—and there is always another hand—the experiences you may have as a channel can be overwhelming and beyond your understanding. Your friends and family may not understand what you're doing, which can cause you to feel isolated.

If you have physiologically based mood swings, opening to channel can push you into greater ups and downs. If you have mental health issues such as schizophrenia, channeling can be dangerous and should be avoided. It can be difficult to discern whether you're reacting to the physical world or the psychic world. A balanced mental and emotional state is necessary to engage in this work. If you want to channel in the hopes that it will help you become more balanced, you're better off working with a channel than becoming one.

How to Channel

Channeling is best learned under the guidance of a teacher. There are many books and teaching institutes you can use (see Appendix B); however, there is no standard approach to finding one. Just be sure whoever you use has a good reputation. Seek out people who have trained with the person and ask questions. Interview the channeler and notice the "vibe" you get. (We'll give you more details on finding the right person in Chapter 19.)

Here's a simple method that may help you decide whether channeling is for you. If so, enjoy your awakening:

Timeless Tips

A great book to help you get started is called *Opening to Channel: How to Connect with Your Guides* by Sanaya Roman and Duane Packard (see Appendix B).

1. Find a quiet, comfortable space where you will be undisturbed. Turn off your cell phone!

2. Accept the possibility that you can channel, and leave your self-doubt outside.

3. Sit comfortably, relax, and take three deep, cleansing breaths—imagining all impurities flowing out with your breath.

4. Use meditation or deep breathing to quiet and focus your mind.

5. Intend to meet your guide, and invite him or her to assist you. Be open to acknowledging a presence. Assume the guide is present even if you can't feel or see one.

6. When your mind is clear, visualize white light surrounding you. Imagine being in the Hall of Records, and visualize threads of light connecting you to the book of your life.

7. Ask a question, either out loud or in your mind. It can be quite simple. Let your mind free-float with no expectations. Pay attention to what you see in your mind's eye, hear inside your head, feel in your heart, and sense in your gut.

8. Write down your impressions, no matter how menial they seem. Keep an ongoing record of your "readings," and you will be surprised how they develop over time as you give yourself the space to discover.

If you get immediate results, that's great. If not, don't worry. Like everything else, channeling takes practice and dedication. Prove to yourself that you have persistence, and stay with it until you achieve the results you're after.

Lucid Dreams

Dreams are a valuable and easy way to contact the Akashic Record. We all gain insight and guidance from our dreams, and using your dreams doesn't require extensive training or psychic ability. Chapter 7 gave examples of scientific breakthroughs, technical insights, and artistic inspiration that came to people through their dreams. Many of these inspirational dreams had something in common (besides revealing information). They happened in a particular type of dream called a lucid dream.

A lucid dream happens when you're aware that you're dreaming in a dream. It can happen spontaneously. You're in the middle of a dream when the dreaming-you suddenly is aware that it's all a dream. The first time it happens, you may be so surprised that the experience immediately returns to a regular dream. With practice, however, you can stay lucid in the dream state and eventually purposefully induce lucid dreams.

You may be wondering what the benefits are. A dream isn't real, so why is it important to be "consciously" asleep? Anything is possible in a dream. You can go anywhere, do anything, and have access to any truth. Dreams happen in delta brain states, a deep and highly connected state. In lucid dreams, we can astral project outside our bodies and go anywhere we wish.

Normally, we're at the mercy of our dreams. What happens in them is outside our conscious control. In a lucid dream, we know we are dreaming and can take control of everything that happens. At a minimum, this is great for overcoming nightmares. No one likes having a bad dream. Taking control and vanquishing your nightmares is a big deal. Once you've become successful at controlling events in your dream, you can use your dreams to access other realms.

Preparing to Dream

The first step to maintaining awareness in dreams is to improve your dream recall. It's a good idea to keep a journal or voice recorder near your bed and get in the habit of noting your dreams. Try to remember between one and three dreams every night. Often after a significant dream, you'll wake up knowing something important happened even if you can't quite remember. Write down what happened right away. You will remember more details as you write.

Writing down your dreams has two functions. First, it helps you become good at dream recall. Second, it increases your awareness of the dream state—something that will help alert you to lucid dreams.

Another preparation technique is called a reality check. In a dream, you think everything is real until something odd happens. The odd thing is a cue to your subconscious mind that you're sleeping. Once you get used to these cues, they'll alert you and you can become conscious in the dream. Odd things such as suddenly flying, putting your hand through a wall, or being in two places at once are cues—as are devices that fail for no reason.

In a dream, a reality check proves to you that you're dreaming. You can train yourself to check reality in your dreams by doing it in your waking state. It sounds weird, but every few hours during the day, stop and make sure you're in the real world. Check the clock, then check again. Make sure doors open in the right direction, and pinch yourself every once in a while!

It may sound silly, but when you "wake up" in a dream, performing a reality check helps you gain control. Making it part of your daily routine carries it into the dream state.

Inducing a Lucid Dream

There are three basic steps to inducing a lucid dream. They're really simple to perform and produce a quick result:

1. **Set an intention.** Every night before you go to bed, intend to wake up in your dream. Hold this intention as you go to sleep.

2. **As you're falling asleep, imagine yourself having a lucid dream.** Imagine being awake in a dream. See yourself, feel the wind, sun, or other elements. Smell where you are; engage all your senses in your imagination. Not only are you supporting your intention, you're also training yourself what to pay attention to when you wake up dreaming.

3. **Practice controlling your dreams.** Do this by remembering a dream you've had, maybe a nightmare, and change the dream in your mind. Take control of it. Doing this helps program you to take control in a lucid dream.

The Benefits of Lucid Dreaming

Tibetan monks consciously dream and call it dream yoga. They believe that awake or asleep, we create reality. Dream yoga is a means of enlightenment. Theosophists such as Charles Leadbeater believe we travel in our dreams to meet with guides, to help souls cross over, and to attend etheric universities. We can meet with higher-dimensional beings, receive healing, and learn new skills and techniques.

> **Timeless Tips**
>
> The Lucidity Institute at Stanford University (www.lucidity.com) covers many tips for learning how to lucid dream. Another great site for information is www.world-of-lucid-dreaming.com.

Lucid dreaming allows you, in complete safety, to explore different realms. You can visit the Akashic Record, meet yourself in a past life, or see future potentials. You can use lucid dreaming to visit people who have passed away and to see the afterlife.

In your dreams, you can create the perfect world of peace and community. You can live the new paradigm, spread light to others, and use all of your abilities. As you learn to create reality in your dreams, you're creating reality in your daily life.

The Least You Need to Know

- Psi phenomena is independent of distance; you can use psychic skills regardless of time and space.
- Quantum mechanics explains psi phenomena with theories of non-locality and entanglement.
- To access the Record, you need to align to higher ideals of compassion and non-judgment while staying neutral and unbiased.
- Remote viewing is a great mind-training technique because you have immediate verification of your success.
- Channeling requires a balanced emotional state to avoid becoming overwhelmed.
- Lucid dreaming is a safe, relatively easy way to access other realms in the Akashic Record.

19

Accessing Your Record

In This Chapter

- ◆ Choosing an approach to the akasha
- ◆ Remembering through regression
- ◆ Intuitive readings
- ◆ Unusual revelations

While you're developing your intuitive skills, you may want to explore the Akashic Record through an akashic reader or a past-life regression therapist. There are various methods available, as we've discussed throughout this book. To achieve the best results, it's important to feel comfortable with both the method and the person you work with. This chapter takes you through what you can achieve and what you can expect with different approaches to your personal Akashic Record.

Appointment with the Akasha

Seeking a reading with the Akashic Record is a big step. Deciding what type of reading you want and who to go to takes research. There are different types of readers and sessions. What you want from the session, how much money you want to spend, and how much time and energy you want to invest will have a big impact on who you decide to see.

There are two main types of sessions: one with a hypnotherapist and one with an intuitive. The first requires your direct involvement in the process. The therapist puts you into a state of deep relaxation using one of several different induction processes. Once you're in an altered state, you're guided by your therapist to one of your past and/or future lives. The therapist can also make a bridge for you to talk directly with your higher self and guides. Visiting a past life through hypnosis is referred to as past-life regression (PLR).

You can also have a session with an intuitive for an Akashic Record reading. A reading doesn't require your direct involvement, and sometimes you don't even have to be in the same room with the intuitive. Although most sessions are done in person, some readers work via the phone or Internet.

> **Library Links**
>
> In this type of work, the terms psychic, seer, intuitive, akashic reader, and channeler may be used interchangeably, even though each has subtle differences.

The reading can involve channeling your guides, angels, or an ascended master. The intuitive may vision your past life by seeing images and receiving psychic impressions. They may provide information, pass on messages from the other side, or give you direction from your guides. A reading can involve the intuitive going into a trance or simply tuning in and aligning with you and your personal Akashic Record.

Who Can Benefit?

Sessions with the Akashic Record are offered to individuals, couples, and families. Those who benefit most are those who are at a turning point in their lives. You may seek a reading knowing what you want to change, or maybe you aren't sure why you're coming but feel compelled by curiosity. You may not know why, but your higher self does. You're being pushed forward because some aspect of your life is ready to shift. People's lives have been completely turned around by a reading they considered "just for fun." The process works regardless of your level of conscious engagement.

Many people seek a session to overcome obstacles in their lives. They may have tried every possible means of shifting the problems to no avail. Sessions can reveal old patterns and limiting beliefs. They can help you understand the obstacles in your path, where they came from, and how to overcome them.

Sessions are geared to encourage and guide your growth and support your best expression in the world. You'll benefit most if you're ready to live your life purpose and fulfill your dreams. If you have a strong desire to grow, you'll receive in-depth information that you'll be ready to use to change your life.

Why Have a Reading?

You can seek a reading to solve any problem you're facing. Issues can revolve around finding your soul mate, career success, or family troubles. No subject is off limits. Sometimes people don't have a specific question but want general guidance to enrich their lives and find more joy and fulfillment.

Readings can be very broad and cover a range of information or be very specific, depending on your objective. Here are some reasons people decide to have a reading:

◆ To obtain specific information on past-life influences in present problems

◆ To learn past-life connections with people in their lives

◆ To investigate a romantic partner and the connections, challenges, and rewards in the relationship

◆ To discover the origin and purpose of health issues and what can be done to correct them

◆ For career direction or business advice

◆ To overcome fears and phobias

◆ For soul growth and spiritual development

◆ To access hidden talents and overcome challenges

Verifying Truth

People who receive past-life regressions and akashic readings often wonder whether they can trust their experience. There are several indications to determine the validity of your session. The most important is this: Has your session helped your life? If it has, trust it.

In general, your emotions are your guide to the truth of your experience. Were your emotions intense? Did your experience provoke more emotional response than those evoked in your everyday life? When the emotions you experience in your past-life regression or akashic reading are powerful and self-validating, they change how you perceive your situation. This is an indication the experience was true.

Your experience is also validated when you're suddenly released from a fear or phobia. If you've been terrified of snakes and after your regression have lost your fear or hated public speaking but after your akashic reading can deliver a speech with ease, then the experience was real. Another indicator is the sudden acquisition of abilities after your session that you didn't learn in this life. Some people find they can play music or draw well, for example. These are indications you've had a true and powerful encounter with the Akashic Record.

Not as verifiable but equally powerful is the recognition in your past life of people you know today. Like the children we discussed in Chapter 3 who recognized their previous families, this can be a dramatic internal demonstration. All in all, if your experience had emotional power, a positive impact, and generated new perceptions and or abilities, you've had a successful and real experience.

Past-Life Regression

A past-life regression is one of the most effective and useful ways to retrieve information from the Akashic Record. If you choose this approach, you'll be directly involved in seeing and feeling your past. Sessions can be highly emotional and very real. Releasing the emotional trauma from past lives will allow you to move on. You'll be free to make new choices instead of repeating old patterns. When past-life trauma is contacted and released, all the energy you used to manage the pattern will be available for living. More than information, past-life regressions provide freedom.

In hypnotic regression, you will be encouraged to process the emotions you encounter. Most hypnotherapists are certified or licensed in some form of counseling. As you would expect, the emotions from past-life sessions can be very intense; otherwise, they wouldn't be an active force in your present life. The fact that emotions from your past still impact your choices, relationships, and phobias shows how powerful they are. If you suffer from an emotional or mental disorder, although a past-life reading can still be helpful, you'll want the regression therapist to be a skilled psychotherapist or psychiatrist for your own safety. All in all, professional guidance can help you get the most from your experience.

The PLR Session

Your session will begin with an interview that may include your past history, both medically and emotionally. It will focus on the issue you want to resolve and how it presents itself in your life. The therapist will want to know your family makeup: how many siblings, basic childhood dynamics, whether you're married, with or without children, and so on.

After the interview, you'll be invited to lie down or sit in a comfortable place. You may have a blanket, pillows, or other items necessary for comfort. The therapist usually sits next to you and guides you into an altered state. Hypnosis involves systematic relaxation of the body and gentle induction to deeper brain wave states. An induction can include counting backward from 10 to 1, visualizing yourself walking down a flight of stairs or floating on a raft in the ocean, or it can focus on listening to a repetitive sound. The therapist will guide the process and add suggestions such as, "You are deeply relaxed," "You are fully supported," "You are floating in complete relaxation and safety," and so on.

Etheric Advisory

Many PLR therapists don't use the term "hypnosis" for fear of conjuring outmoded images. The method is deep relaxation, which changes brain states—allowing alert, relaxed awareness.

Everything the therapist says is an instruction to the subconscious mind. Even while your conscious mind is focused on the therapist's voice, your subconscious mind is following the instructions—and soon you will be in an altered state. In this state, you're deeply relaxed yet mentally alert. You're able to respond to the directions of the therapist, reply to his or her questions, and maintain awareness of your surroundings.

Your PLR Experience

The therapist will make contact with your higher self and ask that your awareness move to the life and situation that holds the key to your present problem. Some people are immediately in the past situation. Others require prompts from the therapist, such as, "Look down at your shoes and describe what they look like," "Is it day or night?", or "Are you alone or with people?" It doesn't take long for you to be submerged in the process. If you recall something traumatic, your therapist will guide you through and help you connect with inner strength and resources you lost touch with in the original trauma. Trust your therapist to keep you safe and don't worry about getting stuck in a trance state. You will always return to everyday reality.

Throughout the regression, you'll be working with your therapist on the emotions that emerge. They'll instruct you in integrating, releasing, and moving on from the past. Lianne Escher is a past-life therapist trained by Roger Woolger, a renowned past-life regression therapist and trainer. In her work she encourages people to fully relive their past-life events no matter how traumatic they were. In doing so, she says, you will completely release them from your body, mind, and soul. You'll never have these influences in your life again.

After the session, more processing may be done with the therapist, or you may journal your ongoing reactions. You may return for several sessions of counseling to fully integrate one PLR experience.

Professional Training in PLR

Hypnosis is usually an adjunct to psychotherapy or psychiatry, but not always. Some people attend the National Guild of Hypnotists (NGH) training seminars, practice for a while on smoking cessation and weight loss, and then continue training in PLR. A PLR training can be a weekend certification, a year-long once-a-month training session, or a formal three-year program. Supervised sessions are often part of the training practice. While there are many skilled and capable people who have been trained through the NGH, if you are new to this you may want the support and safety of a licensed health care professional.

> **Timeless Tips**
>
> Dr. Brian Weiss, Dr. Michael Newton, Dr. Robert Schwartz, Roger Woolger, and Dr. Helen Wambach are good examples of therapists who work with PLR. You can read direct transcripts from their sessions in their books; see Appendix B for their book titles.

Psychotherapists and psychiatrists are licensed professionals who participate in continuing education, professional associations, and professional supervision. They receive hypnosis training as an adjunct to their psychotherapeutic practice. PLR training carries no professional continuing education credits and has no standards of practice or quality control. However, because it is practiced by licensed professionals, it tends to be highly credible.

Pros and Cons of PLR

There are pros and cons to using hypnosis. Many people are concerned they won't be able to be hypnotized. You'll make a good hypnotic subject if you're an open person with a healthy degree of skepticism. Someone who is gullible actually doesn't make a good subject! After your initial interview, your therapist will tell you whether they think you're a candidate.

On the positive side, both hypnotherapy and PLR are very deep and transformative therapies. In one or two sessions, you can come to completion with issues that may have plagued your entire life. You'll have the support of a trained professional as you process difficult emotions. Your direct involvement adds authenticity to the process. Nobody is telling you about yourself; you're directly accessing the information.

Conversely, sometimes hypnotherapy requires several sessions to get to the core of the problem and can be costly. Some people feel traumatized again by experiencing again the events they visit, although a good therapist minimizes this. Your session can initiate introspection and processing, which can impact your relationships. While ultimately positive and certainly what your higher self had in mind, it isn't always welcomed at the time.

You may also be concerned that while in an altered state, you may be influenced by the beliefs of the therapist. It is possible for this to happen—and an important reason why you want to work with a respected professional.

Choosing a Therapist

Deciding on a PLR therapist takes research. If you already see a therapist, ask his or her advice. If friends have been to a PLR therapist, see what they have to say. Word of mouth is often the best source of referral. Escher recommends going to a library and looking at published books. If you find a book that speaks to you, locate the author or someone trained by the author to work with.

If you have no referral sources, go to your local natural food or book store. There are usually magazines and newspapers listing local health practitioners. Some magazines have actual profiles so you can learn about the therapist and how he or she works. If you're drawn to a particular person, call him or her and request an interview. Don't sign up for treatment until you've either met him or her in person or talked over the phone.

Ask about the person's training, experience, work focus, and methods used. Be sure the therapist is licensed. Your comfort with the person is important; trust your gut, and if you have a good or bad feeling, follow it. Once you've found a few people you think would work, check around and see whether anyone knows them or has worked with them. Get some feedback. Once you've found the person, enjoy your process!

Akashic Record Readings

Some people prefer an Akashic Record reading. The information you'll find in an akashic reading is much more than a psychic reading because it deals with your soul's path and purpose. Readings are passive events: all you have to do is provide some basic information, and the intuitive takes over. The reading is set up on a soul level and is geared toward your best good.

You'll be given details on what happened in your past and how it affects you today. The reader will connect the dots and tell you your growth challenges, abilities, and future directions.

Information in a reading is tied up in a neat little package. You can accept what you're told—or not. However, because you don't experience the past life directly, it may not have the same emotional impact. You might think of it as an interesting story. Some people report having their memory jogged as the intuitive talks, seeing images and feeling an emotional connection to what's being said. When it hits just right, things internally shift and the impact is profound.

In an intuitive reading, you can move through extremely challenging events with little re-traumatizing. Rather than shifting patterns through emotional processing, the intuitive shifts patterns by shifting energy. All your memories have an energetic component, and clearing the energy supports the change you are undergoing. We showed you techniques to do this yourself in Chapter 9.

Experiencing an Akashic Reading

You may have had an Akashic Record reading in person, on the phone, or via the Internet. An Internet reading usually involves giving the intuitive some basic information, paying via PayPal, and then receiving a report via e-mail. Sometimes it involves a short phone consultation after you've received the report. Although many people have good experiences, there's a lot of room for fraud in Internet readings, so be careful. Try to get some feedback on the site from people you know.

In both phone consultations and in-person sessions, you'll be asked what you want to focus on and you'll provide basic background information to help the reader connect with your personal record. Whether your reading is via the phone, the Internet, or in person, your reader might ask for your current full name, the name you use (such as nicknames), and your full name at birth. You may be asked your birth date and place as well. They may want a photograph. This is all to help your reader tune in.

While he or she is tuning in to you, the reader relaxes into an altered mind state. Once he or she has contact with the Record, he or she will provide you with details related to your past lives, current issues, and soul growth. The reader may ask you questions to verify the information or to fine-tune the connection. He or she may ask questions to help you connect with the information he or she is giving you. You may be allowed to ask questions throughout the session, but if not, you'll be able to ask questions at the end. You can also ask questions of your higher self for direction and soul growth.

Professional Training for Readers

There are no professional training standards for psychic readers of any kind, including Akashic Record readers. Many claim their psychic ability is a gift and requires no training. Others think it can be taught, but only to people with a knack for it. Still others think anyone can learn to varying degrees.

There are a considerable number of training centers for developing intuitive abilities, including channeling. Although some offer training certificates, because there is no governing body or standard of quality, the certificate is simply a statement that your intuitive attended some type of training. It doesn't tell you how good he or she is or whether he or she stands by the results.

Pros and Cons of Intuitive Sessions

On the positive side, Akashic Record readings don't require you to engage a traumatic memory. Through the energy clearing, you can expect positive results without the work and drama of processing. People often experience positive changes after one reading. Although some people have multiple readings, it isn't usually necessary. You can get what you need in one session.

Conversely, intuitive readings are difficult to verify. The information they give you may not be relevant to where you are today and may not make sense for years to come. Also, it's possible your reading might reflect the bias and mindset of your reader. Because it's not coming from you, it's easy to be unduly influenced. Sessions generally cost from $100 to $200, but sessions with famous readers can cost as much as $650.

There are no standards or ways to validate quality. This doesn't mean there aren't good, unbiased, relevant readers—there are! You just need to be careful who you pick.

Finding Your Intuitive

Because there are no standards, personal recommendations are essential. An Internet search will show you how many psychic readers are available. Many are very good, while others are frauds. A lot of damage can be done by an unscrupulous person, so check out your prospective intuitives carefully. After you've read a few sites, you may get a good feeling about one of them. Follow up and verify what he or she claims. There are many companies who will supply background information on people and businesses; see Appendix B for a few good ones.

Another way to find a reader or training center is through New Age and natural health magazines. You can usually find such magazines in health food stores, book shops, and crystal stores. Look through the advertisements. They're usually filled with local advertisers who are easier to check up on. Ask the shop owners whether they have someone they recommend. Check on quality control websites such as Angie's List (www.angieslist.com). Call and talk to the readers. Trust your gut. If you don't connect, don't make an appointment.

Watch out for anyone who tries to string you along from reading to reading. An unethical reader will hook into a weakness in your psyche and manipulate it. He or she may make you think you need his or her help to make it through some trial; otherwise, something bad will happen. You may have an enjoyable reading with someone only to have that person call you later saying they're worried about you and want you to come in for another reading. Or the reader may start an important piece of information right at the end of a session and leave you hanging, asking you to come back to receive more instruction. These are warning signs that the person is unscrupulous and looking for ways to make more money. No one but you knows your path. Allowing someone to access your Record is a gift. If they abuse it, you have the power to take the invitation back!

> **Etheric Advisory**
>
> Here's a big warning sign that a psychic is probably a fraud: he or she tells you something big is coming, such as an astrological transit, a major life shift, an illness, or a career change, and that you won't make it without his or her guidance. Aside from milking you for money, this is mind control and would never happen in legitimate circles!

Akashic Additions

The Akashic Record holds more than just your past lives. There are many different dimensions to the Record, each with its own lessons and inspiration. Your growth is unlimited, and so is the information you can obtain in the Record. Sometimes you find the information you need accidentally. Your Record is part of you, and it can reveal itself unexpectedly.

Some people find the cause of a present problem to have started in a future life. Sound impossible? Not in the quantum holographic universe. Some people find they are completing a soul mission on Earth that began on another planet. There are more things possible than we can imagine.

Access Through the Body

According to Dr. Candice Pert, author of *Molecules of Emotion: The Science Behind Mind-Body Medicine* (see Appendix B), your body is your subconscious mind. It holds your memories and is your access to universal consciousness. Many people find that bodywork, such as massage or energy balancing, can awaken the memories stored in cells, muscles, and the energy field around your body. It can even open the patterns you carry from a previous life.

Accessing the Akashic Record through bodywork has the advantage of occurring organically. It's always relevant because it's provoked by what you're feeling—the pain you have from an injury or illness, for example. It's your body, and you're in control—and this type of access is empowering. It opens Akashic Record memory while clearing the energy patterns, creating real and lasting change.

You can find a good bodyworker through massage therapy associations. Look for people who advertise emotional process therapy and/or energy balancing. Also, PLR therapists trained by Roger Woolger all have a body approach to their regressions.

Future "Regressions"

Legend has it that the ability to regress into our past lives was discovered by accident. We can imagine the therapist instructing his hypnotized client to "go to the place in your past when this pattern first developed." Surprisingly, the person ended up in a past life! Some people have been "regressed" to the future, where the cause of their problems resides in future-life memories.

It's not as impossible as it seems. Just as with past lives, all you need to do is direct your thoughts to a particular point in time, and you're there. It's intimidating to think of visiting the future that hasn't been written yet, and of course you're only visiting one possible future. If quantum physics is right, all the possible futures happen—just as all the possible presents are happening. The big leap is to get over the idea that time is linear. If the universe is holographic, wouldn't time be holographic, too? Time is a dimension; it doesn't have to be accessed linearly.

Future lives help people see their options, potentials, and abilities more clearly. Here's an example.

Joe was pressured to follow in the family business even though it didn't interest him. What he wanted to study was computer programming. When he was 19, he began having dreams in which he was met by an older man who encouraged him to take computer classes. The man assured Joe he had a happy future ahead if he did.

This was a difficult time in Joe's life. He was conflicted in following his passion versus listening to his father, who distrusted computers. The dreams continued until, against his father's wishes, Joe signed up for a computer class at the local community college. Eventually, his computer skills were called on to save the family business and modernize the store.

Joe didn't think about his dreams again until his fortieth birthday. Reminiscing about his decision to take that computer class, he caught sight of himself in the mirror. With a start, Joe realized he was looking at the dream man from 20 years ago!

Dimensional Access

Other surprises have been revealed through the Akashic Record. People have remembered lives in different dimensions, forms, and on different planets.

Many people remember lives in animal form. Contrary to popular opinion about animals, the lives described were purpose-oriented and assisted global consciousness. In animal form, souls were functioning on much higher levels of awareness than the humans around them. People claim that as animals they operated in dimensional reality and used their senses to perceive more than we do with our human senses. Some used what they learned to become psychic readers in this life. A woman who died in childbirth recounts coming back into animal form in order to guide and watch over her child. We've all heard stories of animals that heroically saved their owners' lives. Is it so hard to consider that might have been their life purpose?

Akashic Wisdom

We need another and a wiser and perhaps a more mystical concept of animals ... We patronize them for their incompleteness, for their tragic fate of having taken form so far below our own. And therein we err, and greatly err. For the animal shall not be measured by man. In a world older and more complete than ours they move finished and complete, gifted with extensions of the senses we have lost or never attained, living by voices we shall never hear. They are not brethren, they are not underlings; they are other nations caught with ourselves in the net of life and time, fellow prisoners of the splendor and travail of the earth.

—From *The Outermost House: A Year of Life on the Great Beach of Cape Cod* by Henry Beston (Holt Paperbacks, 2003)

People report lives on other planets where they're working in a council to integrate humans into the greater universal civilization. Some people remember being "fallen angels," and others remember being guides. Here's one woman's story:

> I was regressed to a past life to find out where my sorrow comes from. I saw myself in the Midwest in what is now Minnesota where the red clay is for the pipes. I saw myself standing in the snow outside my teepee. My family was dead all around me, spread in the snow, surrounded in red. When the therapist asked me why I was still alive, I realized I wasn't. I looked down at my body, I was a man and I was dead, too.
>
> My family had moved on, into the light, but I couldn't. I needed to understand why the White Man had come to our lands and why the Great Spirit was allowing them to destroy his people. I wandered the earth for a hundred years until I understood. But I could not leave until I passed on what I learned so I found three women who could hear me and I whispered into their ears the things I knew. My name was White Eagle and I spoke to these women for many years before I was able to pass on.

Interestingly, there was a spirit called White Eagle who channeled through a British woman named Grace Cook. She formed a teaching institute based on these channeled messages in 1936 called the White Eagle Lodge.

The Least You Need to Know

- There are two types of Akashic Record approaches: hypnosis and intuitive readings.

- Hypnosis requires you to be actively involved in the session and allows you to process the emotions that arise.

- Intuitive readings are passive. The readers provide you with the details from your Record that are of importance to you.

- Past lives aren't the only dimensions that can be accessed in the Record. Animal incarnations, future lives, and lives on other planets have all been found in the Record.

Chapter 20

Evolution of the Record

In This Chapter

- How the past illuminates the future
- The growth of human abilities
- Staying grounded through change
- Finding the new paradigm

The Akashic Record is growing. What form it takes depends not only on us but also on all consciousness in the universe. Is there an end point, a certain number of souls, or a certain level of attainment where the game is over? The mystery of the universe, why it came into existence and how, and the secrets of life are contained within the Record. At some point, we will have the mastery to decode the symbols, glyphs, and mathematics to understand the questions that drive science, philosophy, and society forward. This chapter looks at the evolutionary forces at work in the Record and where they may be heading.

Directions to the New Reality

Author Dr. James Hurtak has stated that cataclysmic changes happen periodically to push the consciousness of the planet forward. He suggests humans are on the verge of mastering the "physical continuum and progressing beyond this world." How do we master the physical, and what exists beyond this world? Chapter 16 revealed prophecies for our planet, but the earth is one small part of the larger consciousness of the Record. If Earth transforms, will that send the entire Record into transformation? What will life be like afterward?

All matter and energy are interconnected, entangled, and able to transmit to each other instantaneously. In quantum mechanics, mastering the physical continuum means losing physical separation between individuals. The observation that we are all connected becomes the greater truth that we are all one. We also lose the temporal separation of events. Time exists simultaneously. The past and the future are now. Right now, right here is the new reality. It already exists—all that's missing is our own awakening and willingness to live in the present moment.

The crux of the matter is this: what is transforming is not the physical world, it is us. The transformation is one of consciousness. What will life be like in a transformed state of mind? We can't possibly know. There's no way to conceive of new consciousness when thinking about it with old consciousness. Maybe that's why Ed Dames's remote viewing group couldn't see past 2012, as we mentioned in Chapter 16. We simply can't know the world we're entering ahead of time. The interconnecting pieces have not yet been seen as what they truly are. As long as we hold on to the old, we cannot see the new.

The Ancient Ones

The Akashic Record readings we've looked at have related primarily to Western civilization. But what about indigenous societies? How do the tribes across the planet fit into the shifting consciousness? They haven't been part of the imbalance of modern society, yet they share the same water, air, and weather. Considered more primitive, these societies may hold the key to our future. The Mayan codices say that "We will return to the wisdom of the past." This doesn't mean returning to the old ways. We're moving into something absolutely new, but the wisdom of the past may be guiding us into the future.

The tribes of the Kogi, Wiwa, Arhuaco, and Kankuamo people live in the Sierra Nevada Mountains in northern Colombia, South America. They live completely removed from modern society at the top of a mountain called the Heart of the World. What's unique is that they've fully developed the psychic senses innate in all humans. Calling themselves the Elder Brothers, from the top of their mountain they have telepathically monitored the progress of humanity for centuries.

In 1991, the Sierra Nevada tribes felt compelled to reveal their existence and issue a message to us, the "younger brothers." The message is simple: the Heart of the World is dying, and so is the planet itself. In 2006, a delegation of their spiritual leaders, called the Mamas, traveled to Washington, D.C., to deliver the message again. We were invited guests.

Like the Tibetans, the Mamas maintain continuous meditative prayer around the clock to help stabilize the planet. In fact, the meditations of the Mamas, the Tibetan monks, the Aborigines, and other people with enhanced awareness may be the force empowering our transformation.

> **Library Links**
>
> You can read the story of the tribes of the Sierra Nevada in the book *The Elder Brothers* by Alan Ereira (see Appendix B) or in the 1991 documentary *Message from the Heart of the World* by the BBC.

Meditating on the New Reality

Peace meditations have been going on for decades. Groups around the world meditate for peace on the same day at the same time. Researcher Lynn McTaggart has demonstrated the effectiveness of this in her intentional meditation experiments discussed in Chapter 16. The impact of meditation on individuals and groups can be scientifically demonstrated.

A PET scan is a brain-imaging technique that can show which parts of the brain are functioning during different activities. PET scans of the brain of yogi Sri Nithyananda Swami, were reported by Dr. Murali Krishna in an article published by The Life Bliss Foundation in 2008, titled "The Mind of a Mystic." It reveals something extraordinary. While the Swami was in gentle meditation, the scans showed a significantly heightened activity in his frontal lobe associated with the functions of intelligence, attention, wisdom, and judgment. In deep meditation, all areas of his brain were quiet except a small portion of the mesial-frontal area corresponding to the mystical "third eye." The third eye is the doorway to spiritual consciousness and divine connection. Stimulation of this area increases dopamine production in the brain and feelings of bliss. It also activates our psychic awareness and the capabilities needed to access the Akashic Record. This research demonstrates that in meditation we can access and connect to a larger reality, an ability that will help us transcend the difficulties we face in the transitions currently underway.

Dr. Ervin Laszlo, scientist and consciousness researcher, has studied the brain waves of people while they are meditating. As we know, the left and right hemispheres of the brain synchronize during deep meditation. Synchronization creates *coherence*, which amplifies the effects of the meditation. More interestingly, when people meditate together, the left and right sides of brain synchronize across individuals. This happens regardless of whether people are meditating in the same room or meditating at different places across the planet.

def•i•ni•tion

Coherence is when two or more waves are in phase with each other. Coherent waves amplify each other.

Quantum physics confirms non-local connections between entangled minds. These experiments indicate that more than information is transferred; states of being are communicated and amplified. Graham Hancock reports that people in altered states induced by the same hallucinogenic drug observe the same alternative realities, indicating they visit an objective and "real" dimension. This is true of people in shared meditation as well. Typically, people who meditate together share a similar internal experience—amplified by the number of people meditating.

The doorway into the world we're moving toward may be held open by the continuous prayers and meditation of the Mamas, Tibetans, and Elders around the world. In fact, they may be holding this reality together long enough for the shift to happen. Where we're going is unchartered territory. The tools to navigate the pathway are being handed down from the "wisdom of the past"—the wisdom that originally understood the balance of life on the planet.

Interspecies Communication

Humans aren't the only intelligent life forms making up the consciousness of the Akashic Record. The Record is clear: we're not alone. The universe, and even our own planet, is flooded with sentient life. On some level, we've always known this. NASA programs such as the Search for Extra-Terrestrial Intelligence (SETI) search the cosmos for intelligent life that science believes is there. However, in our search for other intelligence, we don't need to look off-planet. We have other intelligent life right here on this planet.

Humans overlook animals as the highly intelligent beings they are because they don't act, think, and perceive the way we do. We measure animals against our own credentials and find them lacking when we have no clue as to their true design and capabilities. In fact, if we found intelligent life off this planet, would we even recognize it? Judging by our assessment of animals, probably not.

Evolution of the Record is inclusive of all forms of consciousness. Interaction, communication, and coherence with other life forms, on and off this planet and in or out of this dimension, reflect the expansion of awareness underway. According to ancient native peoples in many continents, the Earth, as well as all celestial bodies, is a conscious being. This is supported by ideas in quantum physics of a conscious universe.

Timeless Tips

Anita Curtis is an animal communicator whose work with all types of intelligence can be read in her book *Animal Wisdom: How to Hear the Animals* (see Appendix B).

The Human Design

We are changing. Our vibration is increasing, and different aspects of reality are opening as we gain new perspectives. This process is called a "quickening," an energetic acceleration whereby we emit a new frequency.

Everyone is experiencing the effects of the quickening. Not everyone is paying attention, and even fewer know what it means—but everyone is undergoing this change. There are different signs along the way that help us navigate the terrain. We may be heading into unchartered waters, but there are signs to follow.

Knowing what to expect can take the shock out of the changes to come. Knowing how to use the signs to accelerate your growth and expansion can give you a leg up in adjusting to the new reality.

Synchronous Dimensions

Have you noticed that synchronicity is occurring more and more frequently? Synchronicity, as you'll recall, is meaningful coincidence. The types of synchronistic events are getting more dramatic as well. For example, in the past a synchronicity might be this: you're yearning to buy a red dress when a friend stops by on her way to the store with a red dress she is returning. Of course, it's the one you want to buy— and it's in your size. In today's synchronicity, add this: your spouse walks into the room and apropos of nothing says, "You know, you'd really look good in a red dress." Synchronicity is resonance. More people are entangled in the same resonance inviting multiple synchronicities. This is a sign that we're all moving together in a forward direction. We all might want to spend more time with like-minded people and enjoy the amplification of synchronicity.

Faster Than Time

Another sign of change is the sense that time is speeding up. Carl Johan Calleman, author of *The Mayan Calendar and the Transformation of Consciousness* (see Appendix B), believes that the Mayan pyramids are coded with information about time periods on Earth. He claims the calendars and pyramids foretell the acceleration of time.

Many people notice that there don't seem to be enough hours in the day to do everything they want to do. Time acceleration, however, has more to do with how much time goes by between conceptualizing something and creating it. Your intentions become reality much faster. The results of your thoughts will provide feedback to you much faster, allowing exponential growth. Every negative thought will have nearly an immediate impact, teaching you the importance of kindness, compassion, and non-judgment. Positive reinforcement will be just as fast. Every thought that sends upliftment into the akasha will bring manifold return in your own spiritual, emotional, mental, and physical well-being.

We're entering the graduate school of training our minds and intentions. This is a great time to join or establish meditation circles and positive intention groups. Start training your mind to move into higher coherence with the resources found in Appendix B. Be aware of new thoughts and perceptions that open you to new possibilities.

Opening Perceptions to Higher Realms

Increasing vibration opens our perceptions to work in higher realms. Moving awareness to the akashic level opens the door to all realms (for a refresher, review Chapter 17). As our vibration accelerates, communication with animals, people who have died, alien intelligence, and spiritual dimensions will increase. This can happen as a stray thought that creates a connection you can't deny. For example, a woman was visiting a horse stable when she suddenly had the thought, "The grass looks very good to eat." Turning sideways, she caught sight of an older horse leaning against a fence as he looked longingly at a patch of grass. An immediate flow of energy passed between them, and she knew the horse had sent the thought she just had. As she gave the horse some grass, an acknowledgement between them cemented her knowing that this type of communication between animals and people would become commonplace.

Not all communication will be this clear. Messages from your departed loved ones may show up as random thoughts leading you to photographs, lost letters, or connections to living family members. They can be more direct; you may hear your loved one's voice giving you a message. You may look in the mirror and see a face behind you, or faces may show up in photographs. This can be a little startling, but there's nothing to fear. As time goes on, communication between dimensions will be as common as picking up the phone to call another country—something unimaginable 100 years ago.

Psi Awakening

The quickening will give us the opportunity to develop the extensions of our senses that have been dormant. Parts of both our brain and genetic structure that have been unused will become activated. Abilities that people spent years in training to develop will become easy to learn and use.

In general, all aspects of psi phenomena are said to be heightened in the quickening, allowing your senses to extend into new domains. You may develop greater awareness of the energy that flows within, around, and between people. The abilities we all have to send healing energy may be more pronounced with greater effectiveness. Telepathy, clairvoyance, and precognition are said to become commonplace. So will the ability for your consciousness to leave your body and travel at will in other realms. As the transformation of consciousness continues, will you even need a body?

> **Akashic Wisdom**
>
> Four decades of laboratory experiments show that "thinking about people at a distance, directing either calm, loving thoughts or aggressive, malevolent thoughts, actually affects their physiology.
>
> —Dean Radin, consciousness researcher

Connecting with the Divine

Stimulating the areas of the brain that open the third eye will bring you into more direct connection with the divine. It's part of remembering that we are first and foremost spiritual beings. Awakening to the divine removes the last vestiges of fear. Take time each day to meditate, to love unconditionally, and to see the positive in life. Connect with your inner divine, and change can be easy and fearless.

The new paradigm will most certainly redefine our concept of what the divine is. The divine itself is not something outside the whole or even the largest component of the whole. It *is* the whole, as ancient teachings like the Tao in Chinese philosophy describe. There is no need to seek an external divinity, because we are living in the divine. We are the knee, the finger, or the eye of the divine. We are part of the whole already, and as we shift our awareness we realize we are the whole.

Surviving Change

Change can be scary, and the first thing to know about navigating the water we're in is that there's nothing to fear. That may sound empty in the face of the difficulties we face socially, economically, and environmentally, but it's true. The skills you need are within, and you'll access and activate them as the energies increase.

The more you open yourself to your spiritual essence, the less there is to fear. With less fear, you can be expansive and of generous spirit in your interactions. To create more ease, be more authentic. Be yourself in all ways. Everybody has both healed and unhealed parts of themselves. Ideas and opinions change. You change. You don't need to protect, defend, or explain your growth or past views. Once you look in the Akashic Record, you see we have all been the best and the worst of humanity. Be in the present, be yourself, let go of the past, and be open to the future. By seeing yourself clearly in the Record, you can choose to be your authentic essence now.

Your body is designed to perceive in the dimension we live in, but it also has the fundamental wiring to perceive in other dimensions as well. Trust your senses and perceptions. Stay grounded and centered. Develop your intuitive capacity. Everything you need, you have.

The Growth of Love

Love is the deepest spiritual truth available to humankind. As we explained in Chapter 12, love is the glue that holds the universe together, and it is the substance of the akashic field. This is not an emotion; the emotion of love is simply our physical experience of the energy of love. Love itself is the force and substance of the universe.

When we become aware of love as a spiritual force, there is nothing we can't do. Growing in love is expanding into universal consciousness. Some people consider universal consciousness to be our original consciousness. Souls originate in the divine and return to the divine at the end of the sojourns of life. Ecstasy is the frequency of universal or original consciousness—the state of being that allows the total flow of love through every fiber of our being and every part of our awareness.

A Path with Heart

Moving with the changes underway requires finding a path with heart. This is the path that excites you, opens your energy flow, and represents your purpose in life. Each of us is here with a particular path to walk and mission to accomplish. No one else can tell you what it is; your path is the one that gives you energy and fulfills your soul. Trust your heartfelt experiences and move forward with confidence.

Road Map to the New Paradigm

The Akashic Record is a dimensional road map. We've spent century upon century exploring a very small area of the map. Limited by our paradigms, our worldviews, we have been unable to see that the map is merely a three-dimensional representation of something much larger. The territory we live in is changing. The shift in paradigms began a full hundred years ago. Since the breakthroughs of Einstein, there has been a slow awakening of humankind to the realization that the world we see is only a small part of reality. There is more in the universe than our skepticism will allow.

The new paradigm embraces the wisdom of the ancient mystics and masters. It encompasses the realization that we're not only interconnected and entangled—we are one. It frees us from the confines of the four dimensions of space and time. It allows us to master the physical continuum. It states that at our core, we are multi-dimensional beings whose minds and hearts together create reality.

Dimensional Consciousness

According to Theosophist Charles Leadbeater, when the Akashic Record is not being observed, it simply forms the background of everything that's happening. It reflects the activity of all consciousness on all planes of reality. We live within the akashic consciousness, and the change in paradigm is allowing access to the other planes we share.

The science of today supports the worldview of the mystics of the past, but it would be a mistake to stop there. Rather than limiting this extraordinary pinnacle we're on to reconstructing the past, we can let a new worldview construct itself from a spiritual matrix. We don't have to do anything except let go of everything we think we know. To find the whole, we have to let go of the little parts of the whole that we know and allow something new to form within.

The Singularity Consciousness

The new paradigm has been named the singularity consciousness. It's the moment when we shift from knowing we are connected to knowing we are one; the moment we shift our perception from being part of the whole to being the whole. The view is unknowable, but we are seeing the many signs of change.

> **Akashic Wisdom**
>
> In the beginner's mind there are many possibilities. In the expert's mind there are few.
> —Shunryu Suzuki, Zen spiritual teacher

As the new paradigm unfolds, more than just our perceptions and abilities are shifting. The biggest change you can directly experience is in our changing attitudes and in our emotional/spiritual growth. If you knew—truly knew—that what you did to another you were doing to yourself, how would your world change? Dannion Brinkley experienced this as part of his life review during his near-death experience. It changed his life completely.

If you knew absolutely that the suffering of one life brought suffering to all lives, would you engage in torture of people and animals? Native American leader Chief Seattle is claimed to have said that "what we do to the earth, we do to the people of the earth." If we live this truth, how would the world change?

It's hard to see in the turmoil of today's headlines, but these changes are underway. Not unexpectedly, change provokes more turmoil—as people who live in fear act in fear. This is why we see so much destructive conflict around us. Leadership at such times can be a blessing or a curse, depending on the awareness level of the leaders. All of us need to take individual responsibility for creating balance and harmony by acting with simple kindness. Personal responsibility is the challenge of this moment.

But here is the truth of the Akashic Record: there are no accidents. The synchronous events that are increasing every day are not mere coincidences. Everything is unfolding according to patterns and designs that we're only beginning to see and feel.

As conflict and fear seem to prevail, we can react with thoughtfulness, calmness, and love. Practice living without fear. Choose to leave your anxious, worried, and angry thoughts outside your mind. Let go of attachments, and open yourself to compassion. Everything we are going through will be used in the creation of the new. So be at peace, be your new self, enjoy the beauty of life, and welcome the evolution of the Akashic Record.

The Least You Need to Know

- The change underway is unknown from where we stand now.

- Ancient cultures that practice perpetual meditation are holding this reality together as we shift into something new.

- As the new paradigm unfolds, your psychic abilities will increase as will paranormal experiences.

- The difficulties we are going through will be used to create something new.

- Everything is moving according to an inner design and pattern.

Glossary

akasha   Translated as ether; one of the five Hindu natural elements of earth, air, fire, water, and ether. It is a non-physical substance that provides the template for physical form.

Akashic Record   A non-physical compendium, or encyclopedia, of the history of the universe that is imprinted on the akasha. It includes all the thoughts and actions of every person throughout time.

astral projection   Leaving the physical body and entering the astral body that is capable of traveling outside it.

Atlantis   Thought to be a mystical continent under the Atlantic Ocean. Atlantis was supposedly created by the Greek god Poseidon. It was popularized by Plato, who believed it was a real place.

aura   Our own personal energy field that maintains our physical form and dimensional awareness. It exists in seven layers, or levels of awareness.

chakra   A Sanskrit word meaning wheel or vortex. It refers to spiritual energy centers in the human body. There are seven main energy centers, each with their own spiritual and developmental lessons.

clairaudience   The ability to hear psychic information and guidance.

clairvoyance   The ability to receive psychic information in the form of visions.

coherence   When two or more waves are in phase with each other. Coherent waves amplify each other.

déjà-vu   The experience of thinking or feeling that a new or current situation has occurred before.

devas   Nature spirits, the essence of plants.

dharma   A religious and spiritual term used in India that means "righteous duty," it can also be translated in some contexts to mean "religion." The straight translation is "that which upholds or supports"; in English, this means "law."

electronic voice phenomena (EVP)   Spirit voice recordings on electronic media, usually tape recorders, with no currently understood physical explanation.

entanglement   A term used in quantum theory to describe how particles of energy or matter become associated to interact with each other regardless of how far apart they are.

extra-sensory perception (ESP)   Also often called "sixth sense." It is sensory information obtained from beyond the known five senses.

higher self   A person's spiritual essence that resides in higher realms and has awareness beyond the physical.

hologram   Comes from the Greek roots "holos" meaning whole and "gramma" meaning message. The process of making a hologram is called holography. When a hologram is made, light from a laser records an image of the desired object on film or a photographic plate.

hypnogogic state   Refers to the time between full wakefulness and sleep when the mind is in an altered state of awareness characterized by alpha and theta brain waves. It is a time when insight and inspiration occur.

Instrumental Transcommunication (ITC)   The practice of electronically capturing voices or images of people who have died.

intuition   At its most essential level, intuition is the gut feeling that guides our perceptions—the basic nature within us all. It's the hunches and insight we gain not from information but from the feel of a situation.

karma   Translates simply as action; a Hindu belief that every action has a consequence. Good and bad karma are the results of good and bad actions.

karmic partnership   A primary relationship that is based on the mutual need of two souls to balance their karma. They help each other by providing the conditions necessary for their karmic lessons.

Lemuria   A hypothetical continent thought by some to be the original home of the lemurs and thought to have existed in the Indian Ocean, where Madagascar is now.

Library of Alexandria   Part of the Alexandrian Museum, a research institute in Alexandria, Egypt. The museum and library were founded around the early third century B.C.E.; the library was the most famous library of classical antiquity.

lucid dream   A dream where you're aware that you are dreaming. They usually reveal significant information for your life, answer a question, or lead you in a better direction.

meditation   The practice of quieting the mind and shifting from our normal state of awareness to a more focused and internal state of awareness.

morphic field   Holds a record of everything learned from each member of a species, including humans, and makes up our collective past. Everything learned or experienced by one of us is available to all of us through a process called resonance.

multiverse   Multiple possible universes (including ours) that together comprise all reality as described by quantum physics. The different universes within the multiverse are sometimes called parallel universes or alternate universes.

near-death experience (NDE)   The mystical experience that occurs when someone dies and is brought back to life through resuscitation.

non-locality   The effect of one object over another at a distance that does not comply with the laws of classical physics.

paradigm   A set of assumptions, concepts, values, and practices that constitutes a way of viewing reality for the community that shares them, especially in an intellectual discipline.

past-life regression (PLR)   Visiting a past life through hypnosis.

precognition   The direct knowledge or perception of the future, obtained through extrasensory means.

premonition   A type of precognition that involves a sense, or feeling, of a future event.

presentiment   A vague thought or feeling that something bad or good is about to happen.

psi phenomena   A variety of paranormal phenomena, which are generally subdivided into two types—extra-sensory perception (ESP) or the paracognitive, and psychokinesis—and are not capable of being explained by accepted principles.

quantum hologram   A unity field that links all creation, also known by some scientists as "nature's mind" and others as "the mind of God." It is the interconnectedness of matter, energy, and consciousness, and there is the supposition that an intelligent self-organizing principle lies at the heart of all creation. This unity field is believed to respond to the things we do, think, and feel.

quantum superposition   The combination of all possibilities for an event existing simultaneously.

quickening   Spiritual acceleration.

reincarnation   Rebirth of the soul in another body.

remote viewing (RV)   The ability to view a distant or unseen target using paranormal means or extra-sensory perception. The object or location can be separated by a great distance. It is thought the distance is immaterial to the ability to view it.

resonance   The transmission and amplification of frequency within a field of energy. You may have experienced this when playing a musical instrument. For example, if you strum the C note on a harp in one octave, all the C notes in all octaves will vibrate.

skrying   The ability to produce visions by staring into shiny, reflective objects such as water, crystal balls, and mirrors. It's a technique used by the Mayans, Aztecs, gypsies, and fortune tellers.

soul group   A metaphysical term meaning a gathering of souls that started out together and evolved at the same rate with past and current dispositions meaningfully appropriate to each other's growth. A collection of naturally complementary souls.

soul mate   Someone with whom one has a natural affinity, deep love, trust, complete compatibility, and intimacy of sexuality and spirituality. It is thought by those who experience this ultimate love friendship and connection that this is the one and only half of one's soul.

stele   An upright stone slab monument inscribed with historical or commemorative information.

synchronicity   The experience of two or more unrelated events occurring together in a meaningful manner.

theosophy   Teachings and beliefs of the Theosophical Society, founded in New York City in 1875. The beliefs incorporate reincarnation and spiritual evolution.

thought experiments   Experiments that can't be conducted in the physical world and can only be demonstrated through the process of thinking.

transmigration   The evolution of a soul from animal to human form.

transmutation   The conversion of bad karma into good karma. In other words, once you've learned what you needed to, you're no longer tied to the condition you created.

twin soul (twin flame)   The ultimate soul mate; the one and only other half of one's soul; the ultimate loving, trusting friendship.

universal consciousness   The interweaving thread, tantra, or bridge that joins all forms of human endeavor with all states and forms of sentient and non-sentient existence. It is the essence of who we are and the synthesis of life itself.

wayeb   A spirit companion. Every person has a personal wayeb. They are often referred to as spiritual doubles or co-essences. It is also the name given to the last five nameless days at the end of the calendar.

Resources

Learn more about the Akashic Record and other topics we discussed in this book with the following books and websites.

Books

Akashic Record

Blavatsky, Helena. *The Secret Doctrine (An Abridgement).* The Theosophical Publishing House, 1966.

———. *The Key to Theosophy (An Abridgement).* The Theosophical Publishing House, 1972.

Carter, Ellen Mary. *Edgar Cayce: Modern Prophet.* Bonanza Books, 1990.

Chaney, Robert. *Akashic Records, Past Lives and New Directions.* Astara Publishing, 1996.

Howe, Linda. *How to Read the Akashic Records: Accessing the Archive of the Soul and Its Journey.* Sounds True, Inc., 2009.

Karlander, Kathy. *Discovering the Essence of Your Soul: Learn How to Facilitate Your Spiritual Growth by Accessing Your Akashic Records.* iUniverse, Inc., 2006.

Laszlo, Ervin. *The Akashic Experience, Science and Cosmic Memory Field.* Inner Traditions, 2009.

———. *Science and the Akashic Field.* Inner Traditions, 2007.

Lumari. *Akashic Records: Collective Keepers of Divine Expression.* Amethyst, 2003.

Martinz, Shaun. *Remember Who You Are: Insights from the Akashic Record.* Infiniti Press International, 2004.

Schwartz, Robert. *Your Soul's Plan: Discovering the Real Meaning of the Life You Planned Before You Were Born.* Frog Books, 2009.

Todeschi, Kevin. *Edgar Cayce on the Akashic Records: The Book of Life.* A.R.E. Press, 1998.

Alien Intelligence

Hopkins, Bud. *Missing Time.* Ballantine Books, 1988.

Jacobs, David. *The Threat: Revealing the Secret Alien Agenda.* Simon & Schuster, 1999.

Mack, John E. *Abduction: Human Encounters with Aliens.* Scribner, 2007.

Ancient Cultures

Andrews, Synthia, and Colin Andrews. *The Complete Idiot's Guide to 2012.* Alpha Books, 2008.

Aveni, Anthony. *Empires of Time.* University Press of Colorado, 2002.

Calleman, Carl Johan. *The Mayan Calendar and the Transformation of Consciousness.* Inner Tradition, 2004.

Childress, David Hatcher. *Technology of the Gods: The Incredible Sciences of the Ancients.* Adventures Unlimited Press, 2000.

Hall, Manly. *The Secret Teachings of All Ages.* Wilder Publications, 2009.

Hancock, Graham. *Supernatural: Meetings with the Ancient Teachers of Mankind.* The Disinformation Company, 2007.

Jenkins, John Major. *Maya Cosmogenesis 2012.* Bear & Company, 1998.

Sitchin, Zecharia. *The Wars of Gods and Men.* Bear & Company, 1992.

Van Daniken, Eric. *Gods from Outer Space.* Bantam Books, 1972.

Consciousness and Science

Bodanis, David. *E=mc²: A Biography of the World's Most Famous Equation*. The Berkley Publishing Group, 2000.

Gribbin, John. *In Search of Schrödinger's Cat, Quantum Physics and Reality*. Bantam Books, 1984.

Grof, Stanislav, and Zina Hal Bennett. *The Holotropic Mind: The Three Levels of Human Consciousness and How They Shape Our Lives*. HarperCollins Publishers, 1990.

Hawking, Stephen. *The Illustrated A Brief History of Time/The Universe in a Nutshell—Two Books in One*. Bantam Books, 2007.

Kafatos, Menas, and Robert Nadeau. *The Conscious Universe: Parts and Wholes in Physical Reality*. Springer, 1999.

Kenyon, Tom. *Brain States*. World Tree Press, 2001.

McTaggart, Lynn. *The Field, A Quest for the Secret Force of the Universe*. Harper Perennial, 2002.

Mitchell, Edgar, and Arnan Dwight Williams. *The Way of the Explorer: An Apollo Astronaut's Journey Through the Material and Mystical Worlds*. New Page Books, 2008.

Pert, Candace. *Molecules of Emotion: The Science Behind Mind-Body Medicine*. Simon & Schuster, 1999.

Radin, Dean. *The Conscious Universe*. HarperEdge, 1997.

———. *Entangled Minds: Extrasensory Experiences in a Quantum Reality*. Paraview Pocket Books, 2006.

Sheldrake, Rupert. *A New Science of Life*. Park Street Press, 1995.

———. *The Presence of the Past: Morphic Resonance and the Habits of Nature*. Park Street Press, 1995.

Talbot, Michael. *The Holographic Universe*. HarperCollins Publishers, 1992.

Targ, Russell. *Mind-Reach: Scientists Look at Psychic Abilities*. Hampton Roads Publishing, 2005.

Targ, Russell, and Jane Katara. *Miracles of Mind, Exploring Non-Local Consciousness and Spiritual Healing*. New World Library, 1998.

Wilbur, Ken. *The Theory of Everything*. Shambhala, 2001.

General

Bach, Richard. *A Bridge Across Forever: A True Love Story*. William Morrow & Co, 1984.

Bolles, Richard N. *What Color Is Your Parachute? 2009: A Practical Manual for Job-Hunters and Career-Changers*. Ten Speed Press, 2008.

Curtis, Anita. *Animal Wisdom: How to Hear the Animals*. iUniverse, Inc., 2001.

Ereira, Alan. *The Elder Brothers*. Knopf, 1992.

Gerber, Richard. *Vibrational Medicine: The #1 Handbook of Subtle-Energy Therapies*. Bear & Company, 2001.

Guiley, Rosemary Ellen. *Harper's Encyclopedia of Mystical and Paranormal Experience*. HarperCollins Publishers, 1991.

Hurtak, James J. *The Book of Knowledge: The Keys to Enoch*. Academy for Future Science, 1987.

Shimo-Barry, Alex, and Christopher Maron. *The Environment Equation: 100 Factors That Can Add to or Subtract from Your Total Carbon Footprint*. Adams Media, 2008.

Shumsky, Susan G., and Dannion Brinkley. *Exploring Auras: Cleansing and Strengthening Your Energy Field*. New Page Books, 2005.

Life After Death and Reincarnation

Bayless, Raymond. *Phone Calls from the Dead*. New English Library Ltd., 1980.

Brinkley, Dannion, and Paul Brinkley. *Saved by the Light*. Villard Books, 1994.

Cerminara, Gina. *Many Lives, Many Loves*. Devorss & Co., 1981.

Head, Joseph, and S.L. Cranston. *Reincarnation: Phoenix Fire Mystery*. The Julian Press Inc., 1979.

Lonnerstrand, Sture. *I Have Lived Before: The True Reincarnation of Shanti Devi*. Ozark Mountain Publishing, 1998.

Macy, Mark. *Spirit Faces: Truth About the Afterlife*. Weiser Books, 2007.

Newton, Michael. *Journey of Souls: Case Studies of Life Between Lives*. Llewellyn Publications, 2002.

———. *Destiny of Souls: New Case Studies of Life Between Lives.* Llewellyn Publications, 2000.

Raudive, Konstantin. *Breakthrough—An Amazing Experiment in Electronic Communication with the Dead.* Taplinger Publishing Company, 1971.

Schwartz, Gary, and William Simon. *The Afterlife Experiments: Breakthrough Scientific Evidence of Life After Death.* Pocket Books, 2002.

Steiner, Rudolf. *Re-Incarnation and Immortality.* Harper and Row Publishers, 1970.

Stevenson, Ian. *20 Cases Suggestive of Reincarnation.* University of Virginia Press, 1980.

———. *Children Who Remember Previous Lives: A Question of Reincarnation.* McFarland & Company, 2000.

Sutphen, Dick. *Soul Agreements.* Hampton Roads Publishing, 2005.

Wambach, Helen. *Life Before Life.* Bantam, 1984.

Weiss, Brian. *Only Love Is Real.* Grand Central Publishing, 1997.

———. *Many Lives, Many Masters.* Simon & Schuster, 1988.

Woolger, Roger. *Other Lives, Other Selves: A Jungian Psychotherapist Discovers Past Lives.* Bantam, 1988.

Remote Viewing and Other Techniques

McMoneagle, Joseph. *Remote Viewing Secrets.* Hampton Roads Publishing, 2000.

Morehouse, David. *Remote Viewing: The Complete User's Manual for Coordinate Remote Viewing.* Sounds True, Incorporated, 2007.

Roman, Sanaya, and Duane Packard. *Opening to Channel: How to Connect with Your Guides.* HJ Kramer, 1993.

Targ, Russell. *Limitless Mind: A Guide to Remote Viewing and Transformation of Consciousness.* New World Library, 2004.

Self-Help

Buckingham, Marcus. *Now Discover Your Strengths.* Free Press, 2001.

Chopra, Deepak. *The Seven Spiritual Laws of Success: A Practical Guide to the Fulfillment of Your Dreams.* Amber-Allen Publishing, 1994.

Dyer, Wayne. *Excuses Begone!: How to Change Lifelong, Self-Defeating Thinking Habits.* Hay House, 2009.

Grason, Sandy. *Journalution: Journaling to Awaken Your Inner Voice, Heal Your Life and Manifest Your Dreams.* New World Library, 2005.

Myss, Caroline. *Sacred Contracts: Awakening Your Divine Potential.* Three Rivers Press, 2003.

Tipping, C. Colin. *Radical Forgiveness, Making Room for the Miracle.* Quest Publishing & Distribution, 2002.

Tolle, Eckhart. *A New Earth: Awakening to Your Life's Purpose.* Plume Books, 2005.

Websites

Akashic Record

Psychics and mediums: www.psychics.co.uk/spiritworld/akashic-record.html; spiritualharmonics.blogspot.com/

Akashic reading: www.mediumfind.net

Douglas Cottrell: www.douglascottrell.com

Consciousness and Science

The Academy for Future Science: www.affs.org

The Association of Research and Enlightenment: www.edgarcayce.org

Center for Akashic Studies: www.akashicstudies.com

The Chopra Center: www.chopra.com

Consciousness and nature: www.grahamhancock.com

Consciousness and Quantum Mechanics: plato.stanford.edu/entries/qm-copenhagen/

Consciousness Research Laboratory: www.deanradin.com/default_original.html

Institute of Consciousness Research: www.icrcanada.org

Institute of Noetic Sciences: www.noetic.org

Intentional Peace Experiment: www.theintentionexperiment.com/the-peace-intention-experiment

International Association for the Study of Dreams: www.asdreams.org/index.htm

Princeton Global Consciousness Project: noosphere.princeton.edu/
www.boundaryinstitute.org/bi/index.html
www.boundaryinstitute.org/articles/timereversed.pdf

Webbot: www.rense.com/general69/webbotrun806.htm

Disclosure and Government UFO

The Disclosure Project: www.disclosureproject.org

The Exopolitics World Network: www.exopoliticsworld.net

The Paradigm Research Group: www.paradigmresearchgroup.org

Finding an Intuitive

Complete Detective: www.completedetective.com

Intelligent consumer (teaches you what you need to check credentials): intelligent-consumer.com/
?kw=Back%20Ground%20Search&gclid=CNWAg_fe75wCFQtN5QodvSSurQ

Net Detective: orders.netdetective.net/cgi-bin/shop.cgi

The Truth Is in Here: www.backgroundsearcher.com/?hop=cbdet12

General

General news topics: www.rense.com

Angel light invention: gizmodo.com/030657/;
perdurabo10.tripod.com/warehousec/id31.html

Brain wave–activating audio programs: www.daael.com/precognition.htm;
www.monroeinstitute.org

Doreen Virtue: www.alleghenycandles.com/doreenvirtueoraclecards.html

Edgar Cayce's Association for Research and Enlightenment: www.edgarcayce.org

Finding purpose: www.soulfulliving.com/bookspurpose.htm;
www.missionstatements.com

Healing Rhythms—Wild Divine: www.wilddivine.com

How to use a journal: www.amanobooks.com/tips.php;
www.affirmations.gems4friends.com/articles/work.html

Inspiration: www.creativethinkingwith.com;
www.abundance-and-happiness.com/inspiration.html

Meaningful coincidences and synchronicity:
www.meaningoflife.i12.com/coincidence.htm

Personality test: www.humanmetrics.com/cgi-win/JTypes2.asp

Positive motivation: vladdolezal.com/blog/2009/the-pain-and-pleasure-principle/

Sacred contracts: www.myss.com

Society of the Inner Light: www.innerlight.org.uk

Spiritual addiction: moonviewsanctuary.com/addiction-treatment/
spiritual-addiction-treatment.html;
www.spiritualresearchfoundation.org

Theosophical Society: theosophical.org; www.blavatsky.net

Life After Death and Reincarnation

Brian Weiss: www.brianweiss.com

Dannion Brinkley: www.dannion.com

EVP recordings: www.trueghosttales.com/how-to-record-evp.php

ITC images: www.worlditc.org

James Leininger: abcnews.go.com/Primetime/Technology/
Story?id=894217&page=1;
lotusborn.wordpress.com/2007/11/02/the-past-life-memories-of-an-ex-pilot-james-leininger-part-i

Mellen-Thomas Benedict: www.near-death.com/experiences/reincarnation04.html

Past-life clues: www.selectsmart.com/pastlives

Past-life stories: www.open-sesame.com/memorybank.html

Nature

Findhorn: www.findhorn.org

Perelandra: www.perelandra.com

A Place Called Hope, Inc.: www.aplacecalledhoperaptors.com

Remote Viewing and Lucid Dreaming

Dream-inspired ideas: www.brilliantdreams.com/product/famous-dreams.htm

Exploration of consciousness: www.monroeinstitute.org

Lucid dreams: www.lucidity.com; www.world-of-lucid-dreaming.com

Remote viewing: www.greaterreality.com/rv/instruct.htm

Remote viewing and crop circle research: www.mountbaldy.com/mbi

Silva UltraMind training: www.ultramind.ws/invention_in_a_dream.htm

Index

Numbers

2012
  consciousness and, 274
  Mayan calendar, 221
  prophecies and predictions, 224
  Remote Viewing Institute, 223
  Tibetan monks, 225

A

abandonment fear, 164
abilities, 166
  at birth from past lives, 116
abuse of children, 161
abuses of past, 218
access to purpose, 148
accessing Akashic Record, 249-251
  channeling, 253-256
  dimensions, 270-271
  direct, 235
  lucid dreaming, 256-258
  meditation, 250
  qualities of a good reader, 250
  targets, 252-253
accessing success, 158
accomplishments, material, 157
actions, guided by Record, 35
activities enjoyed, past lives, 114
ADD (Attention Deficit Disorder), 188
addiction, 190-191
ADHD (Attention Deficit Hyperactive Disorder), 188
advanced civilizations, 81

advanced souls, 105
  Crystal children, 105
  Indigo children, 105
  Rainbow children, 105
advancement to root race, 104
affirmations, 136
AFFS (Academy for Future Science), 241
afterlife
  awareness, 200
  electronic phenomenon, 197
  EVP, 197
  guides, 201
  Halls of Learning, 201
  hell, 196
  hypnotic regression, 196
  life review, 196, 199
  met by God, 202
  NDE (near-death experience), 198-200
  past-life readings, 196
  religion's descriptions, 196
agreements
  sacred, 68
  to suffer, 182
AIDS epidemic, 188
akasha
  as cosmic sky, 5
  as element, 4
  defined, 4
  ether, 4
  space that fills the sky, 5
akashic field of consciousness, 232
akashic imprints, 124
akashic love, unconditional, 168
akashic plane, 233
Akashic Planning, 191-192
Akashic predictions, 212

Akashic Record
  accessing, 249-251
    qualities of a good reader, 250
  as dimensional library, 4
  as dimensional road map, 281-282
  as history of mankind, 8
  descriptions of, 4
  dimensions, 268
    access, 270-271
  direct access to, 235
  evolution of, 8
  imprint of memory, 5
  location, 5
  means, 11
  methods, 11
  planes of reality, 232
  purpose, 6-8
  reading
    benefits, 260
    channeling, 253-256
    experience, 266
    intuitives, 260, 265-267
    lucid dreaming, 256-258
    meditation and, 250
    past-life regression, 260-265
    reasons for, 261
    targets, 252-253
    verifications, 261
  reasons for consulting, 4, 11
  remote viewing, 251-253
  similarity to computer technology, 4
  training for readers, 267
  universal consciousness, 231
alcoholism, pacts and, 68
alien intelligence, 237-241

aliens, 75
    abductees, 238
    abduction, typical
        experiences, 239
    altered consciousness, 240
    ancient astronauts, 237-238
    crop circles, 239
    encounters, 238-239
    governments and, 240-241
    Roswell, New Mexico, 240
    SETI (Search for Extra-
        Terrestrial Intelligence), 276
aligning to highest ideal, 228
alpha brain state, 24
altered states of consciousness,
    235-236
    aliens and, 240
alternate futures, 223
ancestors from the stars
    (Mayans), 87
ancient astronauts, 237-238
ancient civilizations, 83
angels, 59, 89-90
    streams of light, 90
    Virtue, Doreen, 89
animal communication, 278
animal partnerships, 178-180
animal soul mates, 179
animal totems, 59
animals
    as other nations, 270
    communication, 277
    intelligence, 276
    reincarnation, 178-179
    returning as, 270
    souls, 178
anti-Christ (Nostradamus), 222
Anthroposophical Society, 21
archangels, 59, 89-90
architecture, past lives and, 113
art
    da Vinci, Leonardo, 102
    Hall of Artistic Inspiration,
        101

inspired, 101
    past lives and, 113
Art Bell's *Coast to Coast* radio
    show, 223, 226
artist case, Akashic healing, 132
artists, 100
ascended masters, 59, 90-91
Aspect, Alain, 248
assessing success, 158
    external measure, 160-161
    internal measure, 159-160
astral plane, 233
astral projection, 25-26
    Fortune, Dion, 22
astronauts, ancient, 237-238
astronomy discoveries, 97
Atlantis, 7, 82-83
    conflict in, 34
    Cyprus-Atlantis Project, 86
    differences in accounts, 84
    Hall of Records, Sphinx, 87
    hidden records, 85
    soul groups, 82
    souls from end times
        returning, 219
    today's similarities, 219
attunement to information
    sought, 28
Atzlan, 87
auras, 105, 232
    chakras and, 232
    cleansing, 129
authority figures, parents, 57
awareness, 184
    after death, 200
    multidimensional, 236
    shift in, 94
    spiritual, increase in, 220

B

Bach, Richard, 178
bad relationships, 55
Banner of Peace, 101

base chakra, 159
battle within, 219
becoming, 157
Bedouin tribe case, 121-122,
    162-163
behavior changes, 125
believing messages we get, 168
Bell, Art, 223, 226
Benedict, Mellen-Thomas, 200
beta brain state, 24
betrayal in soul mates, 175
Bible
    The Book of Life, 4, 6, 9
    consciousness, 30
    great flood, 82
        Lemurians, 84
    to be shown the truth, 30
Bierman, Dick, 206
Bimini, hidden records of
    Atlantis, 85
birth
    soul consulting Record prior
        to, 48
    timing, 70
Blavatsky, Madame Helena, 10,
    20-21
    afterlife, 196
    Germane, 83
    halls, 94
    Lemuria, 84
blocks to growth, 125
body as subconscious mind, 269
bodywork, 269
bow wave, 75
    Web Bot Project, 75
brain
    as holographic, 235
    meditation group, 276
    synchronizing during
        meditation, 276
brain states, 24
    Wild Divine, 24
brain waves of meditators, 276
breathing practices, Blavatsky,
    Madame Helena, 21

Brinkley, Dannion, 39, 182, 198
  life review, 199
Browne, Sylvia, existence of
  halls, 94
Buddha, 90

C

calculus discovery, 96
calendars, Mayan, 221-222
Calleman, Carl Johan, 278
capacity for love, increasing, 30
careers, past lives and, 115
cataclysmic changes, 273
  as agents of evolution, 225
categories of love relationships,
  170
  animal partnerships, 178-180
  karmic relationships,
    170-173
  soul mate reunions, 173-176
  twin flame soul mates, 177
causal plane, 233
cautions about claims of
  readers, 23
Cayce, Edgar, 7, 10, 20-22
  1998-2010 advancement, 104
  afterlife, 196
  animals, 178
  Atlantis, 82
  diagnosis ability, 126
  Edgar Cayce's Association
    for Research and
    Enlightenment, 21
  Germane, 83
  halls of Akashic Record, 94
  healing of self, 126
  health, 124
  past-life information, 109
  precognitive skills
    development, 207
  predictions, 213-214
  psychic ability increase, 207
  Pyramids of Giza, 86
  reincarnation, 36

soul mates, 52, 173
souls as points of light
  separated from source, 30
celestial plane, 233
Cerminara, Gina, 178
chakras, 159
  1st (base), 159
  2nd (sacral), 159
  3rd (solar plexus), 159
  4th (heart), 159
  5th (throat), 159
  6th (third eye), 159
  7th (crown), 159
  aura and, 232
challenges, 181
  becoming gifts, 164-166
  suffering, 182
  viewing as punishment, 184
Chaney, Robert, akasha as
  cosmic sky, 5
channeling, 25, 253-256
  higher self, Edgar Cayce
    reading Record, 235
characteristics of karmic
  partnership, 171
Chilam Balam, 221
child abuse, 161
child prodigies, 100
childhood
  choices, 161-163
  illness, 187
children
  ADD/ADHD, 188
  abilities at birth, past lives
    and, 116
  Crystal, 105
  Indigo, 105
  past-life memories, 41-42
    Erin, 44-45
    Leininger, James, 43-44
    Shanti Devi, 42
    Stevenson, Dr. Ian, 42
  play, past lives and, 114
  Rainbow, 105
  relationships, 58

choices between material and
  spiritual values, 35
Christian Gnostics, 37
civilizations
  ancient, 83
  Atlantis, 82-83
    Cyprus-Atlantis Project,
      86
    hidden records, 85
    soul groups, 82
  Atzlan, 87
  destruction, 82
  Lemuria, 82-84
    Easter Island heads, 88
  Mayans, 87
  Mu, 83
  Pyramids of Giza, 86
Civil War case, 121
clairaudience, 22, 246
clairvoyance, 22, 246
collapse of dollar, 75
collective intention, 227
communication, 50
  with guides, 90
compassion, 29-30
computer technology's similarity to Akashic Record, 4
concentration camps, 184
conflict
  Atlantis and Lemuria, 34
  Mayans and Spaniards, 34
  Native Americans and
    Europeans, 34
  religion and, 35
connectedness of humankind,
  247
connection through field of
  energy, 95
connections, strong emotions, 67
conscience, undeveloped, 125
consciousness, 11
  2012 and, 274
  akashic field of consciousness,
    232
  altered, aliens and, 240

altered states, 235-236
dimensional, 281
government and, 240
Hinduism, 10
Noetic Science Institute, 247
singularity, 39, 282
universal consciousness, 94
Record as, 231
consciousness scientists, 34
consciousness singularity, 73
consultants, 20
contracts
family, 56
children, 58
choosing, 56
parents, 56
siblings, 57
love, 51-52
difficult relationships,
54-55
lack of relationship, 55-56
soul mates, 52
twin souls, 52-53
unrequited, 53-54
petty tyrants, 62
relationships, 47-51
spiritual, 58
movements, 59
spiritual beings, 59
transmuting accumulated
karma, 60-61
strangers and, 61
work relationships, 62
Cook, Grace, 271
core imprints on Record, 126
Cottrell, Douglas, 82
Easter Island heads, 88
Course in Miracles, 132
creative thinking, 135
crop circles, 239
crown chakra, 159
Crusades case, 121, 162
Crystal children, 105
ADD/ADHD, 188
curing versus healing, 124

current life, moment of death, 47
Cyprus-Atlantis Project, 86

D

da Vinci, Leonardo, 102
Dalai Lama, 103
reincarnation of, 59
Dale, Henry, 99
Dames, Major Ed, 223
Darwin, Charles, 96
déjà-vu, 119
death
fear of, 121
life beyond, 247
moment of, vibrations, 47
deceased loved ones as guides,
59
decision making, foundation
and, 143
decisions
affecting the outcome, 75
intuition and, 206
deep focus/concentration, 94
delta brain state, 24
demons, 91
destruction
as agent of evolution, 225
predictions, 224
detecting one's purpose,
144-149
devas, 92
difficult relationships, 54-55
dimensional consciousness, 281
dimensional library, 4
dimensions
to Record, 268
seven dimensions, 232-233
direct access to Record, 235
discernment of information,
26-27
disease, 186-187
spiritual separation and, 123
divination, 207
dollar collapse, 75

dream yoga, 258
dreams, 97
accessing Record in, 94
lucid dreaming, 256-258
nerve transmission (Loewi),
99
past lives and, 120
lucid dreams, 120
precognitive, 206
Stevenson, Robert Louis, 102
Yesterday, Paul McCartney,
101
duty, 183

E

earth
changes, predictions, 220
crossing plane of Milky
Way, 221
Easter Island heads, 83, 88
Eastern philosophy, Madame
Helena Blavatsky, 21
ecological challenges, 72
economy, world, 71-72
Edison, Thomas
fearful machine invention,
104
infinite laws, 95
inspiration, 95
journaling, 96
on non-violence, 72
Edwards, Harry, 100
rooms in Hall of Learning,
100
effectiveness in life, purpose
and, 143
Egyptians
Hall of Two Truths, 9
judgment, 6
pyramids, 83, 85-86
Sphinx, 86-87
Einstein, Albert
human beings, 8
QM (quantum mechanics),
209

Theory of Relativity, 14
    thought experiments, 98
Elder Brothers, 274
electric phenomenon, 197
electromagnetic energy, 14
elemental beings, 91
elves, 92
emotional matrix, 159
emotions, 90
    Course in Miracles, 132
    fear, 132
    guiding life's path, 159
    love, 132
    strong emotions, 67
    unhealed, next life and, 164
empowerment in this time
    period, 225-226
encounters with aliens, 238-239
end times
    Atlantis/Lemuria, souls
        returning, 219
    current age, 221
    empowerment, 225-226
    Mayans, 221-222
    positive intention, 223
    reconciliation, 221
energy, 14-15
    connection through field of
        energy, 95
    matter and, 73
    sending toward outcome, 74
energy field, 231
energy shift, healing and, 129
energy-enhanced food, 92
entanglement, 248-249
equality in soul mates, 175
ESP (extra-sensory perception),
    23, 74, 246
    entanglement, 248-249
    examples, 246
    simultaneous events, 247
    telepathy, 246
etheric levels, 200
etheric plane, 232
eureka moment, 99

evolutionary advancements, 104
    cataclysmic changes as agent,
        225
    of love, 167
    of Record, 8, 34
    of the soul, 30-31
evolving relationships, 172
EVP (Electronic Voice
    Phenomena), 195-197
excitement, success and, 160
external measure of success,
    160-161

F

Fabricius, Johannes, 97
fairies, 92
fallen angels, 271
false purposes, 145
family, 56
    children, 58
    choices, 161-162
    choosing, 56
    duty and, 183
    learning from, 164
    parents, 56
    siblings, 57
fashion sense, past lives and, 113
fate versus free will, 76-77
Father of Holistic Medicine
    (Edgar Cayce), 22
Father of the New Age (Edgar
    Cayce), 22
fear, 132
    of abandonment, 164
    of death, 121
    past lives and, 117
financial ruin, 189-190
Findhorn (Scotland), 92
five worlds (Mayans), 84
flashes of insight, 90
flow, purpose/path and, 151
flower essences, 68
focusing on path, 150-151
food, energy-enhanced, 92

foot pain case, Akashic healing,
    131, 163
forensic psychics, 247
forgiveness, 35, 68
forming intentions, 135
Fortune, Dion, 20, 22
foundation, purpose and, 143
free will versus fate, 76-77
freedom, relationships and, 50
friends, group karma, 67
Fuller, Buckminster, 102
future, 45, 74
    alternate futures, 223
    existence in Record, 205
    as extension of present, 208
    creating, 226-228
    dreams of, 206
    Heisenberg's Uncertainty
        Principle, 209
    positive intention, 223
    probabilities, 212
    QM (quantum mechanics),
        208-209
    sending energy toward
        outcome, 74
future beings arriving for
    incarnation, 104
future destiny, reading, 27
future lives, 268
future outlook after NDE
    (near-death experience), 200
future regressions, 269-270

G

Galilei, Galileo, 97
Gandhi, Mohandas (Mahatma),
    103
Germane, 83
gifts, 166
Gisin, Nicolas, 248
glowing leaf, 226
glyphs on tablet as memory
    imprints, 5
gnomes, 92

goals
  design, 157
  meaningful, 143
God
  interaction with, 202
  meeting souls, 202
Goldberg, Dr. Bruce, 157, 197
Golden Age of Mayan
  prophecy, 222, 225
government
  aliens and, 240-241
  consciousness and, 240
grace, law of, 40
great flood (Bible), 82
  Lemurians, 84
group karma, 65-66
  changing paradigms, 73
  ecological challenges, 72
  friends, 67
  future, 74
  nations, 69
  pacts, 67-68
  quantum paradigm, 73
  soul groups, 66-67
  today's challenges, 70-71
  vows, 69
  world economy, 71-72
group meditation, brain and, 276
growth
  blocks to, 125
  guides, 202
  of love, 280
  soul mates, 173
  willingness, 129-130
guardian angels, 89-90
Guardians of the Record, 89
guides, 28, 90
  afterlife, 199, 201
  communicating with, 90
  growth, 202
  remembering, 271
  soul groups, 201
  styles, 202
  training for, 203

Guiley, Rosemary Ellen, 206
gut instinct, 90

H

Hall, Manly P., 69
Hall of Artistic Inspiration, 101
Hall of Learning, 94
  language, 102
  rooms for arts, 100
  search for truth of being, 94
Hall of Records, 94
Hall of Records of Atlantis,
  Sphinx and, 87
Hall of Two Truths, 9
Hall of Wisdom, 94
Halls of Learning, 201
Hancock, Graham, 92, 240, 276
Hawking, Dr. Stephen, 185, 187
  multiverse, 234
healing, 123, 184
  Cayce, Edgar, healing self,
    126
  karma and, 123
  physical, 130-131
  process, 126-127
    expand perspective, 129
    find cause, 128
    growth, 129-130
    identify issue, 127-128
    shift energy, 129
  relationships, 133-134
  situational, 132
  TABs, 124
  versus curing, 124
health professionals' challenges,
  182
health tests, 185
  disease, 186-187
  illness, 186-187
    childhood, 187
    terminal, 188-189
  transmuting health karma,
    186

heart chakra, 159
  satisfaction and, 159
Heart of the World, 274
Hein, Dr. Simeon, 26
Heisenberg's Uncertainty
  Principle, 209
hell, 196
heritage, duty and, 183
higher self, 20
  Cayce, Edgar, channeling,
    235
higher-level pacts, 68
highest ideal, aligning to, 228
Hindu
  devas, 92
  karma, 6, 9
  seven dimensions, 232-233
  Upanishads, 9
historical change
  Gandhi, Mohandas
    (Mahatma), 103
  Hitler, Adolf, 103
historical figures, past lives, 112
historical time periods
  past lives, 111
  upheaval, 111
history
  loss of, 6
  of mankind, 8
  patterns in, 34
Hitler, Adolf, 103
hobbies, past lives and, 115
holograms, 16-17
  reality as, 211
holographic brains, 235
honesty in soul mates, 175
Hopkins, Bud, 238
Howe, Elias, 97
human abilities, expansion of, 74
human beings, Albert Einstein
  on, 8
human perception, 219
Hundredth Monkey Effect, 16
Hurtak, Dr. James, 225, 241, 273

hypnagogic state, 96
hypnosis, NGH (National Guild of Hypnotists), 264
hypnotic regression, afterlife, 196

I

ideas erupting across planet simultaneously, 95
illness, 186-187
    childhood, 187
    terminal, 188-189
imprint of memory on Akashic Record, 5
imprints on Akashic Record, 124
    core imprints, 126
increasing vibration, 278
indigenous societies, 274-275
Indigo children, 105
    ADD/ADHD, 188
infinite laws, Thomas Edison, 95
information
    attunement to that sought, 28
    increasing in vibration, 95
    responsibility with, 28
information received, discernment of, 26-27
information retrieval from Record, 128
insight, Silva UltraMind System, 99
inspiration
    Edison, Thomas, 95
    Hall of Learning, 94
    hypnagogic state, 96
    meditative states and, 14
    Shelley, Mary Wollstonecraft, 102
    Stevenson, Robert Louis, 102
inspired artwork, 101
instantaneous transmission of information, 248

instinct, 90
    past lives and, 116
    purpose/path and, 152
Institute of Noetic Sciences, 206
intentional meditation, 275
intentional thinking, 135-136
intentional visioning, 227
intentions
    collective, 227
    forming, 135
    positive actions, 228
    power of, 226-227
    quantum physics, 227
intercessions, 224-225
interconnectedness, 39, 274
    akashic field of consciousness, 232
    aura and, 232
internal imbalance, 182
internal measure of success, 159-160
International Center for Attitudinal Healing, 133
Internet spiders, 75
interspecies communication, 276
intuition, 23, 206, 246
    decisions and, 206
    reading the Record and, 27
intuitives, 260
    locating, 267-268
    pros/cons of sessions, 267
    Record readings, 265-266
inventions, simultaneous, 96-97
inventors, 95
invisible substance universe is made of, 5
ITC (Instrumental TransCommunication), 197

J

James, William, 234
Jampolsky, Dr. Jerry, 133
Jesus, 90

Jewish Kabbalists, 37
journaling, 96, 110
journey, purpose as, 145
journey of love, 168
judgment, 196
    life review process, 199

K

karma, 6, 9, 13
    accumulated, transmuting, 60-61
    behavior changes, 125
    consequences, 125
    creating, 38
    free will versus fate, 76-77
    group karma, 65-66
        changing paradigms, 73
        ecological challenges, 72
        friends, 67
        future, 74
        nations, 69
        pacts, 67-68
        quantum paradigm, 73
        soul groups, 66-67
        today's challenges, 70-71
        vows, 69
        world economy, 71-72
    healing, 123
    misuse, 41
    paths, 182
    physics, 38
    reincarnation, 36
    as retribution, 38, 182
    score card idea, 39
    as teaching tool, 38
    timing of birth, 70
    transmuting, 40
        health karma, 186
        help for humanity, 71
    United States as experiment, 69
    with other people, 39

karmic partnerships, 170
    characteristics, 171
    evolving, 172
    Sharon and John, 171
karmic relationships, 170-173
    Sharon and John example, 171
    soul-mate relationships, 172
karmic shadow, 40
Keepers of the Record, 28
King, Martin Luther Jr., 103

L

lack of relationship, 55-56
language in Hall of Learning, 102
Laszlo, Dr. Ervin, 226, 276
Lavoisier, Antoine, 96
law of grace, 40
Leadbeater, Charles, 178
leaf glowing, 226
learning from family, 164
Leininger, James, 43-44
Lemuria, 7, 82-84
    conflict in, 34
    differences in accounts, 84
    Easter Island heads, 88
    great flood (Bible), 84
    Native Americans, 84
    souls from end times returning, 219
leper colony case, 163
lessons
    akashic imprint, 124
    in life, reincarnation, 36
levels of existence, 89
life
    as an adventure, 144
    beyond death, 246-247
    circumstances, design, 157
    physicality, 169
    on other planets, 271
    plan, 12, 203
    purpose, soul evolution, 30-31
    review, 196, 199

life events
    major, 165
    purpose, 146
life's record, 7
likes/dislikes, past lives and, 117
linear time, 211
Lines of Nazca, 88
literature, Shelley, Mary Wollstonecraft, 102
living in the past, 111
location of Akashic Record, 5
Loewi, Dr. Otto, 99
loss of history, 6
lost civilizations, 7, 81
love, 51-52, 132
    access, 29
    addiction, 191
    as basis for all you create, 169
    capacity for, 30
    conflict, 35
    difficult relationships, 54-55
    evolution of, 167
    growth of, 280
    journey of, 168
    lack of relationship, 55-56
    losing, 52
    romantic, experience of spirituality, 168
    selfless, animals, 178
    soul mates, 52
    as spiritual truth, 167
    spirituality, 168
    twin souls, 52-53
    unconditional, 168
    unrequited, 53-54
    wholeness, 168
love relationships, 170
    animal partnerships, 178-180
    karmic relationships, 170-173
    soul mate reunions, 173-176
    twin flame soul mates, 177
low-level impulses, 183
lower-level agreements, breaking free, 68

loyalty, misplaced, 183
lucid dreaming, 90, 120, 256-258

M

Mack, Dr. John, 238
Macy, Mark, 197, 201
major life events, 165
manifesting purpose, 153
Many Worlds Theory (MWT), 234
Marcel, Jesse, 240
Martinz, Shaun, 188
material accomplishments, 157
material values, choice between spiritual, 35
material wealth, 158
matter, energy and, 73
Mayans, 87
    ancestors from the stars, 87
    astronomical skills, 88
    calendar, 88, 221
    Chilam Balam, 221
    codices, 9
    conflict with Spaniards, 34
    five worlds, 84
    mathematical skills, 88
    Milky Way and, 221
    predictions, 70
    prophecies, 221-222
    pyramids
        time periods, 278
McCartney, Paul, *Yesterday*, 101
McTaggart, Lynne, 226, 275
meaning in life, purpose, 142
meditation, 24, 250
    Blavatsky, Madame Helena, 21
    brain synchronization, 276
    brain waves of meditators, 276
    group, brain and, 276
    inspiration during, 14
    intentional, 275

peace meditations, 275
PET scans, 275
transformation and, 275
meeting people, past lives and, 116
Melchizedek, 90
memories
  brain and, 235
  imprint on Akashic Record, 5
  past encounters, 48
  past lives of children, 41-42
    Erin, 44-45
    Leininger, James, 43-44
    Shanti Devi, 42
    Stevenson, Dr. Ian, 42
  Pribram, Dr. Karl, 16
  storage, 5
mental plane, 233
mental telepathy, 74
messages from other side, 195
messages from the departed, 278
metaphysical thought,
  Blavatsky, Madame Helena, 21
migration from Atlantis, 83
Military Remote Viewing
  Project, 223
Milky Way, Mayans and, 221
mind effects, 247
mind-matter interaction, 246
mind's abilities, 246
mirrors, relationships as, 50
misplaced loyalty, 183
mission statement for purpose, 150
Mitchell, Dr. Edgar, 23, 226
moment of death, vibrations
  set up, 47
Moody, Dr. Raymond, 197
morphic fields, 15-16, 248
  resonance, 15
morphic-resonant field, 95
  information increasing in
    vibration, 95
motivation, purpose and, 144

movements, spiritual contracts, 59
MS (Multiple Sclerosis), 189
Mu, 83
multidimensional awareness, 236
multiverse, 233-234
musicians, 100
  child prodigies, 100
MWT (Many Worlds Theory), 234
Myss, Caroline, 61
mystics, 10
myths, 91

N-O

nation's karma, 69
Native Americans
  conflict with Europeans, 34
  Lemurians, 84
  White Eagle, 271
natural disaster, 191
Nazca lines, 88
NDE (near-death experience),
  94, 198-200. *See also* afterlife
nerve transmission (Loewi), 99
New Era, wisdom of the past, 222
Newton, Dr. Michael, 197, 201
Newton, Sir Issac, 96
NGH (National Guild of
  Hypnotists), 264
Noetic Science Institute, 247
non-locality, 248
non-violence, Thomas Edison, 72
Nostradamus, 207
  nuclear bomb prediction, 224
  predictions, 222

owning your shadow, 125
oxygen discovery, 96

P

pacts, 67-68
  alcoholism, 68
  higher impulses, 67
  higher-level, 68
  lower impulses, 67
pandemic, 75
paradigms
  changing, 73
  definition, 71
  quantum, 73
parallel universes, 233
paranormal
  abilities, 246
  fear of, 246
  researches, 247
parents, 56
  choosing, 162-163
partnerships
  animal, 178-180
  karmic, 170
    characteristics, 171
    evolving, 172
    Sharon and John, 171
passions, past lives and, 118
past encounters, memories of, 48
past issues, resolving, 163
past lives, 12
  abilities born with, 116
  activities, 114
  alienation from present, 109
  architecture and, 113
  art, 113
  artist case, 132
  Bedouin tribe case, 121
  benefits from information, 108
  careers, 115
  children's play, 114
  Civil War case, 121
  Crusades, 121
  Crusades case, 162
  déjà-vu, 119

dreams, 120
fashion sense, 113
fears, 117
feelings after discovery, 108
foot pain case, 131, 163
historical figures, 112
historical time periods, 111
hobbies, 115
horses/desert case, 121
instant recognition, 119
instincts, 116
leper colony case, 163
likes/dislikes, 117
living in the past, 111
meeting someone for the
  first time, 116
note taking, 110
passions, 118
personality types, 115
phobias, 117
physical problems, 117
physical sensations, 116
  back pain case, 121
places drawn to, 112
preferences, 110-111
reading, 27
reasons for wanting to know,
  107
recognizing instantly, 119
recurring patterns, 118
religious beliefs, 109
Revolutionary War soldier
  case, 131, 163
risk-taker husband case, 133
unintended consequences
  from learning, 109
past-life memories of children,
  41-42
  Erin, 44-45
  Leininger, James, 43-44
  Shanti Devi, 42
  Stevenson, Dr. Ian, 42
past-life readings, 196

past-life regression, 260-263
  pros/cons, 264-265
  therapist choice, 265
  training in, 264
path, 142
  awareness, 184
  duty, 183
  emotions, 159
  flow, 151
  focusing on, 150-151
  healing, 184
  instincts, 152
  rebalancing, 182
  resistance, 152
  sacrifice, 184
  service, 185
  synchronicities, 151
paths of karma, 182
patterns
  changing, 134
  in history, 34
  recurring, past lives and, 118
Peace Intention Experiment, 227
peace meditations, 275
peer relationships, siblings, 57
people, purpose of, 49
perception
  human ability, 219
  of reality, 234-236
Perelandra flower essences, 68
Perelandra (Virginia), 92
personal crises, 189
  addiction, 190-191
  financial ruin, 189-190
  mass murder, 191
  natural disaster, 191
  war, 191
personal precognition, 206-207
personality tests, 115
personality types, past lives, 115
perspective, purpose and, 144
Pert, Dr. Candice, 269
PET scans on meditators, 275
petty tyrants, relationships, 62

phobias, past lives, 117
physical healing, 130-131
physical plane, 232
physical problems, past lives, 117
physical sensations, past lives,
  116
  back pain case, 121
  Civil War case, 121
physicality of life, 169
places, past lives, 112
plan, design, 157
planes
  of existence, 232
  multidimensional awareness,
    236
  of reality, 232
planning life, 191-192, 203
plastic bags predictions (1970s),
  218
Plato, Atlantis, 82
play in children, past lives, 114
political dynasties, 183
positive actions, 228
positive intentions, 223, 228
power
  of intention, 226-227
  in relationships, 50
precognition, 206-207, 246
predictions, 212
  2012, 224
  Cayce, Edgar, 213-214
  destruction, 224
  fear of, 207
  Nostradamus, 222
  nuclear bomb, 224
  probable outcomes, 220
preferences, past lives and,
  110-111
preparations for next life, 156
  abilities, 166
  childhood, 161-164
  family, 161-164
  gifts, 166
  guidance and planning, 157

life events, 165
material accomplishments, 158
present-time similarities to Atlantis, 219
Presley, Reg, 100
Pribram, Dr. Karl, 16, 235
Priestly, Joseph, 96
prime directive in Akashic Record, 167
Princess Diana's funeral, random generators, 227
Princeton global consciousness project, 76
privacy, Keepers of the Record, 28
process of healing, 126-127
    expand perspective, 129
    find cause, 128
    growth, 129-130
    identify issue, 127-128
    shift energy, 129
progression of relationships, 169
prophecies, 207
    2012, 224
    Mayan, 221-222
psi phenomena, 246
    categories of abilities, 246
    quickening and, 279
psychiatrists, 264
psychic abilities
    Elder Brothers, 274
    learning, 249
    teachers, 249
psychics, forensic, 247
psychotherapists, 264
punishment, viewing challenges as, 184
purpose, 142
    access to, 148
    connecting to, 141
    detecting, 144-147, 149
    direction, 143
    effectiveness, 143

exercises, 148
false purposes, 145
flow, 151
focusing on path, 150-151
instincts, 152
as journey, 145
life span, 146
manifesting, 153
meaning in life, 142
mission statement, 150
motivation, 144
perspective, 144
quality of life, 146
resistance, 152
synchronicities, 151
purposeful life, 143
purpose of Akashic Record, 6-8
purpose of life, 12, 30-31
purpose of people, 49
Puthoff, Harold, 223
pyramids of Egypt, 83, 85-86
Pyramids of Giza, 86

Q

QM (quantum mechanics), 208-209
    Heisenberg's Uncertainty Principle), 209
    holographic reality, 211
    particles, 209
    Schrödinger's Cat, 211
    subatomic particles, 247-248
    waves, 209
quantum holography, 16-17, 73
quantum paradigm, 73
quantum physics, 73
    entangled minds, 276
    intention, 227
    Mayans, 221
    multiverse, 234
    new realities, 233
quantum superposition, 210

quickening, 277
    psi phenomena, 279
    surviving change, 280
    time speeding up, 278

R

Radin, Dr. Dean, 34, 73-74, 206, 226, 247
    entanglement and psychic abilities, 249
    telepathy, 246
Rainbow children, 105
Randall, Lisa, 234
random generators, 227
readers of the Record, 20
    Andrews, Colin, 27
    Blavatsky, Madame Helena, 20-21
    cautions, 23
    Cayce, Edgar, 20-22, 235
    experience of reader, 71
    Fortune, Dion, 20-22
    Steiner, Rudolf, 21
reading the Record, 246
    benefits, 260
    experience, 266
    intuitives, 260
        pros/cons, 267
    past-life regression, 260-265
    qualities of a good reader, 250
    reasons for, 261
    training for readers, 267
    verifications, 261
reality
    as hologram, 211
    multiple, 236
    perceptions, 234-236
rebalancing, 182
recognizing instantly, past lives, 119
reconciliation, end times, 221
Record Keepers, 28, 89

recurring patterns, past lives
  and, 118
recurring thoughts, 90
reincarnation, 12, 36. *See also*
  current life
  animal, 178-179
  Cayce, Edgar, 36
  Christian Gnostics, 37
  cursing of by Council of
    Churches, 37
  Dalai Lama, 59
  history, 37
  Jewish Kabbalists, 37
  karma, 36
  lessons in life, 36
  memories of past encounters,
    48
  misconceptions, 37
  past-life memories of
    children, 41-42
      Erin, 44-45
      Leininger, James, 43-44
      Shanti Devi, 42
      Stevenson, Dr. Ian, 42
  Theosophical perspective, 37
relationships, 13, 47-49
  animal partnerships, 178-180
  communication, 50
  death of person, 49
  difficult, 54-55
  as doorway to Record, 168
  freedom, 50
  goals, 51
  healing, 133-134
  karmic partnerships, 170
    characteristics, 171
    Sharon and John, 171
  lack of, 55-56
  letting go, 51
  love, categories, 170-180
  as mirrors to soul, 49-50
  objectives, 51
  petty tyrants, 62
  power, 50

progression of, 169
purpose of people, 49
respect, 49
seeking wholeness through,
  168
things learned in, 48
work relationships, 62
religion
  afterlife descriptions, 196
  conflict and, 35
religious beliefs, past life
  information and, 109
Remote Viewing Institute, 223
remote viewing (RV), 26, 223,
  251-253
resistance, purpose and, 152
resonance, 15
respect in relationships, 49
responsibility
  with information, 28
  spiritual mastery, 169
retribution, karma as, 182
retrieving information from
  Record, 128
revelations, 90
review of life, 196
Revolutionary War soldier case,
  131, 163
Ring of Fire, 88
risk-taker husband case, 133
Robbins, Tony, 164
Roerich, Nicholas, 101
root race, advancement to, 104
Roswell, New Mexico, 240
Royal, Lyssa, 82-83
royal dynasties, 183
Russell, Ron, 26
RV (remote viewing), 223

S

sacral chakra, 159
sacred agreements, 68
sacred sites, Lemuria, 84
sacrifice, 184

saints, 59
Scheele, Carl Wilhelm, 96
Scheiner, Christopher, 97
Schrödinger's Cat, 211
Schwartz, Dr. Gary, 226
Schwartz, Robert, 188, 201
science, 13-14
  forward movement, 217
scientists
  consciousness scientists, 34
  creative thinking and, 98
score card view of karma, 39
search for truth of being, Hall
  of Learning, 94
self as active element in Record,
  35
self-awareness of Record, 34
selfless love, animals, 178
September 11 attacks
  random generators and, 227
  Web Bot Project, 76
service, 185
SETI (Search for Extra-
  Terrestrial Intelligence), 276
seven dimensions, 232-233
sewing machine invention, 97
Shanti Devi, 42
Sheldrake, Rupert, 15, 95, 248
Shelley, Mary Wollstonecraft,
  102
shift in awareness to access
  Record, 94
sibling relationships, 57
Sierra Nevada tribes, 275
Silva UltraMind System, 99
simultaneous inventions, 96, 97
singularity consciousness, 39, 282
situational healing, 132
sixth sense, 23
skrying, 222
Sleeping Prophet (Edgar Cayce),
  22
Society of the Inner Light, 21
society's transformation, 225
solar plexus chakra, 159

Solon, 83
  Atlantis, 82
soul groups, 66-67
  Atlantis, 82
  development, 157
  guides, 201
soul mates, 52. *See also* twin
  flame soul mates
  animal soul mates, 179
  attracting, 175-176
  betrayal, 175
  Cayce, Edgar, 52, 173
  conflict, 175
  development, 157
  end of relationship, 52
  equality, 175
  growth, 173
  honesty, 175
  issues, 52
  multiple, 174
  myths about, 174
  recognizing, 176
  reunions, 173-176
  seeking, 174
  soul groups, 66
  unavailability, 174
souls
  advanced, 105
  animals, 178
  as cells in body of Record, 35
  consulting Record before
    birth, 48
  evolution, 30-31
  human form, 202
  lessons, 36
  from other planets, 104
  as points of light separated
    from source, 30
  purpose, reading, 27
  relationships as mirrors to, 49
  responding to collective
    need, 102
speed of thought, 247
speeding up of time, 278

Sphinx, 86
  age, 87
  Hall of Records of Atlantis,
    87
spiders, Internet, 75
spiritual awareness, increase
  in, 220
spiritual beings, 89
spiritual contracts, 58
  movements, 59
  spiritual beings, 59
  transmuting accumulated
    karma, 60-61
spiritual discernment and
  Record access, 23
spiritual guides/guardians,
  58-59
spiritual identity, 31
spiritual mastery, 169
  responsibility and, 169
spiritual possession, addiction,
  190
spiritual separation as cause of
  disease, 123
spiritual source sending
  transmissions, 219
spiritual truth of love, 167
spiritual values, choice between
  material, 35
spirituality
  aliens and, 75
  love and, 168
  romantic love and, 168
Sri Lanka, 227
St. Germain, 90
Star nations, 238
starting point, 33
Steiner, Rudolf, 21, 92
  afterlife, 196
  awareness of Akashic realms,
    235
stele, 87
Stevenson, Robert Louis, 102
strangers, 61
streams of light, angels, 90

strengths, purpose and, 147
string theory, 235
strong emotions, 67
strong feelings, sudden, 90
subatomic particles, 247-248
subconscious, body as, 269
substance abuse, 190
success
  accessing, 158
  assessing, 158
  external measure, 160-161
  internal measure, 159-160
sudden strong feelings, 90
suffering, agreement to, 182
Sundrum, Raman, 234
sustainable living practices, 75
synchronicity, 277
  path and, 151

T

TABs (thoughts, attitudes, and
  beliefs), 124
  healing and, 124
Talbot, Michael, 73
talents, purpose and, 147
Targ, Russell, 223, 247
targets when reading Record,
  252-253
teachers of psychic abilities, 249
technology
  Atlantis, 83
  forward movement, 217
  past civilizations, 84
  people reincarnating for
    creation, 116
telepathy, 246
  ESP and, 246
  Lemurians, 84
  Radin, Dean, 246
template plane, 233
terminal illness, 188, 189
Tesla, Nikola, 105
  on inventing, 97

The Book of Life, 4, 6, 9
The Twelve Principles of
    Attitudinal Healing, 133
theory of non-locality, 248
Theory of Relativity, 14
    Einstein's imaginings, 98
Theosophical Society, 10
    Blavatsky, Madame Helena,
        21
    website, 21
Theosophists, 5, 10
    animal souls, 178-179
    reincarnation, 37
therapist choice for PLR, 265
theta brain state, 24
thinking
    affirmations, 136
    creative thinking, 135
    intentional, 135-136
third eye chakra, 159
thoughts
    experiments, Albert
        Einstein, 98
    recurring, 90
    speed, 247
    spontaneous, 90
throat chakra, 159
Tibetan monks
    2012 and, 225
    dream yoga, 258
time and space, 73
time periods, past lives, 111
time speeding up, 278
today's challenges, karma and,
    70-71
Todeschi, Kevin, 212
Tolle, Eckhart, 144
training for Record readers, 267
training in PLR (past-life
    regression), 264
transformation
    consciousness, 274
    meditation and, 275
    of society, 225

transmigration, 178
transmission of information, 248
transmissions from spiritual
    source, 219
transmuting karma, 40
    help for humanity, 71
twin flame soul mates, 177
    as final test, 177
    recognizing, 177
twin souls, 52-53
    development and, 157

U

UFOs, 237
unconditional love, 168
undeveloped conscience, 125
unhealed emotions, next life
    and, 164
United States' karma, 69
universal consciousness, 94
    Record as, 231
universes, parallel, 233
University of Amsterdam, 206
unrequited love, 53-54
Upanishads, 9

V

vibration
    of energy field, 232
    increasing, 278
victims, 181, 192
    childhood, 161
viewing remotely, 26
Virtue, Doreen, 89
volcanic ring, 88
von Leibniz, Gottfried
    Wilhelm, 96
vows, 69

W–X–Y–Z

Wallace, Alfred Russel, 96
Wambach, Dr. Helen, 197
wars, 111, 191
Washington snipers, 27
wayeb, 59
wealth, material, 158
Web Bot Project, 75
    September 11 attacks, 76
    trends noticed, 75
Weiss, Dr. Brian, 173
West, John Anthony, 87
White Eagle, 271
White Eagle Lodge, 271
wholeness, 168
Wilbur, Ken, 234
Wild Divine, 24
Winfrey, Oprah, 165
wisdom of the past, New Era,
    222
work relationships, 62
world economy, 71-72
Wright brothers, 102
writers, 100
WWII concentration camps,
    184